OXFORD ENGLISH MONOGRAPHS

General Editors

British Modernism and the Anthropocene

Experiments with Time

DAVID SHACKLETON

Great Clarendon Street, Oxford, OX2 6DP,
United Kingdom

Oxford University Press is a department of the University of Oxford.
It furthers the University's objective of excellence in research, scholarship,
and education by publishing worldwide. Oxford is a registered trade mark of
Oxford University Press in the UK and in certain other countries

Published in the United States of America by Oxford University Press
198 Madison Avenue, New York, NY 10016, United States of America

British Library Cataloguing in Publication Data

Data available

Library of Congress Control Number: 2023910872

ISBN 978-0-19-285774-3

DOI: 10.1093/oso/9780192857743.001.0001

Printed and bound by
CPI Group (UK) Ltd, Croydon, CR0 4YY

To Anne and Arthur

Acknowledgements

Writing a book about time has taught me many things, including that the tortoise does not, in fact, win the race. However, while the course has been long, it has also been rewarding, and I am very grateful to those who have helped me along the way.

This book started as a doctoral dissertation at the University of Oxford, where I am very grateful for the brilliant guidance and example of my supervisor, Michael Whitworth. His patience, intellectual generosity, and willingness to push the argument laid the foundations for this project. For their sustaining conversation and friendship in Oxford, thanks to Philip Burnett, Oren Goldschmidt, Calum Mechie, Alys Moody, Camilla Mount, Carla Neuss, Courtney Nimura, Robert Rapoport, Becky Roach, Stephen Ross, Lialin Rotem-Stibbe, John Scholar, Yasmine Shamma, David Soud, Lisa Terris, Luke Williamson, and Michelle Witen. Thanks specially to Lisa for educating me about J. R. R. Tolkien, and to Michelle and her students for hosting me so beautifully at the University of Basel. My admiration goes to the staff of the Bodleian Libraries, who have endured my presence in the Upper Reading Room, and allowed me to play for the Bodleian Cricket Club for a number of years.

Whilst teaching as a Lecturer in English Literature at the University of Exeter, I was grateful for the hospitality and friendship of John Bolin, Beci Carver, James Fraser, Jana Funke, Vike Plock, and James Williams. In particular, for their warmth and good humour on an icy picket line, thanks to James and James. At Cardiff University, I am lucky to have wonderful colleagues and friends, including Alix Beeston, Jamie Castell, Jess Cotton, Josie Cray, Ailbhe Darcy, Sarah Daw, Derek Dunne, Holly Furneaux, Corin Gilchrist, Mark Llewellyn, Anna Mercer, Meredith Miller, Becky Munford, Irene Morra, Josh Powell, Josh Robinson, Ceri Sullivan, Aidan Tynan, and Martin Willis. Particularly inspiring having been the various activities and events organized through Cardiff Environmental Cultures. For being an excellent mentor and friend since his time as a Visiting Professor at Cardiff University, and for his inspiring example as a scholar-activist, I am grateful to Allen Webb. For their invaluable feedback on various parts of this book, thanks to Alix Beeston, Colin Burrow, Bart van Es, Jana Funke, Jane Garrity, Caroline Hovanec, Mark Llewellyn, Meredith Miller, Becky Munford, Rachel Murray, and Josh Robinson. For her love and support over many years which has made this project possible, thanks to my mother, Caroline Shackleton. And finally, for her unwavering support and encouragement during the slow crawl to the finish line, thank you to Anne.

This research has been generously supported by the Arts and Humanities Research Council with a Studentship Award at the University of Oxford; by St Catherine's College with a Graduate Scholarship (Arts); and by the British Society for Literature and Science with a grant to present research at the Radclyffe Hall Symposium, Birkbeck, University of London. At Oxford University Press, I would like to thank Ellie Collins and Karen Raith for being wonderful editors, and Alexander Hardie-Forsyth for seeing the book so smoothly through production. I am also extremely grateful to my two reviewers, whose generous comments have improved this book beyond measure.

Material from this book has previously been published as 'The "bare germs of things to come": H. G. Wells's Utopias, Ecological Risk, and the Anthropocene', *Modernism/modernity Print Plus*, 2 (2022); 'Olive Moore, Queer Ecology, and Anthropocene Modernism', *Modernism/modernity*, 28/1 (2021), 35–76; 'H. G. Wells, Geology, and the Ruins of Time', *Victorian Literature and Culture*, 45/4 (2017), 839–55; and 'The Pageant of Mutabilitie: Virginia Woolf's *Between the Acts* and *The Faerie Queene*', *Review of English Studies*, 68/284 (2017), 342–67. I would like to thank the editors of these journals and Johns Hopkins University Press, Cambridge University Press, and Oxford University Press for permission to reproduce this material. Finally, thanks to the Society of Authors as the literary representative of the Estate of Virginia Woolf for permission to quote from the Monks House Papers.

Contents

List of Figures

Introduction

Modernism and the Anthropocene

In Virginia Woolf's *Orlando* (1928), the narrator ponders over the 'extraordinary discrepancy between time on the clock and time in the mind'.[1] The distinction is a suggestive one, yet it is curiously unable to account for much of what is most striking about the work's experiment with time: that Orlando lives through centuries, changes sex, and witnesses fluctuations in climate. Indeed, the young Orlando's imminent marriage is interrupted in the Jacobean age by the sudden appearance of 'the Great frost': birds 'froze in mid-air and fell like stones to the ground', and the King holds a carnival on the Thames which had 'frozen to a depth of twenty feet and more for six or seven miles on either side' (24–5). His plans to elope with Princess Sasha are confounded when she disappears during the sudden thaw, as people are swept out to sea on fragments of ice (44–5). Later, at the start of the nineteenth century, Orlando watches as a 'small cloud gathered behind the dome of St Paul's'; it darkens and spreads until a 'huge blackness sprawled over the whole of London': a 'change seemed to have come over the climate of England' (156–7). 'Climate' is used here in a capacious sense to include furniture and fashion, and as throughout the work, shifts in climate reflect ways of writing about weather as much as the weather itself: in this case, the target of parody is John Ruskin's 'The Storm-Cloud of the Nineteenth Century' (1884). Yet the shifts also correspond to real climatic changes. The 'Great frost' is based on those that occurred in the seventeenth century as part of 'The Little Ice Age', and the dark cloud reflects the London Fog which was caused principally by the burning of coal in domestic fires and industry. Woolf's playful conceit in which Orlando's life stretches across centuries queerly disrupts the conventions of biography, and makes visible major changes in climate which are now deemed to characterize the Anthropocene.

The Anthropocene is the name of a proposed geological epoch in which humans have fundamentally changed the Earth System and altered the course of the Earth's geological evolution. Having been used by the ecologist Eugene Stoermer in the 1980s, the term 'Anthropocene' was popularized by the atmospheric chemist Paul Crutzen at the beginning of the twenty-first century.[2] Crutzen argued that it

---

[1] Virginia Woolf, *Orlando*, ed. Brenda Lyons (London: Penguin, 2000), 68.
[2] See Will Steffen and others, 'The Anthropocene: Conceptual and Historical Perspectives', *Philosophical Transactions of the Royal Society A*, 369 (2011), 842–67, 843.

British Modernism and the Anthropocene. David Shackleton, Oxford University Press. © David Shackleton (2023).
DOI: 10.1093/oso/9780192857743.003.0001

'seems appropriate to assign the term "Anthropocene" to the present, in many ways human-dominated, geological epoch, supplementing the Holocene'.[3] That is, the Anthropocene would succeed the Holocene which began some 12,000 years ago, and become the most recent geological epoch in the Earth's 4.5 billion year history. There has been much debate about when the epoch should be thought to have started. Crutzen proposed the latter part of the eighteenth century, as the time of the Industrial Revolution and growing global concentrations of carbon dioxide and methane. Other proposals include an 'early Anthropocene' beginning with the spread of agriculture and deforestation about 8000 years ago; a date of 1492 or 1610 to correspond with the 'Columbian Exchange' of species following the colonization of the Americas; or a mid-twentieth century date to coincide with the 'Great Acceleration'—a period marked by rapid industrialization and population growth, the development of new plastics and persistent organic pollutants, and nuclear testing.[4] For geologists and Earth System scientists trying to ratify the Anthropocene as a geological epoch, the decision involves various technical considerations such as identifying a suitable stratigraphic marker—a physical trace that is left in the geological record. Although the epoch has yet to be formally ratified by the International Commission on Stratigraphy, in 2016 the 'Anthropocene Working Group' voted to accept the Anthropocene as stratigraphically real, and favoured a mid-twentieth century start date whose primary signal would be plutonium fallout.[5]

The recent concept of the Anthropocene provides an opportunity to return to modernism and assess what might retrospectively be identified as some of its environmental concerns, and its environmental politics. Partly, this involves reading modernism in relation to a set of contexts that includes fossil fuel energy systems, plantation labour and monocultures, climate change, and species extinctions. In turn, this book argues that some of the underappreciated environmental concerns of modernism promise to inflect the way that the current environmental crisis is conceived. Indeed, I introduce the term 'Anthropocene modernism' to describe a version of literary and cultural modernism that registers the environmental transformations such as climate change that are now considered to characterize the Anthropocene, and offers the possibility of rethinking the pressing environmental concerns of the present.

British Modernism and the Anthropocene thereby forms part of a recent ecocritical turn in modernist studies. At first sight, it might seem that modernism has little to offer to those concerned about the environment. As Anne Raine remarks,

---

[3] Paul J. Crutzen, 'Geology of Mankind', *Nature*, 415 (2002), 23; see also Paul J. Crutzen and Eugene F. Stoermer, 'The "Anthropocene"', *Global Change Newsletter*, 41 (2000), 17–18.
[4] For an overview of these proposals, see Colin N. Waters and others, 'The Anthropocene Is Functionally and Stratigraphically Distinct from the Holocene', *Science*, 351/6269 (2016), 137.
[5] See Jan Zalasiewicz and others (eds), *The Anthropocene as a Geological Time Unit: A Guide to the Scientific Evidence and Current Debate* (Cambridge: Cambridge University Press, 2019), 10.

ecocritics have been slow to come to modernism, partly because the movement was seen to define itself in opposition to 'nature', and to the literary genres of realist prose and romantic nature poetry that ecocritics tend to champion.[6] Similarly, Joshua Schuster notes that far less ecocritical attention has been devoted to modernism than to British and American romanticism and to environmentalist writing since the 1960s, and highlights the fact that certain modernists and members of the avant-garde showed patent environmental disregard. For example, the Italian Futurists and London-based Vorticists shared the sense that 'urban grime, smokestacks, and industrial waste, far from being debilitating, actually are energizing, invigorating, aesthetically promising manifestations of the modernist celebration of the new'.[7] If, as Michael Rubenstein and Justin Neuman suggest, modernist texts invite being read in relation to the 'environmental unconscious', then Futurism and Vorticism might be seen as expressions of modernism's ecological death drive.[8] Similar problems arise in relation to the modernist novel. In *The Great Derangement* (2016), Amitav Ghosh argues that the novel as a cultural form has failed to deal adequately with the phenomenon of climate change, and more alarmingly, that its representational failures have made it complicit with the expansion of the fossil fuel economy: its failure 'will have to be counted as an aspect of the broader imaginative and cultural failure that lies at the heart of the climate crisis'.[9] If realist novels—which are Ghosh's most immediate concern—are to be indicted for their failure to represent climate change, then modernist novels might be held even more culpable, insofar as they renounce the representational ambitions of realism to focus on psychological interiority. As Andrew Kalaidjian puts it, 'modernism's focus on interiority, the inner life, seems particularly ill-suited to illuminate the exterior world'.[10]

However, there has recently been a surge of ecocritical interest in modernism. For example, following Bonnie Kime Scott's and Alison Lacivita's single-author studies of Virginia Woolf and James Joyce, Kelly Sultzbach has brought a host of ecocritical approaches to bear on British modernism, and finds in the breaks and fissures of these works an awareness of the non-human world and an environmental consciousness; Kalaidjian adopts a complementary approach but pays greater attention to early environmentalist movements in identifying sites of environmental exhaustion and recovery; Jesse Oak Taylor highlights a distinctive 'climatic

---

[6] Anne Raine, 'Ecocriticism and Modernism', in *The Oxford Handbook of Ecocriticism*, ed. Greg Garrard (Oxford: Oxford University Press, 2014), 98–117, 99.

[7] Joshua Schuster, *The Ecology of Modernism: American Environments and Avant-Garde Poetics* (Tuscaloosa: University of Alabama Press, 2015), 7, 2.

[8] Michael Rubenstein and Justin Neuman, *Modernism and Its Environments* (London: Bloomsbury, 2020), 14.

[9] Amitav Ghosh, *The Great Derangement: Climate Change and the Unthinkable* (Chicago: University of Chicago Press, 2016), 61, 11, 8.

[10] Andrew Kalaidjian, *Exhausted Ecologies: Modernism and Environmental Recovery* (Cambridge: Cambridge University Press, 2020), 19.

modernism' as part of his wider study of the representation of the London Fog in literature; and a growing number of critics address modernism in relation to the Anthropocene.[11] In contributing to this ecocritical turn, this book seeks to follow Sultzbach's example of not providing 'a glossy patina of celebratory green' over works of modernism, and obfuscating 'the very conflicted reactions to environmental relationships and human responsibility that make them so productively messy'.[12] Clearly, not all modernists present us with perfectly ethical relationships to the non-human, just as not all modernists embrace pollution. Here, the recent debates about the Anthropocene provide a model for assessing the environmental politics of modernism.

In this study, part of the usefulness of the concept of Anthropocene lies in the fact that it has provoked such controversy. The concept has been fiercely debated outside geology and the Earth sciences, where it has gained a new life in the social sciences, the humanities, and the media. There, versions of the Anthropocene have been advanced that are less tied to the dictates of stratigraphy, but tend in wider senses to describe the impact that humans have had on the planet, including transformations of the landscape, urbanization, species extinctions, resource extraction, and waste dumping.[13] In his taxonomy of the grand narratives of the Anthropocene, Christophe Bonneuil identifies what he calls the 'dominant' version in which humans as a species are seen to have altered the Earth System at a geological scale, and distinguishes a techno-utopian variant that hopes for a 'good Anthropocene' to be realized through technology and geoengineering projects.[14] These narratives have been criticized for being universalist and technocratic, and alternative ways of conceptualizing environmental crisis have been advanced in their place. Donna Haraway proposes replacing 'Anthropocene' with 'Chthulucene' as the name of the epoch in which humans and non-humans are

[11] See Bonnie Kime Scott, *In the Hollow of the Wave: Virginia Woolf and Modernist Uses of Nature* (Charlottesville: University of Virginia Press, 2012); Alison Lacivita, *The Ecology of* Finnegans Wake (Gainesville: University of Florida Press, 2015); Kelly Sultzbach, *Ecocriticism in the Modernist Imagination: Forster, Woolf and Auden* (Cambridge: Cambridge University Press, 2016); Kalaidjian, *Ecologies*; Jesse Oak Taylor, *The Sky of Our Manufacture: The London Fog in British Fiction from Dickens to Woolf* (Charlottesville: University of Virginia Press, 2016); Rubenstein and Neuman, *Modernism*; Jon Hegglund and John McIntyre (eds), *Modernism and the Anthropocene: Material Ecologies of Twentieth-Century Literature* (Lanham: Lexington Books, 2021); Peter Adkins, *The Modernist Anthropocene: Nonhuman Life and Planetary Change in James Joyce, Virginia Woolf and Djuna Barnes* (Edinburgh: Edinburgh University Press, 2022); and Jeremy Diaper (ed), *Eco-Modernism: Ecology, Environment and Nature in Literary Modernism* (Clemson: Clemson University Press, 2022).
[12] Sultzbach, *Ecocriticism*, 6.
[13] See Clive Hamilton, Christophe Bonneuil, and François Gemenne, 'Thinking the Anthropocene', in *The Anthropocene and the Global Environmental Crisis: Rethinking Modernity in a New Epoch*, ed. Clive Hamilton and others (Abingdon: Routledge, 2015), 1–13, 3.
[14] Christophe Bonneuil, 'The Geological Turn: Narratives of the Anthropocene', in *The Anthropocene and the Global Environmental Crisis*, 17–31, 18–26. As Bonneuil points out, Anthropocene narratives 'preclude or promote some kinds of collective action rather than others', and so 'the kind of stories we tell ourselves today about the Anthropocene can shape the kind of geohistorical future we will inhabit' (30, 17).

inextricably linked in tentacular practices, and advocates multispecies feminist practices of 'making kin'.[15] Jason Moore develops the idea of the 'Capitalocene' and world-ecology, which holds that capitalism—rather than an undifferentiated 'mankind'—has caused environmental destruction over a period of several hundred years.[16] Combining a world-ecological approach with a tradition of Black radicalism, Françoise Vergès calls for a conception of the 'racial Capitalocene' that would pay especial attention to the devastation produced by colonialism and racial capital.[17] And Malcom Ferdinand champions a version of the 'Plantationocene' to highlight the destructive transformations wrought by the Caribbean plantation system.[18] Others would dispense with the concept and its variants altogether, arguing that they diminish rather than improve the chances of equitable and efficacious responses to ecological crisis.[19]

Here, my approach is to use the debates about the Anthropocene as a means of assessing the environmental politics of modernism. The range of positions within the Anthropocene debates serves as a useful model for distinguishing the environmental politics of different modernists. For example, we will see that H. G. Wells anticipates optimistic accounts of a 'good Anthropocene' by acknowledging that humans have caused environmental destruction on geological and planetary scales, but holding that they could redirect their power to utopian ends through suitable cosmopolitan projects. By contrast, the other modernists addressed here implicitly or explicitly depart from Wells's confidence in progress, and provide alternative ways of thinking about environmental history. Partly, to draw parallels between modernism and recent narratives of the Anthropocene serves to highlight aspects of modernist experiments with time and history that have been overlooked. Yet once recognized, these experiments provide rich resources for rethinking the current environmental crisis.

Modernism and the politics of time

This book explores how H. G. Wells, D. H. Lawrence, Olive Moore, Virginia Woolf, and Jean Rhys undertook experiments with time in their novels that refigure history and the historical situations into which they were thrown. Much as Woolf

---

[15] See Donna Haraway, *Staying with the Trouble: Making Kin in the Chthulucene* (Durham, NC: Duke University Press, 2016).

[16] See Jason W. Moore (ed), *Anthropocene or Capitalocene?: Nature, History, and the Crisis of Capitalism* (Oakland: PM Press, 2016); and Jason W. Moore, *Capitalism in the Web of Life: Ecology and the Accumulation of Capital* (London: Verso, 2015).

[17] See Françoise Vergès, 'Racial Capitalocene', in *Futures of Black Radicalism*, ed. Gaye Theresa Johnson and Alex Lubin (London: Verso, 2017), 72–82.

[18] See Malcom Ferdinand, *Decolonial Ecology: Thinking from the Caribbean World*, trans. Anthony Paul Smith (Cambridge: Polity, 2021).

[19] See Jeremy Davies, *The Birth of the Anthropocene* (Oakland: University of California Press, 2016), 51–5.

plays with the conventions of biography to imagine Orlando living through several historical ages and witnessing changes in climate, so the other writers addressed here experiment with types of time that underpin various conceptions of history. Wells humanizes and politicizes geological time by plotting history against vast temporal expanses. Lawrence adapts Friedrich Nietzsche's thought of eternal recurrence to portray new forms of temporal experience and wider epochal schemes of history. Moore imagines a queer environmentalism that put into question the reproduction of the conditions of production of a fossil fuel capitalism. And Rhys creates melancholic narratives that refuse to forget the historical losses sustained on Caribbean plantations. In addressing such experiments with time, this book turns its attention away from the short timespans across which the individual life is lived, to the longer timespans across which history unfolds. Moreover, it turns from individual to communal temporal experience: away from private individual consciousness as the privileged site of temporality, to forms of time that can bring a community together in a shared sense of time and history. And finally, it moves its focus from the sense of meaning that arises from the pattern or shape of an individual life, to the sense of meaning that arises from the pattern and shape of history.

It might sound strange to talk about types of modernist time that open onto schemes of history given that, as Adam Barrows explains, there is a long critical tradition that portrays the modernist concern with time as an escape from history.[20] To recapitulate briefly, this tradition interprets modernist experiments with time in terms of what is described as 'subjective', 'interior', or 'private' time, which is counterposed to 'objective', 'exterior', or 'public' time. If a philosophical account is invoked to explicate this opposition, it is most commonly Henri Bergson's distinction between *durée* and clock-time. Modernist writers are seen as deploying innovative narrative strategies to explore varieties of private time as a response to an increasingly homogeneous public time, in a manner that has been both derided and celebrated. György Lukács famously criticized the modernist novel for forsaking the realist ambition of situating its protagonists within the 'objective time' of history, and attempting instead to portray 'subjective time' in which the individual turns away from society and retreats into the inner world of their consciousness.[21] More sympathetically, Randall Stevenson has recently argued that modernist explorations of time in the mind provide 'Utopian compensation' for newly standardized times and the pressures of history.[22]

[20] Adam Barrows, *The Cosmic Time of Empire: Modern Britain and World Literature* (Berkeley: University of California Press, 2011), 4–13, 54–60.
[21] Georg Lukács, *The Meaning of Contemporary Realism*, trans. John and Necke Mander (London: Merlin Press, 1963), 38. As Barrows points out, Lukács's critique has contributed towards the common view of modernist time as a 'reactionary cultural formation' expressing a 'deliberate retreat from crassly material or "political" engagements' (*Cosmic Time*, 4).
[22] See Randall Stevenson, *Reading the Times: Temporality and History in Twentieth-Century Fiction* (Edinburgh: Edinburgh University Press, 2018), 26.

The distinction between public and private time—which corresponds closely to that in *Orlando* between 'time on the clock' and 'time in the mind'—has great explanatory value. However, among its disadvantages are that it tends to obscure the communal and historical dimensions of modernist experiments with time, and to lead to misrepresentations of the politics of these experiments. Indeed, many recent studies of modernist time displace such a distinction, and provide revised accounts of the politics of modernist time. For example, Barrows foregrounds the distinction between national and global time to explore the relationship between time and empire; Paul Saint-Amour addresses interwar structures of anticipation in relation to total war; Jesse Matz argues that modernists sought to cultivate a range of temporal environments; Charles Tung allies modernism with time travel fiction to argue that both defamiliarize time in order to produce 'heterochrony' and reconceive historicity; Kate Haffey identifies instances of queer temporality; and Beryl Pong advances a compelling account of Second World Wartime.[23] This book contributes to what Pong describes as the revisionist effort to demonstrate that politics are at the heart, rather than periphery, of modernist experiments with time.[24] In order to elucidate the communal and historical aspects of modernist time, I will turn to Martin Heidegger's account of temporality and Paul Ricoeur's theory of threefold mimesis. Barrows has argued that it is 'possible and productive to rethink the politics of modernism through the politics of time.'[25] This book undertakes this task with appeal to Heidegger and Ricoeur, although with a narrower focus on environmental politics: it is an attempt to rethink the environmental politics of modernism through the politics of time.

In the second division of *Being and Time* (1927), Heidegger advances an account of different levels of temporality—ecstatic-horizonal temporality (*Zeitlichkeit*), historicality (*Geschichtlichkeit*), and within-timeness (*Innerzeitigkeit*)—that can be used to theorize time in the modernist novel. *Being and Time* is particularly useful for rethinking modernist time outside the confines of the distinction between 'subjective' and 'objective' time, as it is driven by the attempt to break free from a metaphysics that is bound by the subject/object dichotomy. Most immediately, 'historicality' provides a means of elucidating the historical and communal aspects of modernist experiments with time. Much as Heidegger characterizes 'historicality' as a temporal structure in which Dasein 'stretches' itself

---

[23] See Paul Saint-Amour, *Tense Future: Modernism, Total War, Encyclopedic Form* (New York: Oxford University Press, 2015); Jesse Matz, *Modernist Time Ecology* (Baltimore: John Hopkins University Press, 2018); Charles Tung, *Modernism and Time Machines* (Edinburgh: Edinburgh University Press, 2019); Kate Haffey, *Literary Modernism, Queer Temporality: Eddies in Time* (Cham: Palgrave Macmillan, 2019); and Beryl Pong, *British Literature and Culture in Second World Wartime: For the Duration* (Oxford: Oxford University Press, 2020). See also Jean-Michel Rabaté and Angeliki Spiropoulou (eds), *Historical Modernisms: Time, History and Modernist Aesthetics* (London: Bloomsbury, 2022).

[24] Pong, *Wartime*, 19.

[25] Barrows, *Cosmic Time*, 4.

between birth and death and across history, so modernists experimented with different types of 'temporal stretching' in their novels.[26] Here, Orlando's stretching across centuries of history might be compared to the way that the audience stretches between the acts of history as portrayed by Miss La Trobe's pageant in Woolf's last novel; Ruth's life is queerly stretched in Moore's *Spleen* (1930), as she tries to live outside the conventional markers of birth, adolescence, marriage, birth, old age, and death; and Anna's identity is dislocated in Rhys's *Voyage in the Dark* (1934), as she is stretched between her past in Dominica and her present in England.

Concurrently, Heidegger's account of levels of temporality can be used to characterize temporal consciousness in the Anthropocene. His analysis of 'within-timeness' supplies a vocabulary for describing the sorts of 'reckoning with time' that are required by challenges such as global warming, and his conception of 'historicality' provides a way of characterizing shifting forms of historical consciousness in the Anthropocene.[27] The fact that Heidegger accords priority to the future in his account of temporality proves to be a virtue in this context: it enables explication of anticipatory aspects of temporal consciousness in the Anthropocene, including future-oriented structures of risk-consciousness, and associated affective states such as eco-anxiety.[28] Perhaps counter-intuitively, it also proves to be a virtue of Heidegger's analysis of temporality that—like other philosophical approaches in the phenomenological tradition to which it belongs—it struggles to account for conceptions of time employed in the natural sciences, including geological time.[29] For our purposes, the levels of temporality described by Heidegger can be set against an incommensurate geological time, as a characterization of the temporal situation in the Anthropocene.

While Heidegger's account of temporality provides a means of theorizing time in the modernist novel and in the Anthropocene, it can be supplemented by Ricoeur's celebrated account of the way that narrative shapes people's experience of time through 'threefold mimesis'. For Ricoeur, 'mimesis 1' refers to the way that

---

[26] See Martin Heidegger, *Being and Time*, trans. John Macquarrie and Edward Robinson (Oxford: Blackwell Publishing, 2006), 425–7. The priority that Heidegger accords to 'Being-with' over 'Being-alone' might redirect attention to communal aspects of modernist temporality (156–7).

[27] In an article in which he expresses his regret that Heidegger's later work has been embraced by eco-critics, Greg Garrard remarks suggestively in a footnote that it is 'unfortunate . . . that Heidegger's early philosophy of temporality . . . which presents some intriguing ideas to a pragmatic ecocriticism, has been more or less wholly eclipsed by his later, far more involuted "homey murmurings"' ('Heidegger Nazism Ecocriticism', *ISLE*, 17/2 (2010), 251–71, 269).

[28] Heidegger flags that in contrast to the way that time is ordinarily understood on the basis of the 'Present', ecstatico-horizonal temporality 'temporalizes itself *primarily* in terms of the *future*' (*Being and Time*, 479).

[29] Tellingly, Heidegger remarks in a footnote to *Being and Time* that the connections between 'world-time as calculated astronomically, and the temporality and historicality of Dasein need a more extensive investigation' (499). Similarly, Edmund Husserl struggles to reconstruct a 'world-time' on the basis of an internal time-consciousness, and Maurice Merleau-Ponty boldly contends that it is philosophically meaningless to talk about 'the world before man's appearance on it' (*Phenomenology of Perception*, trans. Colin Smith (London: Routledge, 2002), 502).

a person understands action and orients themselves in time; 'mimesis 2' concerns the way that narratives imitate action, and in so doing 'configures' time in particular ways; and 'mimesis 3' describes the way that engaging with a narrative can 'refigure' the way that a person orients themselves in time. The three types of mimesis form stages in a circular process: the way that a person orients themselves in time is shaped by the narratives that they have encountered previously; each time they encounter a new narrative, their temporal understanding of the world is slightly modified.[30] Noting that Ricoeur analyses three modernist novels to illustrate narrative's ability to represent time, Matz extends this account of threefold mimesis to provide a broader explication of time in the modernist novel. For Matz, modernist novels are remarkable for their attempts to refigure their readers' experience of time, and to 'cultivate our temporal environment'.[31] It can be added that they do so by exploring temporal possibilities not just on the individual level but also on the historical: they refigure their readers' experiences of historical time, and shape the time of modernity.

Notably, modernist novels can register and inflect different temporal experiences of modernity. Drawing on Heidegger, Reinhart Koselleck offers an analysis of the temporal structure of modernity. He combines a reconstruction of the semantic prehistory of the term '*Neuzeit*' (literally, 'new time')—a German term for modernity which is found in its composite form only after 1870—with a characterization of the temporal form of modernity that is closely modelled on Heidegger's conception of ecstatic-horizonal temporality: modernity is a new form of historical consciousness that is structured by the tension between a 'space of experience' and a 'horizon of expectation'.[32] Peter Osborne emphasizes that there is not just one temporal structure of modernity, but rather that modernity contains 'a range of possible temporalizations of history within its fundamental, most abstract temporal form'. He adds that the competition between these temporalizations gives rise to the idea of a 'politics of time'.[33] Ricoeur's theory of threefold mimesis suggests how modernist novels can register various temporal experiences of modernity (mimesis 2), and refigure those experiences in political ways (mimesis 3). For example, we will see that Wells's utopias distend the horizon of expectation by imagining future ecological hazards, and Rhys's melancholic narrative refigures the time of modernity by refusing to forget historical losses sustained in the Caribbean.

---

[30] See Paul Ricoeur, *Time and Narrative*, trans. Kathleen McLaughlin and David Pellauer, 3 vols (Chicago: University of Chicago Press, 1984–88), I, 52–87.

[31] Matz, *Time Ecology*, 10–13, 48.

[32] Reinhart Koselleck, *Futures Past: On the Semantics of Historical Time*, trans. Keith Tribe (Cambridge: MIT Press, 1985), 259–61. For Koselleck, 'it is the tension between experience and expectation which, in ever-changing patterns, brings about new resolutions and through this generates historical time' (262).

[33] Peter Osborne, *The Politics of Time: Modernity and Avant-Garde* (London: Verso, 1995), 116.

Using the idea of a 'politics of time', it is possible to assess the environmental politics of modernism by evaluating its competing temporalizations of history. To return to the example of Futurism: F. T. Marinetti's proclamation of a radical break with the past, and an embrace of the future in the form of machines and pollution, constitutes one avant-garde temporalization of history. But it contrasts with other strains of modernism whose environmental politics are expressed in the contrasting attitudes that they adopt towards modernity and history. Ironically, it is partly because modernism embraces the temporal logic of modernity in its drive to innovate and experiment that it provides such rich resources for rethinking environmental crisis. Fredric Jameson argues that the modernist desire to 'make it new' follows the logic of the commodity form and the market.[34] Yet within the innovative narrative forms of modernist novels are encoded various critiques of the temporal logic of modernity, and alternative temporalizations of history that register the environmental destruction caused by the modern world-system.

Ricoeur's theory of threefold mimesis can also be applied to narratives of environmental crisis, including the grand narratives of the Anthropocene. It is particularly useful in this context, as it is an account of narrative's ability to mediate between lived and cosmic time. Ricoeur argues that there are deep and likely intractable differences between 'phenomenological' and 'cosmological' accounts of time, but that the opposition can be bridged by narrative, which inscribes lived time onto cosmic time in the form of historical time.[35] He investigates the aporias of time within a philosophical tradition, yet similar aporias have resurfaced with the concept of the Anthropocene, which pits human history against the expanses of geological time. His analysis thereby intimates the importance of narrative in negotiating what Dipesh Chakrabarty describes as the situation in which 'the geologic now of the Anthropocene has become entangled with the now of human history'.[36] Indeed, the recent proliferation of grand narratives of environmental crisis— including techno-utopian, feminist, Marxist, and decolonial variants—might be seen as competing ways of situating humans meaningfully within geohistory. Ricoeur's notion of a 'semantics of action' can be used to articulate the political stakes of such narratives.

Environmental narratives refigure what Ricoeur describes as people's understanding of the 'meaningful structures' of action. For Ricoeur, narratives modify the 'structural' as well as the 'temporal' aspects of their readers' worlds of action, including their understanding of agents, events, goals, interaction, and responsibility.[37] This function of narrative is particularly significant in the context of

---

[34] Fredric Jameson, *A Singular Modernity: Essay on the Ontology of the Present* (London: Verso, 2002), 151–4.

[35] Ricoeur, *Time and Narrative*, III, 4, 99.

[36] Dipesh Chakrabarty, *The Climate of History in a Planetary Age* (Chicago: University of Chicago Press, 2021), 36.

[37] Ricoeur, *Time and Narrative*, I, 54–6.

the Anthropocene.[38] For example, Chakrabarty influentially argues that the idea that humans have become a geophysical force necessitates rethinking the concept of human agency: 'the current conjuncture of globalization and global warming leaves us with the challenge of having to think of human agency over multiple and incommensurable scales at once.'[39] Indeed, scholars have drawn on a host of critical discourses, including actor–network theory, the new materialisms, and object-oriented ontology, to theorize agency at the time of the Anthropocene.[40] While acknowledging the value of such theorizations, we should also recognize that the concept of agency is shaped by narratives of environmental crisis. The concept is progressively inflected by the stories that are told about the Anthropocene, in a cyclical process of threefold mimesis. In turn, the stories that are told about environmental crisis open and close various possibilities of political action.

This book borrows its subtitle from J. W. Dunne's An Experiment with Time (1927). It redeploys 'experiments with time' to describe both the well-known preoccupation with time shared by many writers and artists in the early twentieth century—a preoccupation that Wyndham Lewis attacks with gusto in Time and Western Man (1927)—and the way that grand narratives of the Anthropocene resituate human history within geological time. Yet it also describes the way that reading modernist novels alongside narratives of the Anthropocene can produce new understandings of the environmental crisis. For example, reading the two together can refigure our conceptions of human and non-human agency. More generally, the ability of modernist novels to inflect the conceptual-temporal structure of modernity has particular significance at a time when the speed and scale of environmental shifts occurring on Earth demand nothing less than a complete rethinking of modernization and modernity.[41] The exceptional ability of modernist novels to refigure time and meaningful structures of action allows a way of reconceptualizing the environmental crisis, and rethinking issues of scale, agency, and responsibility in the Anthropocene.

Paradoxically, it is the representational failures of modernist novels that are most significant in the context of environmental crisis. The early twentieth century was marked by environmental transformations that were so complex and

---

[38] Matz flags the latent political significance of Ricoeur's conception of the 'semantics of action'. He points out that although Ricoeur's phenomenological hermeneutics 'does not dwell on situated practice', it 'remains to apply his approach to what we might call the *happenstance* of narrative temporality—the actual occasions on which the circle of time and narrative comes around to contingent social action and shared human understanding' (*Time Ecology*, 28).

[39] Dipesh Chakrabarty, 'Postcolonial Studies and the Challenge of Climate Change', *New Literary History*, 43/1 (2012), 1–18, 1.

[40] See, in particular, Bruno Latour, 'Agency at the Time of the Anthropocene', *New Literary History*, 45/1 (2014), 1–18; Jane Bennett, *Vibrant Matter: A Political Ecology of Things* (Durham, NC: Duke University Press, 2010); and *New Materialisms: Ontology, Agency, and Politics*, ed. Diana Coole and Samantha Frost (Durham, NC: Duke University Press, 2010). The new materialisms, including their reconceptualizations of agency, have been adapted in literary studies by 'material ecocriticism': see *Material Ecocriticism*, ed. Serenella Iovino and Serpil Opperman (Bloomington: Indiana, 2014).

[41] See Hamilton, Bonneuil, and Gemenne, 'Thinking the Anthropocene', 5.

happened on such great scales that they defied representation. Modernist novelists responded with a range of innovative narrative forms that start to make environmental crisis on a planetary scale visible, yet it is their failures to represent such a crisis that achieve the greatest success. The following chapters explore how British modernists employed types of narrative breakdown—including fragmentation and faltering passages devoid of events—to expose the limitations of human schemes of meaning, negotiate the relationship between different scales and types of time, produce knowledge of ecological risk, and register various forms of non-human agency.

Chapter 1 addresses H. G. Wells's engagements with geology and ecology. Although often confined to the peripheries of modernism, Wells drew on his scientific training to develop literary and historiographic forms that start to make phenomena such as climate change and mass species extinctions visible. The chapter starts by placing *The Time Machine* (1895) in the context of geological literature, showing how Wells reworks the conceit of time travel, tropes of ruin, and a fragmentary aesthetic to imagine the effects of human agency over vast timescales. It then analyses the politicization of geological time in his universal histories, *The Outline of History* (1920) and *A Short History of the World* (1922). Therein, Wells reframes history on geological and planetary scales, and seeks to redirect the destructive power of humans to positive ends through the formation of a cosmopolitan World State. Turning to his 'discovery of the future', the chapter finishes by considering three of his utopias, in which he imagines societies that have overcome the threat of extinction to achieve efficient control over non-human species and the planet's natural resources. In doing so, Wells mirrors the anthropocentrism and human exceptionalism of early ecological science, and anticipates some recent accounts of the Anthropocene. However, the value of his utopias lies less in their proposed environmental solutions than in the ability of their aesthetic form to produce knowledge about ecological risk.

Chapter 2 examines D. H. Lawrence's creative adaptations of Friedrich Nietzsche's thought of eternal recurrence in his coalfield fiction. It charts how Lawrence uses Nietzsche's thought to imagine various forms of rupture in historical time, and the inauguration of a new age. Much like the epochal shift marked by the Anthropocene, Lawrence's visions of historical transformation express an environmental politics. In *Women in Love* (1920), the thought is used to portray mechanical repetition and Gerald's ruthless industrial spoliation of the earth, whereas in *Lady Chatterley's Lover* (1928) it is reimagined as part of Connie and Mellors's desire for a green revaluation of the earth. Rather than involving a retreat from politics and history, Lawrence uses sex and the body to explore intertwined social and environmental crises, and to imagine a transition beyond an industrial system based on the exploitation of workers and the extraction of fossil fuels.

Chapter 3 addresses Olive Moore's novel *Spleen* (1930), in which the main character Ruth is thrown into crisis by her pregnancy and struggles against a conception of 'nature' that dictates that her role as a woman is to be a mother. Instead, she cultivates a 'queer environmentalism' that rejects reproductive futurism, and includes her attempt to counteract the pollution that she encounters in London. The novel, tightly focalized around Ruth, does not provide a comprehensive representation of London's changing climate. Nevertheless, the very limitations of its representation—the partial glimpses it affords of fume-filled alleys and bedraggled hunger marchers—point towards wider historical transformations: of a fossil fuel industry that led to starvation for many of its workers, and that drove climate change on a planetary scale. Reading the novel in the context of early twentieth-century environmental movements, highlighting its literary impressionism, and drawing on more recent queer theory, this chapter argues that *Spleen* should be recognized as a subversive work of Anthropocene modernism. Like other works of modernist queer ecology, it offers anticipatory illuminations of a queer environmental politics and activism that is not yet here.

Chapter 4 argues that Virginia Woolf's fiction provides a model for rethinking agency in the Anthropocene. Drawing attention to her abiding interest in the way that history is written, this chapter compares *To the Lighthouse* (1927) to the experimental historiography of the Annales school. Woolf and the Annalistes share a distaste for 'great men' conceptions of history, and both turn to different scales and types of time to displace emphasis from individuals and events. Yet whereas the Annalistes reject narrative as unsuitable for history on medium and long timescales, Woolf experiments with quasi-plots to convey a sense of history as composed of multiple processes unfolding at different speeds and on different scales. The chapter then turns to *Between the Acts* (1940), in which Woolf uses the affordances of drama to explore the relationship between human and natural history at a time of historical crisis. Throughout, Woolf's fiction achieves what might be called a 'feminist scale critique': her narrative experiments with scale unsettle familiar conceptions of human agency, and displace 'great men' from the centre of history and fiction. Her representations of agency contrast markedly with those of Wells, and might be redeployed to counteract recent masculinist strains of Anthropocene discourse.

Chapter 5 reads Jean Rhys's *Voyage in the Dark* (1934) in light of Simon Lewis and Mark Maslin's account of the Anthropocene, which dates the epoch as starting at the time of the 'Columbian Exchange' of biotas following the colonization of the Americas. On the surface, Rhys's novel seems ill-equipped to register the environmental transformations that are now deemed to characterize the Anthropocene. However, this chapter argues that by rendering Anna's states of distraction through an innovative narrative form, Rhys's novel opens up a historical counter-narrative in which the Caribbean plantation system and its brutal regimes of labour are seen to have underpinned modernity. Having read Anna's states of distraction in the context of attempts to mitigate 'wasted time' on Caribbean plantations through the imposition of time discipline and the use of hurricane insurance, the chapter suggests that recognizing the importance of the Caribbean plantation system necessitates a rethinking of literary history and the scope of Anthropocene modernism.

Channelling a critical counter-mood from the previous chapter, the book concludes by calling for a modernist world-ecology. In response to recent calls for 'weak theory' to be used to generate a strong field of modernism, this conclusion argues that environmental approaches to modernism are better served by using unfashionably 'strong theory'. Specifically, it appeals to the Warwick Research Collective's theory of world-literature as a means of scaling-up environmental approaches to modernism. It is not just a question of how certain writers represent (or fail to represent) environmental transformations that occur on a planetary scale, but also of comparing how writers from different locations in the world register that crisis. By virtue of their concerns with time and history that makes them so adept at rendering different experiences of modernity, works of modernist world-literature promise to enrich the understanding of the environmental crisis supplied by the Capitalocene and the Plantationocene, in what would constitute a distinctively modernist world-ecology. Reading works of modernist world-literature can thereby open better ways of being in the world, and better possibilities of political action.

It should be acknowledged that, in assessing the environmental politics of modernism, this book restricts its scope to focus on a range of (largely) canonical British modernists. It addresses novels at the expense of poetry and other art forms, on the grounds that novelistic narratives are particularly adept at configuring time. And as it is animated by the conviction that analysing these configurations can lead to an understanding of the politics of modernism and reshape the time of modernity, it approaches a small number of novels on what Saint-Amour calls the 'middle scales', as opposed to the microscales associated with topic modelling keyed to particular stems, terms, titles, and devices, or to the macroscales associated with distant reading and quantitative approaches to large literary corpuses.[42]

It should also be flagged that, by reading modernist novels alongside narratives of the Anthropocene, this book departs from some of the protocols of a historicist literary criticism. The concept of the Anthropocene is a recent one, and so modernism falls before the period that Kate Marshall describes as the 'reflexive phase' of the epoch, in which writers self-consciously engage with the concept.[43] To talk about modernism in relation to the concept is to risk anachronistically imposing a recent set of concerns onto an earlier period. This is perhaps nowhere more evident than in my use of the term 'environmental politics', given the significant differences in the ways that 'environments' were conceived then and now,

---

[42] See Paul Saint-Amour, 'The Medial Humanities: Toward a Manifesto for Meso-Analysis', *Modernism/modernity* Print Plus, 3/4 (2019). <https://doi.org/10.26597/mod.0092>

[43] Kate Marshall, 'What Are the Novels of the Anthropocene? American Fiction in Geological Time', *American Literary History*, 27/3 (2015), 523–38, 525.

and in the priorities of early and recent 'environmentalist' movements.[44] However, the desire of this book to read modernism in relation to the environmental concerns of the present necessitates some methodological departures from a historicist approach, which might be described by redeploying its understanding of time and narrative to literary history.

Combining Heidegger's account of temporality with Ricoeur's theory of narrative provides a model for returning to modernism, and re-reading it in light of the pressing environmental concerns of the present. Heidegger characterizes historicality as a structure in which past possibilities of being can be retrieved and repeated, and describes such repetition as 'the possibility that Dasein may choose its hero'.[45] Ricoeur argues that literary works 'unfold' worlds with particular temporal structures, and so can be thought of as repositories of past ways of 'being-in-the-world'.[46] Heidegger's notion of repetition can be redeployed to literary history, and to the novels that—according to Ricoeur—configure time in various ways and thereby contain past possibilities of being. Analysing the rich timescapes of modernist novels, and reading them alongside recent narratives of environmental crisis, promises to refigure our temporal consciousness in the Anthropocene. Learning from the heroic achievements—and villainous failings—of modernist novels allows us to refigure Anthropocene time, cultivate new structures of environmental care and concern, and open new possibilities of political action.

---

[44] See Schuster, *Ecology*, 3, 8; and Rubenstein and Neuman, *Modernism*, 4–7.
[45] Heidegger, *Being and Time*, 437.
[46] Ricoeur, *Time and Narrative*, I, 78–81.

1

H. G. Wells, Geology, and Ecological Risk

In H. G. Wells's short story 'A Vision of the Past' (1887), the narrator dreams that he was 'borne rapidly through a swiftly changing scene' to the remote geological past, where he encounters some reptile-like creatures conversing about their position in the universe. Pointing to the strata displayed in a nearby cliff and the 'facts which they record of the past history of this earth', the creatures congratulate themselves on being the 'culminating point of all existence'. To the obvious displeasure of the creatures, the narrator interjects that they will be wholly extinct in 'a few million years', and that instead it is his kind who 'through the endless æons of the future, will never cease their onward march towards infinite perfection'.[1] The joke is—presumably—that the narrator is just as guilty of arrogance in thinking that he is the summit of creation as the amphibians. The story is an early example of one of Wells's abiding concerns: to situate humans within the perspectives of deep time (and more generally within the cosmos as it was described by contemporary science), and to explore whether within these new perspectives—as two friends argue in another of his early stories—'man' is to be conceived as 'altogether the biggest thing in [the] world', or 'less than an iota in the infinite universe'.[2]

Wells's project of imagining humans in relation to deep time has much in common with the more recent discourse of the Anthropocene. The Anthropocene conceives the present geological epoch as one in which humans have emerged as a planetary force or agent, comparable to other geophysical forces such as the asteroids, ocean currents, or volcanoes that have in the past precipitated climate change or mass extinctions, leaving their traces in the geological record. The concept thereby powerfully assigns culpability to humans for their role in phenomena such as climate change and species extinctions, highlights the vulnerability of humans to such large-scale changes, and opens an ethical or political horizon for taking action on these issues. Yet, as Dipesh Chakrabarty observes, '[t]o call human beings geological agents is to scale up our imagination of the human': it 'leaves us with the challenge of having to think of human agency over multiple and incommensurable scales at once'.[3] While this challenge might be taken up by

---

[1] H. G. Wells, 'A Vision of the Past', in *Early Writings in Science and Science Fiction*, ed. Robert M. Philmus and David Y. Hughes (Berkeley: University of California Press, 1975), 153–7, 153, 155–6.

[2] H. G. Wells, 'A Talk with Gryllotalpa' [1887], in *Early Writings*, 19–21, 20.

[3] Dipesh Chakrabarty, *The Climate of History in a Planetary Age* (Chicago: University of Chicago Press, 2021), 31; 'Postcolonial Studies and the Challenge of Climate Change', *New Literary History*, 43/1 (2012), 1–18, 1.

British Modernism and the Anthropocene. David Shackleton, Oxford University Press. © David Shackleton (2023). DOI: 10.1093/oso/9780192857743.003.0002

philosophers, historians, writers, and artists, Ursula Heise notes that literary critics have been giving serious attention to how existing forms of literature might provide models for this imaginative task. Immersed in the nineteenth-century science in which modern conceptions of geological time were formed, Wells created a number of such models: his writing provides resources for—as Heise puts it—'telling the story of our climate-changed presents and futures'.[4]

Well's experiments with deep time thereby form an important part of Anthropocene modernism. Mark McGurl calls 'posthuman comedy' those works of fiction, and particularly science fiction and horror, that are 'willing to risk artistic ludicrousness' in their representation of the spatiotemporal vastness of the non-human world.[5] Certainly, it is not difficult to detect the ludicrousness of 'A Vision of the Past', in which three-eyed amphibians from the remote geological past talk to each other in a faux-archaic dialect. Such ludicrousness might be seen as a reason for excluding Wells from the hallowed precincts of modernism. However, taking *The Time Machine* as a central case study and building on a longer trend of expanding modernism to include what were once considered disreputably 'low' forms of culture, Charles Tung makes a compelling case for including time travel fiction within modernism. Bringing genre fiction's badness together with what he calls 'long-range modernism', he argues that 'the period's explorations of inhuman time are examples of baddest modernism'.[6] Similarly, Sarah Cole notes that Wells's project of overlaying 'the age and size of the universe onto all of his writing', and his belief that writing 'could and should change the course of history', set him at odds with many of his modernist contemporaries, but argues that both should be understood as part of a 'broader and more capacious modernism'. This chapter follows Cole's counsel that returning to Wells becomes especially pertinent 'as the geological scales governing the earth come into vivid focus in our era of climate peril'.[7] While it will remain attentive to the ludicrousness of Wells's writing as his various forms bend and buckle under the demands of representing spatiotemporal vastness, it will also attend to the political dangers of some of his later engagements with deep time. If, as Chakrabarty suggests, the Anthropocene challenges us to scale up our imagination of the human, then Wells's later visions of deep time stand as a warning of the political dangers that can accompany such a rescaling.

Reading Wells alongside other Anthropocene modernists such as Virginia Woolf allows both to be seen as responding to similar problems of scale. In her essay 'Poetry, Fiction and the Future' (1927), Woolf remarks that modern writers

[4] Ursula K. Heise, 'Science Fiction and the Time Scales of the Anthropocene', *ELH*, 86/2 (2019), 275–304, 278–9.
[5] Mark McGurl, 'The Posthuman Comedy', *Critical Inquiry*, 38/3 (2012), 533–53, 537–9.
[6] Charles Tung, 'Baddest Modernism: The Scales and Lines of Inhuman Time', *Modernism/modernity*, 23/3 (2016), 515–38, 518.
[7] Sarah Cole, *Inventing Tomorrow: H. G. Wells and the Twentieth Century* (New York: Columbia University Press, 2019), 2, 4, 9.

are 'forcing the form they use to contain a meaning which is strange to it': lyric poetry, for example, is unsuited to express the 'unmanageable emotions' connected with the belief that 'the age of the earth is 3,000,000,000 years; that human life lasts but a second; that the capacity of the human mind is nevertheless boundless'. She predicts instead that '[t]hat cannibal, the novel, which has devoured so many forms of art will [...] [devour] even more', and by so doing may 'serve to express some of those feelings'.[8] Woolf's account of the emergence of new literary forms can be applied to Wells's experiments with genre, as well as to her own. In *The Time Machine* (1895)—his most significant early experiment with deep time— Wells rescales the novel to the level of deep time by incorporating forms of science as well as of art.[9] Specifically, he redeploys strategies that geologists used to facilitate the imagination of deep time as part of their project of historicizing the Earth. Having traced his configuration of geological time in *The Time Machine* and his universal histories, *The Outline of History* (1920) and *A Short History of the World* (1922), this chapter turns to Wells's 'discovery of the future', and his engagement with biological and ecological science in his utopias.

The imaginative resources that Wells reworks from geological, biological, and ecological science might seem strangely familiar, given that they recur in the discourse of the Anthropocene. This is because, like the novel on Woolf's assessment, Anthropocene discourse exhibits cannibalistic tendencies. Driven by the scale and complexity of phenomena like climate change and the inability of existing disciplines to address such challenges adequately in their own terms, Anthropocene discourse is a hybrid cultural form that develops with ever-new iterations—the Chthulucene, Capitalocene, and Plantationocene—by devouring elements from a range of other disciplines, including science and literature. To recognize that Anthropocene discourse draws on literary strategies in its imagination of deep time is not to discredit it, as if that were to make it improperly scientific, or tainted by the merely literary.[10] On the contrary, it is to situate Anthropocene discourse within a longer history of reciprocal exchange between science and literature in the imagination of geological time. Moreover, it is to highlight the ability of literature and literary narratives to represent deep time, and to refigure readers' experience of time. That is, it is partly through its incorporation of literary strategies and forms

[8] Virginia Woolf, 'Poetry, Fiction and the Future', in *The Essays of Virginia Woolf*, 6 vols, ed. Andrew McNeillie (London: Hogarth Press, 1994), IV, 428–41, 429, 435.

[9] In a complementary manner but focusing on forms of art rather than science, Aaron Rosenberg argues that *The Time Machine* repurposes the conventions of the romance as a means of narrating expansive temporal scales ('Romancing the Anthropocene: H. G. Wells and the Genre of the Future', *Novel*, 51/1 (2018), 79–100).

[10] Heise draws attention to the anterior future perspectives that abound in both science fiction and Anthropocene discourse, and suggests that the Anthropocene itself is a science fiction idea ('Science Fiction', 300–1; *Imagining Extinction: The Cultural Meanings of Endangered Species* (Chicago: University of Chicago Press, 2016), 215–20). See also Rebecca Evans, 'Nomenclature, Narrative and the Novum: The "Anthropocene" and/as Science Fiction', *Science Fiction Studies*, 45/3 (2018), 484–99.

of imagination that the Anthropocene refigures historical time, and shapes new types of historical consciousness.

Geological time travel

The Time Machine has hitherto been read in two principal scientific contexts: those of evolutionary biology and thermodynamic physics. Critics have demonstrated that the future world that the Time Traveller visits is one beset by evolutionary retrogression in which humanity has degenerated into two species before suffering extinction, and one approaching heat-death as a consequence of the second law of thermodynamics.[11] That is, they have shown how, by drawing on discourses of evolutionary biology and thermodynamic physics, Wells fashioned his own narrative of a degenerating humanity and a slowly dying Earth.

However, while critics often turn to evolutionary biology and thermodynamic physics, they have paid less attention to geology. Certainly, critics such as Frank McConnell and Simon James mention geology and geological time in their discussions of the romance. McConnell suggests that '[w]hat Wells manages to do in *The Time Machine* is to articulate, for the first time and decisively for his age, a vision of the abyss of geological time', and James points out that '*The Time Machine*'s engagement with Victorian science draws not only on biology's reimagining of human physiology, but also on geology's expansion of the Victorian sense of time'.[12] More broadly, Cole highlights geology as one of a number of disciplines that informed Wells's experiments with time.[13] Yet beyond such references, there has not been a sustained discussion of *The Time Machine* in the context of geology. This comparative neglect is characteristic of wider trends in the history of science and literary studies. In the former, as Martin Rudwick points out, geology's historicization of the Earth 'has generally been treated as a mere prelude to the better-known story of the "Darwinian revolution"', and in the latter, as Adelene Buckland remarks, geology has until recently received something of a 'raw deal', tending to be cast as a mere handmaiden of evolutionary biology.[14]

---

[11] For example, on evolutionary biology, see Steven McLean, *The Early Fiction of H. G. Wells: Fantasies of Science* (Basingstoke: Palgrave Macmillan, 2009), 11–40; on thermodynamic physics, see Allen MacDuffie, *Victorian Literature, Energy, and the Ecological Imagination* (Cambridge: Cambridge University Press, 2014), 234–51.

[12] Frank McConnell, *The Science Fiction of H. G. Wells* (New York: Oxford University Press, 1981), 82; Simon J. James, *Maps of Utopia: H. G. Wells, Modernity, and the End of Culture* (Oxford: Oxford University Press, 2012), 56–7.

[13] Cole, *Inventing Tomorrow*, 8–9, 43.

[14] Martin J. S. Rudwick, Bursting the Limits of Time: The Reconstruction of Geohistory in the Age of Revolution (Chicago: University of Chicago Press, 2005), 7; Adelene Buckland, Novel Science: Fiction and the Invention of Nineteenth-Century Geology (Chicago: University of Chicago Press, 2013), 24.

The oversight is surprising, given Wells's expertise in geology. He studied the subject at the Normal School of Science—where he is pictured in Figure 1.1—sitting examinations in the subject in 1886 and 1887. Although he failed the latter exam, he later took 'first place in second class honours in geology' in his B.Sc. degree from London University in 1890, and subsequently taught geology classes at the University Tutorial College.[15] He co-wrote a textbook for students called *Honours Physiography* (1893), which covered geology, astronomy, and meteorology. As its preface claims, 'Honours Physiography involves a sound knowledge of geological structures in general, and the forces moulding them'; the book includes a section on 'The Age of the Earth', and a final chapter on the 'Distribution of Life in Space and Time'.[16] In 1894, Wells reviewed T. G. Bonney's *The Story of Our Planet* (1893), which advertises itself as a non-technical and accessible introduction to geology in the tradition of James Hutton and Charles Lyell's uniformitarianism. Wells praised this book as an 'able and popular exposition of modern geology', and predicted that it would 'be very widely read'.[17] More generally, by late-Victorian times, geology had become an established scientific discipline of considerable prestige and authority, and featured prominently in the work of major scientific popularizers such as T. H. Huxley, who famously taught Wells at the Normal School of Science.[18]

Regardless of the reasons for its neglect, situating *The Time Machine* in the context of geology is rewarding. Wells redeploys various strategies from geological literature and culture—the conceit of time travel, tropes of ruin, and fragmentary narrative form—to create a new type of 'scientific romance', which is capable of representing human agency over vast timescales.[19] These strategies not only enable a way of representing temporal vastness in the novel, but they also involve recasting an aesthetic of the sublime from geological literature as a way of negotiating the structures of feeling—including what Woolf describes as the 'unmanageable emotions'—that accompanied the new and sometimes vertiginous temporal scales.

In *The Time Machine*, the Time Traveller makes two principal journeys into the future before returning home: firstly to the year 802,701 AD and secondly to 'more than thirty million years hence'.[20] The device of time travel which is central

[15] H. G. Wells, *Experiment in Autobiography: Discoveries and Conclusions of a Very Ordinary Brain (Since 1866)*, 2 vols (London: Victor Gollancz and The Cresset Press, 1934), I, 233.
[16] R. A. Gregory and H. G. Wells, *Honours Physiography* (London: Joseph Hughes, 1893), i.
[17] H. G. Wells, 'Reminiscences of a Planet', *Pall Mall Gazette*, 15 January 1894, 4.
[18] Ralph O'Connor, *The Earth on Show: Fossils and the Poetics of Popular Science, 1802–1856* (Chicago: University of Chicago Press, 2007), 436–9.
[19] Wells credits Grant Allen with originating the 'field of scientific romance with a philosophical element' (*H. G. Wells's Literary Criticism*, ed. Patrick Parrinder and Robert M. Philmus (Brighton: Harvester, 1980), 225). See Rosenberg, 'Romancing', 83.
[20] H. G. Wells, *The Time Machine*, ed. Roger Luckhurst (Oxford: Oxford University Press, 2017), 30, 78. Unless otherwise specified, all further references are to this edition, which is based on the 1895 book version published by William Heinemann. An early version of the romance, *The Chronic Argonauts*,

Figure 1.1 H. G. Wells at the Normal School of Science
Reproduced with permission from Alpha Historica/Alamy Stock Photo.

to this romance finds a precedent in what Ralph O'Connor calls 'geological time travel', which became commonplace in geological literature and culture.[21] Wells adapted the conceit. Whereas geological time travel involved an imaginative journey in which the geologist is able to behold the changes wrought on the landscape with the mind's eye, the Traveller is literally able to watch these changes from his machine. And whereas geological time travel involved being carried back into antiquity, Wells's Traveller sets out into the future.

In particular, the Traveller's first voyage resembles the geological time travel described in Lyell's *Principles of Geology* (1830–33). Setting out on his time machine, the Traveller records how he:

> saw trees growing and changing like puffs of vapour [...] they grew, spread, shivered, and passed away. I saw huge buildings rise up [...] and pass like dreams. The whole surface of the earth seemed changed—melting and flowing under my eyes. (22)

Lyell had portrayed the geologist as imagining physical changes through time in a similarly visual and dynamic manner:

> to trace the same system through various transformations—to behold it at successive eras adorned with different hills and valleys, lakes and seas, and peopled with new inhabitants, was the delightful meed of geological research.[22]

This type of visual imagination was central to Lyell's aim of gaining widespread acceptance for the idea of a vast geological time: as Martin Rudwick argues, although many of his scientific colleagues already accepted such an idea as an intellectual working assumption, Lyell 'seems to have recognized that it was their scientific *imagination* that needed transforming'.[23] The 'melting and flowing' of the surface of the Earth in *The Time Machine* also echoes a verse from Alfred Tennyson's *In Memoriam* (1850) that Wells copied into the manuscript of the romance, in which the hills 'flow' and 'melt like mist':

> The hills are shadows, and they flow
> From form to form, and nothing stands;

---

appeared in *The Science Schools Journal* in 1888; *The Time Machine* was published in serial form in the *National Observer* in 1894 and in the *New Review* in 1894–5.

[21] O'Connor, *Earth*, 372–4.

[22] Charles Lyell, *Principles of Geology: Being an Attempt to Explain the Former Changes of the Earth's Surface, by Reference to Causes Now in Operation*, 3 vols (London: John Murray, 1830–33), I, 25. In his Autobiography, Wells recorded his interest in the geology 'of that great generation which included Lyell' (I, 228).

[23] Martin J. S. Rudwick, 'The Strategy of Lyell's *Principles of Geology*', *Isis*, 61/1 (1970), 4–33, 11; see also *Worlds Before Adam: The Reconstruction of Geohistory in the Age of Reform* (Chicago: University of Chicago Press, 2008), 255–6, 304.

> They melt like mist, the solid lands,
> Like clouds they shape themselves and go.[24]

This stanza displays Lyell's influence on *In Memoriam*, and was itself later quoted in geological works. For example, in *The Story of Our Planet* (1893) Bonney used the first two lines to conclude his chapter on the geological construction of the British Isles, where they complement his point that the Earth's surface is 'never at rest' but 'rises and falls, as if it were the breast of some huge monster, slowly breathing as it sleeps'.[25] During his return voyage, the Traveller records that '[t]he fluctuating contours of the land ebbed and flowed' (86), and in the *National Observer* version he witnesses the hills being eroded: 'I noticed the hills grow visibly lower through the years with the wear of the gust and rain'.[26] The time machine allows the Traveller to watch the infinitesimally slow changes of geology and astronomy that normally, as he points out, remain 'imperceptible in a hundred human lifetimes' (58). This way of making slow change visible through vast periods of time is a fictional equivalent of Lyell's geological imagination and his advocacy of reckoning the 'myriad of ages' not by 'arithmetical computation' but by 'a train of physical events': 'signs which convey to our minds more definite ideas than figures can do, of the immensity of time'.[27]

In line with the uniformitarian geology of Lyell and others, geological change in *The Time Machine* consists of small alterations over vast periods as opposed to dramatic changes wrought by violent geological catastrophes. Having arrived in the year 802,701, the Traveller notices subtle topographical changes. The 'Thames had shifted, perhaps, a mile from its present position', and when he reaches the Palace of Green Porcelain he 'was surprised to see a large estuary, or even a creek, where [he] judged Wandsworth and Battersea must once have been' (30, 61). In an abandoned draft chapter, he overshoots his mark on the return journey and ends up in the remote geological past. He worries that he would 'stop when the country was submerged, & sink plump into the water of some of those vanished oceans whose sediments form the dry land of today', although fortunately he comes to rest on the bank of a prehistoric river delta.[28] In the world approaching heat-death, although his machine has not moved through space, he finds himself on

---

[24] Alfred Tennyson, *In Memoriam*, ed. Susan Shatto and Marion Shaw (Oxford: Clarendon Press, 1982), 123, 5–8. See H. G. Wells, *The Time Machine: An Invention*, ed. Stephen Arata (New York: Norton, 2009), 18.

[25] T. G. Bonney, *The Story of Our Planet* (London: Cassell, 1893), 448, 221.

[26] Wells, *Early Writings*, 64.

[27] Lyell, *Principles*, I, 25.

[28] H. G. Wells, *The Definitive Time Machine: A Critical Edition of H. G. Wells's Scientific Romance*, ed. Harry M. Geduld (Bloomington: Indiana University Press, 1987), 184–6. In the book versions, it is left to the frame-narrator to speculate on the fate of the Traveller in the geological past, including the possibility that he fell 'into the abysses of the Cretaceous Sea' (87). In his *Autobiography*, Wells recalls his excitement at realizing, while standing on the brow of Telegraph Hill and looking across the weald to the North Downs, that 'I was standing on the escarpment of a denuded anticlinal, and that this stuff of the pale hills under my feet had once been slime at the bottom of a vanished Cretaceous sea' (I, 144).

the edge of a sloping beach by a sea (77). A process of geological change has taken place incrementally over the intervening timespan, much like that highlighted in Tennyson's *In Memoriam*:

> There rolls the deep where grew the tree.
> O earth, what changes hast thou seen!
> There where the long street roars, hath been
> The stillness of the central sea. (123, 1–4)

Bonney quotes this stanza in *The Story of Our Planet*, and comments that '[t]he poet uttered no dreamer's words, but simple scientific truth'.[29] In Tennyson's poem, the poet thinks that 'where the long street roars, hath been/ The stillness of the central sea', while in *The Time Machine*, what had been central London comes in the distant geological future to be covered by a freezing sea.

More generally, the conceit of time travel makes the scientific romance adept at depicting slow changes—including those caused by humans—that normally elude representation in novels. While some changes such as the fluctuating contours of the land and the shifting of constellations in the sky become perceptible to the Traveller on his voyage, he notices others on his arrival in the future, including climate change and species extinctions. He notices 'how warm the air was' in the world of the Eloi and Morlocks, and later emphasizes 'how much hotter than our own was the weather' of this future age (25, 44). This climate change seems not to be anthropogenic: although the Traveller cannot fully account for it, he speculates that it has happened in conformity with George Darwin's theory that the planets will fall back into the sun and cause it to 'blaze with renewed energy' (44). This temporary warming is followed by a cooling, as he discovers when he travels further into the future and discovers the frozen beaches of a world approaching heat-death. However, other changes have apparently been caused by humans, such as the extinction of various species.[30] The Traveller finds no evidence of contagious diseases in the future, and notices that the 'air was free from gnats, the earth from weeds or fungi; everywhere were fruits and sweet and delightful flowers; brilliant butterflies flew hither and thither'. He surmises that these changes are the result of the careful readjustment of 'the balance of animal and vegetable life to suit our human needs' (33).[31] This hypothesis accords closely to the scenario of 'ethical evolution' that Huxley envisaged, in which humans might defy the 'cosmic process' and the coarse struggle for existence by creating artificial conditions for humans: 'hygienic precautions' would check or remove the natural causes of

[29] Bonney, *Planet*, 222.
[30] As Rosenberg points out, *The Time Machine* registers 'the planetary impact of the human species as a massive agential force' ('Romancing', 93).
[31] In the *New Review* version, he believes that 'man had killed out all the other animals, sparing only a few of the more ornamental' (*Early Writings*, 97).

disease, and 'every plant and every lower animal should be adapted to human wants, and would perish if human supervision and protection were withdrawn.'[32] Later, the Traveller discovers that 'horses, cattle, sheep, dogs, had followed the Ichthyosaurus into extinction' (29).

The Traveller's second voyage through time to 'more than thirty million years hence' resembles more sublime forms of geological time travel. It was not just the ability to imagine that played an important role in scientific discourses such as geology and astronomy, but also the failure to imagine as a constitutive part of an aesthetic of the sublime. As O'Connor points out, the new school of geology, often by drawing on astronomy—'the sublime science *par excellence*'—partook of 'an aesthetic of wonder by which unlimited immensity (spatial or temporal) bewildered the mind into a temporary and pleasurable loss of rationality.'[33] A famous example of sublime geological time travel is John Playfair's description of an imaginative journey through time at Siccar Point, which was inspired by a boat trip with James Hutton, illustrated in Figure 1.2.[34] The rock formations at Siccar Point are an example of what Hutton called 'angular junctions' or what soon became known as unconformities. Although several earlier naturalists had described such formations, Hutton reinterpreted them to confirm his theory of a 'succession of worlds' in which successive rock masses are uplifted then worn down in a cyclical

From a Painting by James Hall, Esq.   Engraved by S. Williams.

Figure 1.2 'Siccar Point, Berwickshire'
Reproduced from Lyell, Charles (1851). *Manual of Elementary Geology*. London: John Murray.

---

[32] Thomas H. Huxley, *Evolution & Ethics and Other Essays* (London: Macmillan, 1894), 19–20.
[33] O'Connor, *Earth*, 153.
[34] John Playfair, 'Biographical Account of the Late Dr James Hutton, F. R. S. Edin.', *Transactions of the Royal Society of Edinburgh*, 5/3 (1805), 39–99, 72. Hutton's work and its 'influence on the growth of the Science of Geology' is the subject of the first chapter of R. D. Roberts's *The Earth's History* (1893), a work to which Wells and Gregory refer their readers in *Honours Physiography* (118).

process.[35] Playfair records his impressions of listening to Hutton lecturing on the rocks:

> [w]hat clearer evidence could we have had of the different formation of these rocks, and of the long interval which separated their formation, had we actually seen them emerging from the bosom of the deep? We felt ourselves necessarily carried back to the time when the schistus on which we stood was yet at the bottom of the sea, and when the sandstone before us was only beginning to be deposited, in the shape of sand or mud, from the waters of a superincumbent ocean. An epoch still more remote presented itself [...] Revolutions still more remote appeared in the distance of this extraordinary perspective. The mind seemed to grow giddy by looking so far into the abyss of time. (72–3)[36]

Contemplating the rock strata, the imaginative journey back into 'the abyss of time' takes the form of a sublime experience. The 'mind seemed to grow giddy' and imagination is overwhelmed: 'we became sensible how much farther reason may sometimes go than imagination can venture to follow'.[37]

The Traveller's journey into the distant future bears some striking similarities to Playfair's description of the mind's journey back through geological time. Although voyaging into the future rather than the past, the Traveller's 'great strides of a thousand years or more' on his machine parallel Playfair's description of feeling 'carried back to the time when the schistus on which we stood was yet at the bottom of the sea', then to '[a]n epoch still more remote', and again through '[r]evolutions still more remote' which 'appeared in the distance of this extraordinary perspective' (78). Standing on the desolate beach in the distant future, the Traveller grows 'giddy'; overwhelmed, he gets off his machine to recover and stands 'sick and confused', 'incapable of facing the return journey' (79). This giddiness is most immediately explained by the disorienting rocking of his machine and the thinness of the air. Yet it also echoes Playfair's description of the extremity of his imaginative voyage back through time: '[t]he mind seemed to grow giddy by looking so far into the abyss of time'. In the *New Review* version, the Traveller had described his planned journey into the extreme future in terms which again echo Playfair: 'I resolved to run on for one glimpse of the still remoter future—one peep into the deeper abysm of time—and then to return to you and my own epoch'.[38] Playfair's 'abyss of time' becomes Wells's 'abysm of time', and his visual metaphor of 'looking' becomes Wells's 'glimpse' and 'peep'. The Time Traveller's terminus, at which he

---

[35] See Rudwick, *Bursting*, 168–9.
[36] According to Rudwick, the 'idea of time as an abyss was borrowed from [Georges] Buffon, but it encapsulates what Playfair's generation (and others since) found most striking about Hutton's system' (*Bursting*, 169).
[37] Playfair, 'Hutton', 73.
[38] Wells, *Early Writings*, 99.

grows giddy and needs to return, is both the extreme point to which he can travel into a world that is increasingly unable to support life, and also parallels the limit at which the imagination becomes overwhelmed in a sublime confrontation with deep time, before needing to return to the present day.

The ruins of time

The world that the Traveller encounters in the year 802,701 is one of ruins. Much of the architecture of the future age is neo-Classical: there are 'huge buildings with intricate parapets and tall columns', a seat with arm rests carved as griffins' heads, and scattered cupolas and obelisks (24, 31–2). Many of the buildings are decaying or ruined and the landscape is overgrown. There were 'great palaces dotted about among the variegated greenery, some in ruins', as well as 'abundant ruins', 'abandoned ruins', and 'splendid palaces and magnificent ruins' (32, 34, 73). The Traveller pursues several of his adventures amongst the ruins: the first thing he sees on arriving is a weather-worn statue of a Sphinx; at one point he pursues a Morlock through heaps of fallen masonry in a 'colossal ruin'; and he later explores the Palace of Green Porcelain, a deserted Victorian-style museum 'falling into ruin' (44, 61).

Patrick Parrinder advances an influential reading of these ruins, which he sees as a key to the time-scheme of *The Time Machine*. He points out that 'the ruined buildings of the age of the Eloi and the Morlocks are, however implausibly, culturally continuous with our own civilisation', and goes on to argue that 'we can understand *The Time Machine* better by seeing both an '"800,000-year" and an "800-year" timescale at work in it': '[t]he two scales, those of historical time measured by the rise and fall of cultures and civilisations, and of biological time measured by the evolution and devolution of the species, are superimposed upon one another'. For Parrinder, these timescales 'come into conflict' when the Traveller arrives at the Palace of Green Porcelain, an episode that supposedly involves 'chronological incongruities'.[39] While the Palace would have made sense on the historical timescale, on the evolutionary timescale it is implausible: 'the decay ought to have gone very much further'.[40]

However, it is not the case, as Parrinder argues, that '[w]ithout the 800-year timescale we cannot easily explain such crucial details as the survival of the

---

[39] See Patrick Parrinder, 'From Rome to Richmond: Wells, Universal History, and Prophetic Time', in George Slusser, Patrick Parrinder and Daniele Chatelain (eds), *H. G. Wells's Perennial Time Machine* (Athens: University of Georgia Press, 2001), 110–21, 116; and *Shadows of the Future: H. G. Wells, Science Fiction and Prophecy* (Liverpool: Liverpool University Press, 1995), 41–2. As McLean points out, 'Parrinder's idea that there are two timescales at work in *The Time Machine* [has been] generally accepted' (*Fantasies*, 12).
[40] Parrinder, *Shadows*, 73.

unmistakably classical forms of architecture into the far future.[41] They can be explained by reference to geological literature, and to the examples and tropes of ruin that were commonly used by geologists. Wells redeployed these tropes in his scientific romance to mediate human and geological history and articulate a new conception of deep time. Like ruins in recent Anthropocene discourse, Wells's ruins stand as monuments to human destruction on a geological scale.

While Chakrabarty argues that the concept of the Anthropocene brings together the times of human history and of the Earth, geologists had long sought to align the two as part of their project of historicizing the Earth.[42] One common strategy used to bridge the two sorts and scales of time were discussions and figures of architectural ruin, around which ideas of geological time clustered.[43] For example, Lyell used ruins prominently in his *Principles*, most notably with his discussion of the (so-called) Temple of Serapis and his frontispiece—reproduced in Figure 1.3—which depicts a man meditating on its ruins.[44] He used the example of this 'celebrated monument of antiquity' to support his local argument that the level of the land constantly changes in relation to the sea. More generally, it emblematized his attempt to historicize the Earth, as the history of the geological changes at Pozzuoli could be reconstructed in coordination with archaeological evidence and written accounts of the Temple.[45] The frontispiece to the *Principles* thereby, as Rudwick puts it, 'neatly encapsulated Lyell's ambition to integrate geohistory with human history.'[46] In part, it does so by deploying a familiar aesthetics of the sublime. By depicting a solitary romantic figure contemplating ruined columns, it invites the reader to consider the work's conception of geohistory—which stretches back through vast tracts of time—on the model of a sublime meditation on classical ruins.

Ruins in *The Time Machine* function in a similar manner to ruins in geological literature. On a hill overlooking the ruined city of the future, the Traveller contemplates the vast spans of time that he has traversed and the changes that have happened during that period:

all the activity, all the traditions, the complex organizations, the nations, languages, literatures, aspirations, even the mere memory of Man as I knew him, had been swept out of existence. (58)

---

[41] Parrinder, *Shadows*, 42.

[42] Dipesh Chakrabarty, 'Anthropocene Time', *History and Theory*, 57/1 (2018), 5–32.

[43] As part of his wider argument that geology and Romantic literature were mutually constitutive discourses that shared a common idiom of landscape aesthetics, Noah Heringman has shown that geologists and Romantic poets borrowed tropes of ruin from each other (*Romantic Rocks, Aesthetic Geology* (Ithaca, NY: Cornell University Press, 2004), 180–1, 234–6).

[44] See also the extended conceit in which Lyell compares geological history to the architectural history of Egypt, with its 'pyramids, obelisks, colossal statues, and ruined temples' (*Principles*, I, 26–8).

[45] Lyell, *Principles*, I, 449.

[46] Rudwick, *Adam*, 299.

Figure 1.3 'Present state of the Temple of Serapis at Puzzuoli'

Reproduced from Lyell, Charles (1830). *Principles of Geology*, I. London: John Murray

Although situated in the future, the meditative Traveller resembles Lyell's solitary Romantic figure in the frontispiece of the *Principles*.[47] Just as Lyell's ruins prepare his reader to join him in his meditation on geohistory, so ruins in *The Time Machine* provide the Traveller and the reader with a means of comprehending the immensity of geological time, and the course of the Earth's history which unfolds over such time.

---

[47] Wells and Gregory referred to the Temple of Serapis in their *Honours Physiography* (122). Bonney also discussed this 'often quoted' example in *The Story of Our Planet*, and provided an alternative illustration of the ruined columns (*Planet*, 222–6).

Yet more than this, the ruined monuments of the future register the agency of humans on a geological scale. The first thing that the Traveller encounters on arriving in the future is a 'colossal figure, carved apparently in some white stone [...] It was of white marble, in shape something like a winged sphinx' (24). Much critical attention has been devoted to the sphinx, which Matthew Beaumont describes as 'an obdurately overdetermined symbol'.[48] One such determinant is Percy Bysshe Shelley's 'Ozymandias' (1818).[49] The verbal echoes between the poem and *The Time Machine* are marked: Shelley's 'colossal wreck' corresponds to Wells's 'colossal figure'; just as Shelley's statue displays a 'frown/ And wrinkled lip and sneer of cold command', so too is there 'the faint shadow of a smile on the lips' of Wells's statue; and, as Shelley's statue displays a 'hand that mocked' and bears an inscription counselling despair, so Wells's Traveller feels that 'the sphinx [...] seemed to smile in mockery of [his] dismay' and later wakes beneath the sphinx to feel 'a profound sense of desertion and despair' (24, 36–7).[50] The Traveller's anticipations of future posterity, like those of Ozymandias, prove misfounded: as he 'was led past the sphinx of white marble' the 'memory of [his] confident anticipations of a profoundly grave and intellectual posterity came, with irresistible merriment, to [his] mind' (27). Shelley's 'traveller from an antique land' becomes Wells's Traveller of the future.

The Ozymandias motif is reinforced when the symbol is paired with perhaps its single most important determinant: the riddle of the Sphinx of Huxley's essay 'The Struggle for Existence in Human Society' (1888).[51] In this essay, Huxley suggests that the 'true riddle of the Sphinx' is to know how to escape from the conditions of an unchecked evolutionary struggle for existence. Should this fail, he warns of the bifurcation of society into a wealthy positive pole and a miserable poor pole, after which each nation will 'sooner or later be devoured by the monster [that it] has generated'.[52] Wells's society of the Morlocks and Eloi is a nightmarish imagination of a society that has failed to solve Huxley's riddle of the Sphinx. In this society, which the Traveller at first mistakenly thinks of as a golden age, humanity has degenerated and split into two poles: the decadent Eloi and cannibalistic Morlocks. The sphinx statue, combining the senses of Shelley's anticipations and Huxley's failure to resolve the evolutionary struggle for existence, stands as a symbol of the arrogance of humans in believing themselves to be assured a long evolutionary prosperity.

---

[48] Matthew Beaumont, *The Spectre of Utopia: Utopian and Science Fictions at the Fin de Siècle* (Oxford: Peter Lang, 2012), 229.

[49] Michael Page notes the allusion to 'Ozymandias' (*The Literary Imagination from Erasmus Darwin to H. G. Wells: Science, Evolution and Ecology* (Farnham: Ashgate, 2012), 158–9).

[50] Percy Bysshe Shelley, *The Major Works*, ed. Zachary Leader and Michael O'Neil (Oxford: Oxford University Press, 2009), 198.

[51] See John Prince, 'The "True Riddle of the Sphinx" in *The Time Machine*', *Science Fiction Studies*, 27/3 (2000), 543–6.

[52] Huxley, *Evolution*, 212.

While the Sphinx ironically symbolizes humans' capacity to destroy themselves, the Palace of Green Porcelain stands as a monument to the destruction
that humans have wrought on other species. Exploring the ruins of this 'latter-
day South Kensington', the Traveller identifies 'the Palaeontological Section, and
a very splendid array of fossils it must have been' (61–2). In the *Origin of Species*
(1859), Charles Darwin drew attention to the 'paltry display' that is found even in
'our richest geological museums' in order to illustrate his contentions that only a
small part of the geological record has survived, and that we have only fragmentary evidence of the 'infinite number of generations' that 'must have succeeded
each other in the long roll of years'.[53] In his essay 'On Extinction' (1893), Wells
echoed Darwin by noting that '[i]n the long galleries of the geological museum
are the records of judgements that have been passed graven upon the rocks': '[t]he
long role of palæontology is half filled with the records of extermination'. He adds
that humans have driven many species to extinction: in 'the last hundred years
the swift change of condition throughout the world, due to the invention of new
means of transit, geographical discovery, and the consequent "swarming" of the
whole globe by civilised men', has destroyed 'dozens of genera and hundreds of
species'.[54] In *The Time Machine*, Wells extends Darwin's conceit by depicting a
Victorian-style museum and its already-poor palaeontological collection as having
undergone a further, second-order process of decay: the fossils and skeletons—
which themselves are vestiges from the geological past—have once again become
subject to processes of decay since being exhibited (64–5). Moreover, the Palace
likely contained records of the species that have become extinct in the far future,
including those that had been purposefully eradicated by humans, although the
Traveller regrets that the animals and plants have disintegrated in the natural
history section and so he cannot 'trace the patient readjustments by which the
conquest of animated nature had been attained' (62). The Palace thereby stands as
a mausoleum-like monument to mass extinction and the destruction that humans
have wrought on a geological scale.

If there remains an implausibility in Wells's ruins of the future, it is an aesthetic
and formal discontinuity that registers the incommensurability of the temporal
scales that the romance sets out to negotiate. While architectural ruins were commonly used in geological literature to mediate historical and geological time, there
is something incongruous about Wells's projection of what so closely resemble
Victorian buildings into the distant future. This incongruity is one that reveals
what Tung calls 'the heterochronic multiplicity of scalar zoom'.[55] In this case, the

[53] Charles Darwin, *On the Origin of Species by Means of Natural Selection, Or the Preservation of Favoured Races in the Struggle for Life* (London: John Murray, 1859), 287.
[54] H. G. Wells, 'On Extinction', in *Early Writings*, 169–72, 169–70.
[55] Charles Tung, 'Second Modernism and the Aesthetics of Scale', in Jon Hegglund and John McIntyre (eds), *Modernism and the Anthropocene: Material Ecologies of Twentieth-Century Literature* (Lanham: Lexington Books, 2021), 133–50.

romance's scalar zooming is accompanied by jumps and discontinuities that are registered as representational failures: the disappearance of the fossils and natural history exhibits in the Palace makes what was already a partial record of an incomplete history even more limited, and that history even more difficult to reconstruct. Complementing the sublimity of the ruined museum (which deploys an aesthetic suited to convey overwhelming vastness), the Palace signals the romance's failure to tell the longer story of extinction that has unfolded over the years that the Traveller has traversed, and to depict the full damage wrought by humans on a geological scale.

By signalling human destruction on a geological scale, the ruins of *The Time Machine* anticipate those of Anthropocene discourse. Establishing the Anthropocene as a geological time unit involves thinking about what traces humans will leave in the rock layers that are being laid down. These might include the presence of 'technofossils', composed from materials such as aluminium and plastic that will be left in particularly high density in urban areas.[56] Such traces invite figuration in terms of ruin. For example, Jan Zalasiewicz and Kim Freedman imagine a future geologist discovering the 'ruins of the Urban Strata that hugely expanded in the last century'.[57] The trope of ruin here conveys the incompleteness of the rock strata that will survive in the future, but also evokes the environmental ruination that has left its traces in the geological record. More generally, Gerry Canavan suggests that '[f]rom the point of view of the Anthropocene all structures are Ozymandian, always premediated as ruins, as if watching history on fast-forward'.[58] The Traveller's watching London fall into ruin before seemingly disappearing from the shifting geological landscape stands as a precursor to such Anthropocene forms of imagination.

Ultimately, the ruins of *The Time Machine* are more sublime than those of Lyell's uniformitarian geology.[59] For Hutton and Lyell, the processes of ruin to which the Earth was subject were counterbalanced by processes of renewal. For instance, Hutton's confidence in geological renovation led to the famous conclusion of his *Theory of the Earth* (1795) that 'we find no vestige of a beginning,—no prospect of an end'.[60] However, Wells's romance, reflecting later developments in evolutionary biology and thermodynamic physics, imagines a bleaker future. Evolutionary

---

[56] See Jan Zalasiewicz and others, 'The Technofossil Record of Humans', *The Anthropocene Review*, 1/1 (2014), 34–43.

[57] Jan Zalasiewicz and Kim Freedman, *The Earth After Us: What Legacy Will Humans Leave in the Rocks?* (Oxford: Oxford University Press, 2008), 212.

[58] Gerry Canavan, 'Memento Mori: Richard McGuire's *Here* and Art in the Anthropocene', *Deletion*, 13 (2017). <https://www.deletionscifi.org/episodes/episode-13/memento-mori-richard-mcguires-art-anthropocene/> [last accessed 25 January 2023].

[59] In this sense, they complement the 'neocatastrophism' that has gained ascendancy in Earth Sciences in recent decades. See Jeremy Davies, *The Birth of the Anthropocene* (Oakland: University of California Press, 2016), 9–10.

[60] James Hutton, *Theory of the Earth, with Proofs and Illustrations*, 2 vols (Edinburgh: William Creech, 1795), I, 200.

biology embraced the extended timescales of geologists such as Lyell but raised the possibility that humans might suffer biological retrogression or degeneration. Physical theorists such as William Thomson argued that the Earth was younger than geologists claimed, and—contravening Hutton's optimistic conclusion that we find 'no prospect of an end'—that it was undergoing physical decay through the 'dissipation of mechanical energy'.[61] *The Time Machine* combines the vastly-extended geological time of Hutton and Lyell with an evolutionary scenario in which humanity has degenerated into distinct species, and a thermodynamic scenario in which the Earth suffers a heat-death. These two forms of decay over deep time become part of the meaning of the ruins that the Traveller visits, partly through the depiction of the terminal beach.

The Traveller's journey to the desolate beach is one of sublime horror. He finds no easily-recognizable descendants of humans—not even the degenerate Eloi and Morlocks of the year 802,701. Instead, he encounters a 'thing like a huge white butterfly' and 'monstrous crab-like [creatures]'. Travelling further into the future, even this 'crawling multitude of crabs' has disappeared, and the beach appears 'lifeless'. The physical effects brought about by the dissipation of energy are similarly nightmarish, and the Traveller watches 'the life of the old earth ebb away' with a 'strange fascination' that turns to horror. He describes how a 'horror of this great darkness came on me', and of how in the 'rayless obscurity' he was struck by a 'terrible dread of lying helpless in that remote and awful twilight'. His experience is described in the lexicon of the sublime: 'obscurity', 'horror', 'terrible', 'dread', 'awful' (77–80). It adds a sublime dimension to the deep time of the romance that was absent from Hutton's and Lyell's conceptions of geological time.

In turn, the sublimity of the desolate beach feeds back into the sublimity of the ruins of the future age. By foreshadowing the destruction of the Earth, Wells's ruins more closely resemble those deployed in an apocalyptic tradition of nineteenth-century geology, than those of Lyell's *Principles*. For example, in Andrew Ure's *A New System of Geology* (1829), the 'mighty ruins' of the Earth 'serve to rouse its living observers from their slumberous existence', leading them 'to meditate seriously on the origin and end of terrestrial things'. Geological ruins prophetically point forward to the eschaton: 'the very stones cry out' and 'we feel transported along with them to the judgment-seat of the Eternal'.[62] Despite being set within a tale underpinned by a secular cosmology, the ruins of *The Time Machine* also function prophetically. Emblematic of the processes of biological and physical decay, they anticipate not the Day of Judgement imagined by Ure, but the frozen waste beaches of a slowly dying Earth.

[61] William Thomson, 'On a Universal Tendency in Nature to the Dissipation of Mechanical Energy', in *Mathematical and Physical Papers*, I (Cambridge: Cambridge University Press, 1882), 511–14, 511.

[62] Andrew Ure, *A New System of Geology* (London: Longman et al., 1829), liii, 505.

Narrative unconformities

The Time Machine employs narrative strategies suggested by geology to render deep time. It pursues what Gillian Beer identifies as 'the problem of finding a scale for the human', although its literary form is inspired not so much by evolutionary theory as by geology, which—as Adelene Buckand has shown—offered Victorian novelists a useful form for narrative breakdown.[63] Wells replicates the fragmentary form of the geological record in a manner that pushes the romance to its limits. Indeed, it is the points where the narrative fails that most effectively render a non-human time that lies outside the meaning-making structures of the romance, and intimate its failure to establish an appropriate scale and place for the human. Ultimately, the sublime geological time of the romance decentres humans, leaving them—as Wells put it in his early short story—'less than an iota in the infinite universe'.

The Time Machine is a variable internally focalized narrative, consisting of the autodiegetic narrative of the Traveller and a frame-narrative told by one of his guests. The narratives of the various versions are, in different ways, fragmentary. In the *National Observer* version, the Traveller's narrative of his voyage into the future is repeatedly interrupted by objections and comments from his sceptical audience, to the extent that he at one point breaks off his story. We learn how he was eventually appeased and 'produced some few further fragments of his travel story'.[64] In the book versions, the Traveller's narrative is embedded within the frame-narrative as the incomplete fragment of a greater story, the rest of which has been lost by his failure to return from his second voyage. The frame-narrator recalls how he was left 'waiting for the second, perhaps still stranger story' (86). These fragmentary narrative forms reflect Lyell's and Darwin's views of the narratives that could be told about the geological and biological past.

Geologists and natural scientists commonly figured the Earth as a fragmentary book. Such figures form part of a wider phenomenon that occurred as part of geologists' historicization of the Earth in which, as Rudwick puts it:

[i]deas, concepts and methods for analyzing evidence and for reconstructing the past were deliberately and explicitly *transposed* from the human world into the world of nature, often with telling use of the metaphors of *nature's* documents and archives, coins and monuments, annals and chronologies.[65]

[63] Gillian Beer, *Darwin's Plots: Evolutionary Narrative in Darwin, George Eliot, and Nineteenth-Century Fiction*, 3rd edn (Cambridge: Cambridge University Press, 2009), 233; Buckland, *Novel Science*, 26–7. Buckland argues that geology justifies formal breakdown rather than narrative organization: '[t]ell stories they might, but the gaps and blanks of the stratigraphic column could usefully suggest dark and disturbing ruptures in the continuous flow of the plot' (27).
[64] Wells, *Early Writings*, 71.
[65] Rudwick, *Bursting*, 6.

Indeed, in a variation of the older 'book of nature' metaphor, geologists often fig-ured the landscape as a text from which the Earth's past could be read. Lyell, for instance, contended that the ancient history of the globe was for classical geolo-gists a 'sealed book'.[66] Wells employed his own version to describe the task of the geologist in his review of Bonney's *Story of Our Planet*:

> [t]he geologist [...] scrutinizes this round respectable planet of ours with a trained and penetrating eye, and where the common man sees only a haphazard arrange-ment of hills and valleys [...] he reads, as plainly as if it were print, the story of this or that vicissitude our mother earth has experienced.[67]

From such metaphors, it is a short step to figure the incomplete geological record as a fragmentary archive or book. Lyell and Darwin both stressed that our knowl-edge of the geological past is incomplete. For Lyell, this was important as part of his defence of his 'doctrine of absolute uniformity', and for Darwin, the 'extreme imperfection of the geological record' was needed to explain what was otherwise 'the most obvious and gravest objection which can be urged against [his] theory' of evolution by natural selection: that there is no evidence of the 'innumerable transitional links' between different stages of evolving species.[68] Lyell evoked the 'great chasm in the chronological series of nature's archives', and in the *Origin of Species*, Darwin wrote that:

> following out Lyell's metaphor, I look at the natural geological record, as a history of the world imperfectly kept [...] [O]f this history we possess the last volume alone, relating only to two or three countries. Of this volume, only here and there a short chapter has been preserved; and of each page, only here and there a few lines.[69]

That is, far from resulting in a complete narrative of the Earth's geohistory, the metaphor of legibility leads to an incomplete 'history of the world imperfectly kept'.[70]

Wells reflected Lyell and Darwin's idea of a fragmentary history of the world in *The Time Machine*. He employs a type of narrative breakdown to replicate what

---

[66] Lyell, *Principles*, I, 20.
[67] Wells, 'Reminiscences', 4.
[68] Lyell, *Principles*, I, 87; Darwin, *Origin*, 279–80.
[69] Lyell, *Principles*, I, 159; Darwin, *Origin*, 310.
[70] In *The Story of Our Planet*, Bonney reiterated Darwin's emphasis on the inherent imperfection of the geological record: he pointed out that though 'it is now a quarter of a century since Darwin wrote that well-known chapter' on the subject in the *Origin of Species*, and 'though since that time the labour of numerous indefatigable writers has filled many a gap and supplied many a link for which he had vainly sought, yet even now the lacunae are very great, and the materials at the disposal of the geologist can never be anything but fragmentary'. He advanced his own variants of the metaphor, for example figuring a gap in the geological record as a page having been 'torn out of the volume' (369, 8).

Buckland calls the 'anti-narrative' of geologists such as Lyell.[71] Just as the geological record provides only a fragmentary history of the past, so the Traveller's narrative provides only a fragmentary account of the future. The frame-narrator draws attention to the gaps left by the Traveller's narrative: 'to me the future is still black and blank—is a vast ignorance, lit at a few casual places by the memory of his story' (87). The description of the deep future as 'blank' echoes Darwin's frequent descriptions of the geological past containing blank periods, often of enormous duration. For instance, he writes that 'there will be blanks in our geological history', and that 'between each successive formation, we have, in the opinion of most geologists, enormously long blank periods'.[72] Again, the narrator's metaphor of illumination resonates with a nexus of similar Enlightenment metaphors in geological literature of research illuminating sections of the otherwise obscure geological past.[73] Wells later used such metaphors in *The Discovery of the Future* (1902). Whereas previously the remote past had been a blank 'darkness', this all changed with the comparatively recent discovery of 'the geological past' by 'modern science': rock formations 'became sources of dazzling and penetrating light,—the remoter past lit up and became a picture'.[74] For the frame-narrator, the Traveller's fragmentary narrative illuminates a few places of the deep future, just as for geologists the fragmentary geological record illuminates sections of the geological past.

The fragmentary form of Wells's romance mirrors both the history of the world imagined by Darwin, with its various chapters and pages missing, and the incomplete geological record for which Darwin's book is a figure. In the latter case, the gaps in Wells's narrative function like geological unconformities (albeit unconformities that point towards the future as well as to the past): like the gaps in the rock formations at Siccar Point, these 'narrative unconformities' point towards enormous lapses of time for which no record has been left. These unconformities are—like their geological counterparts—open to a variety of interpretations. The guests who think that the Traveller's story is an elaborate hoax are like the ancients whom Lyell criticized in the *Principles* for being unable to read the history of the Earth, despite it being clearly written in the geological landscape 'in characters of the most imposing and striking kind'.[75] By contrast, the frame-narrator who believes the Traveller and interprets the disappearance of the second part of his story as evidence of the truth of his tale, is like the modern geologist who

[71] Buckland, *Novel Science*, 110.

[72] Darwin, *Origin*, 173, 284.

[73] For instance Roderick Murchison, to whom Wells pays tribute in his autobiography as one of the 'great generation' of geologists alongside Lyell (I, 228), remarked that some geologists contend that 'as yet we gaze but dimly into the obscure vista of [the] early periods' in which the first crystalline rocks were formed (*The Silurian System*, 2 vols (London: John Murray, 1839), I, 12).

[74] H. G. Wells, *The Discovery of the Future* (London: T. Fischer Unwin, 1902), 41, 47, 43, 49.

[75] Lyell, *Principles*, I, 20.

appreciates the temporal significance of the landscape, and can interpret geological unconformities as revealing the great age of the Earth.

The fragmentary form of the romance contributes to its articulation of a non-human geological time. Paul Ricoeur offers the following 'paradox':

> [t]he length of time of a human life, compared to the range of cosmic time-spans, appears insignificant, whereas it is the very place from which every question of significance arises.[76]

He adds that the 'full significance of this paradox is revealed only when narrative, understood as a mimesis of action, is taken as the criterion for this meaning'.[77] That is, narrative plays a key role in establishing the significance of humans against cosmic timespans because it promises to inscribe lived time onto cosmic time. By emplotting the Traveller's adventures in deep time, *The Time Machine* might seem to be a work of fiction that is exceptionally able to bridge human and cosmic time. Yet its fragmentary narrative form ultimately frustrates such a bridge. Indeed, the romance's representational failures are what most effectively convey the quality and vastness of a geological time that cannot be contained within its human meaning-making structures.[78] The intimation of such a time shifts the romance from being human-centred to being—to use terms that Chakrabarty borrows from Zalasiewicz—planet-centred.[79] Wells's romance does not allow a 'poetic' resolution for humanity, dwarfed by the abyssal geological time of Hutton and Lyell.[80] Rather, it emphasizes humanity's insignificant and precarious position within a hostile universe, encapsulated by its closing image of the Traveller lost somewhere in the vast expanses of time.

The romance's decentring of humans is reinforced by its aesthetic of the sublime. Chakrabarty points out that historical and geological time engage very different types of affect. Human historical time is an affectively-charged structure, with its horizons of expectation and experience often accompanied by affects such as hope or anxiety. By contrast, geological time is not a lived form of time and so does not display this affective structure, although it does invite affective responses.[81] Indeed, geologists commonly employed an aesthetic of the sublime to shape affective responses to geological time and to mediate humans' position within the

---

[76] Paul Ricoeur, *Time and Narrative*, trans. Kathleen McLaughlin and David Pellauer, 3 vols (Chicago: University of Chicago Press, 1984–8), III, 90.

[77] Ricoeur, *Time and Narrative*, III, 298.

[78] Parrinder's argument that there are two different timescales at work in *The Time Machine* conceals a deeper tension: that the romance stages the clash between two incompatible sorts of time—human and geological. As Ricoeur warns, the notion of timescale can introduce an abstract factor of commensurability that takes into account only the comparative chronology of the processes considered (*Time and Narrative*, III, 90).

[79] Chakrabarty, 'Anthropocene Time', 21–2.

[80] Ricoeur, *Time and Narrative*, I, 6.

[81] Chakrabarty, 'Anthropocene Time', 13, 16–17.

cosmos. For example, Rudwick argues that Lyell's frequent analogy in the *Principles* between time and Newtonian space 'added the dimension of geological time to the sublime vision of a universe of perfect and wise design, a universe fully under the dominion of providential natural laws'.[82] Later, although writing in the era of thermodynamic physics, Archibald Geikie similarly employed an aesthetic of the sublime to incorporate geological time into a view of a harmonious (albeit not obviously theistic) world. His *Scenery of Scotland* (1865), to which Wells and Gregory refer their readers in *Honours Physiography*, concludes:

> scenery [...] leads us back farther than imagination can well follow, and, with an impressiveness which we sometime [sic] can hardly endure, points out the antiquity of our globe [...]. [I]t is the little changes which by their cumulative effects bring about the greatest results [...] with a nicely balanced harmony and order, forming out of the very waste of the land a kindly soil, which [...] [ministers] to the wants and the enjoyment of man.[83]

Like Playfair's imaginative journey at Siccar Point, Geikie offers a conceit of geological time travel that bears familiar traits of the sublime: imagination is overwhelmed and the experience is almost unendurable. However, the experience leads Geikie to the vision of a world of 'balanced harmony and order' which ministers 'to the wants and enjoyment of man'. The sublimity of geological time thus serves to heighten the wonder of an orderly and harmonious world, much as had the natural sublime of eighteenth-century theorists such as Joseph Addison. By helping to reconcile humanity's place in a harmonious universe, the sublimity of Lyell's and Geikie's geological times contrasts with that of the deep time of Wells's romance.

In *The Time Machine*, the sublime aesthetic is used to portray a universe that is anything but hospitable to humanity. Working in concert with the conceit of time travel and the ruins of the future age, the romance's fragmentary narrative form contributes to the sublimity of its deep time. While the frame-narrator's depiction of the deep future as 'black and blank' echoes similar metaphors in geological discourse about the geological past, it is also one of obscurity, which had long played an important role in conceptualizations of the sublime. For example, Edmund Burke held that 'terror is in all cases whatsoever, either more openly or latently the ruling principle of the sublime', and that '[t]o make any thing very terrible, obscurity seems in general to be necessary'.[84] The deep future of the romance becomes, in Burke's terms, 'very terrible'. The geological past is similarly portrayed as terrible,

---

[82] Rudwick, 'Strategy', 33.
[83] Archibald Geikie, *The Scenery of Scotland Viewed in Connection with Its Physical Geology*, 2nd edn (London: Macmillan, 1887), 419–20; Gregory and Wells, *Physiography*, 138.
[84] Edmund Burke, *A Philosophical Enquiry into the Origin of Our Ideas of the Sublime and Beautiful*, 2nd ed. (London: R. and J. Dodsley, 1759), 97, 99.

as the frame-narrator speculates on the fate of the Traveller in various geological periods: it may be that he fell 'into the abysses of the Cretaceous Sea; or among the grotesque saurians, the huge reptilian brutes of the Jurassic times' (87). Rather than reconciling humans' place in the cosmos, the romance's sublimely vast and obscure geological time decentres humans in what amounts to a vision of cosmic pessimism.

Cosmic pessimism and beyond

For Huxley and Wells, viewing humans within the perspectives of geological time could motivate the project of ethical evolution. Huxley opened the 'Prolegomena' (1894) to his essay 'Evolution and Ethics' (1893)—whose influence on Wells is widely acknowledged by critics—by invoking vast expanses of geological time to unsettle the belief that 'the state of nature' is somehow permanent.[85] Though such an air of permanence might arise from our 'customary standards of duration' and from considering that, for instance, many of the same plants that are found in Britain today would have been found two thousand years ago, this belief is deceptive:

> measured by the liberal scale of time-keeping of the universe, [the] present state of nature, however it may seem to have gone and to go on for ever, is but a fleeting phase of her infinite variety; merely the last of the series of changes which the earth's surface has undergone in the course of the millions of years of its existence.[86]

Making vivid such a geological perspective, he points out that to '[t]urn back a square foot of the thin turf' and to expose the chalk that lies beneath is to yield 'full assurance' that the sea once covered the site of the supposedly 'everlasting hills', and that between the time the chalk was formed and the turf came into existence 'thousands of centuries elapsed'. In the essay, he explores a similar temporal perspective by quoting from Blaise Pascal's *Pensées* (1669):

> [l]'homme n'est qu'un roseau, le plus faible de la nature, mais c'est un roseau pensant. Il ne faut pas que l'univers entier s'arme pour l'écraser. Une vapeur, une goutte d'eau, suffit pour le tuer. Mais quand l'univers l'écraserait, l'homme serait encore plus noble que ce qui le tue, parce qu'il sait qu'il meurt; et l'avantage que l'univers a sur lui, l'univers n'en sait rien.[87]

---

[85] For example, Page singles out this essay as of 'great significance to the evolutionary vision found in Wells's early scientific romances' (*Imagination*, 151).

[86] Huxley, *Evolution*, 2–3.

[87] Huxley, *Evolution*, 3, 115–16. 'A human being is only a reed, the weakest in nature, but he is a thinking reed. To crush him, the whole universe does not have to arm itself. A mist, a drop of water,

The quotation comes from a section of the *Pensées* that concerns the 'disproportion of man' in the universe, while addressing the question: 'in the end, what is humanity in nature?' Pascal depicts humanity as suspended between the extreme scales of infinite space and the smallest things in nature:

> [w]hoever looks at himself in this way will be terrified by himself, and, thinking himself supported by the size nature has given us suspended between two gulfs of the infinite and the void, will tremble at nature's wonders.[88]

He describes such a vertiginous perspective as a 'new abyss', and repeatedly records his terror of infinite space: '[t]he eternal silence of these infinite spaces terrifies me'. However, this perspective is palliated for Pascal by the fact that humanity thinks and comprehends. One of his previous *pensées*, entitled 'Thinking reed', holds: '[i]t is not in space that I must look for my dignity, but in the organization of my thoughts [...]. Through space the universe grasps and engulfs me like a pinpoint; through thought I can grasp it'. Thus, in what might seem like a paradox, Pascal claims that 'Man's greatness lies in his capacity to recognize his wretchedness'.[89]

Huxley resituates Pascal's thought within the context of nineteenth-century natural science. Whereas Pascal had generated an abyssal perspective by placing humans against infinite space, Huxley generates a similarly vertiginous perspective by positioning them against vast stretches of geological time: Pascal's 'abyss' of nature becomes Playfair's 'abyss of time'. Further, Pascal provides a fitting precedent for Huxley's conception of ethical evolution. Huxley writes:

> [t]he history of civilization details the steps by which men have succeeded in building up an artificial world within the cosmos. Fragile reed as he may be, man, as Pascal says, is a thinking reed: there lies within him a fund of energy, operating intelligently and so far akin to that which pervades the universe, that it is competent to influence and modify the cosmic process.[90]

He here aligns Pascal's idea that man is a 'thinking reed' with his own doctrine of ethical evolution: that man 'is competent to influence and modify the cosmic process'. His citation of Pascal is adroit given that Pascal made a similar move from man's nature as a 'thinking reed' to the need to act ethically:

---

is enough to kill him. But if the universe were to crush the reed, the man would be nobler than his killer, since he knows that he is dying, and that the universe has the advantage over him. The universe knows nothing about this' (Blaise Pascal, *Pensées and Other Writings*, ed. Anthony Levi, trans. Honor Levi (Oxford: Oxford University Press, 2008), 72–3).

[88] Pascal, *Pensées*, 66–7.
[89] Pascal, *Pensées*, 67, 73, 36.
[90] Huxley, *Evolution*, 83–4.

[a]ll our dignity consists therefore of thought. It is from there that we must be lifted up and not from space and time, which we could never fill. So let us work on thinking well. That is the principle of morality.[91]

Just as Pascal located man's dignity in the thought through which he could grasp the immensity of nature and based morality in 'thinking well', so Huxley put great faith in the 'intelligence' by which humans could understand the cosmic process and seek to combat it through an ethical process.[92]

Wells generates similar temporal perspectives to those of Huxley in *The Time Machine* by having the Traveller voyage through geological time. However, while Pascal had salvaged dignity for humans by their ability to comprehend their position in nature, and Huxley had hoped that through such comprehension they could delay their inevitable cosmic fate, Wells offers no such consolation. As critics such as Mark Hillegas and Page have shown, *The Time Machine* dramatizes humans' fate having failed the Huxleyan challenge of evolving ethically, and to that extent its vision is one of cosmic pessimism.[93] As part of this failure, the romance conveys the loss of humans' self-awareness regarding their position in the cosmic process. For Huxley, the 'highly developed sciences and arts of the present day' already allow a great 'command over the course of non-human nature', and there is increasingly 'a right comprehension of the process of life and of the means of influencing its manifestations'.[94] Yet such a comprehension eludes the Eloi, who do not realize the significance of the fossils in the Palace of Green Porcelain, using them simply to make decorative necklaces: '[h]ere and there I found traces of the little people in the shape of rare fossils broken to pieces or threaded in strings upon reeds' (62). Whereas the Traveller can appreciate the pathos of the Eloi and their precarious position in a dying universe, this is an awareness that escapes the decadent and childlike people of the future who are completely oblivious to their impending extinction.

While *The Time Machine* envisages humans' failure to evolve ethically, Wells devoted much of the rest of his career to a political project of trying to secure such an evolution. Indeed, John Partington convincingly argues that Huxley's notion of ethical evolution influenced Wells not just in his early scientific writings but throughout his lifetime, and that it stands as 'the unifying principle' behind his later political commitments.[95] This principle generates many parallels between Wells's writing and more recent Anthropocene discourse. Certainly, the principle of ethical evolution does not define a geological or historical epoch

[91] Pascal, *Pensées*, 73.
[92] Huxley, *Evolution*, 84.
[93] Mark R. Hillegas, *The Future as Nightmare: H. G. Wells and the Anti-Utopians* (New York: Oxford University Press, 1967), 30; Page, *Imagination*, 153.
[94] Huxley, *Evolution*, 84.
[95] John S. Partington, *Building Cosmopolis: The Political Thought of H. G. Wells* (Aldershot: Ashgate, 2003), 37, 2.

and is less concerned with attributing responsibility to humans for major environmental damage. However, it is similar in that it conceives of humans on evolutionary and geological timescales; flags their vulnerability to phenomena such as climate change, overpopulation, and extinction; and acknowledges their capacity to imperil the conditions of their existence.[96] Most saliently, both open an ethical-political horizon for action. This is the sense of the Anthropocene as a moral-political issue in which scholars and activists 'seek in the crisis of global warming an ethical horizon for the future of humanity as a whole'.[97] Influenced by Huxley's conception of ethical evolution, Wells moved beyond his early cosmic pessimism to explore a similar moral-political horizon for the future of humanity. While *The Time Machine* presents a bleak picture in which humans have failed to evolve ethically before falling extinct, the later works convert the threat of extinction into an impetus to political action, and translate the possibility of ethical evolution into a series of political imperatives.

Plotting deep history

Wells's universal histories *The Outline of History* (1920) and *A Short History of the World* (1922) set themselves the ambitious task of telling 'truly and clearly, in one continuous narrative, the whole story of life and mankind so far as it is known today'.[98] They share with *The Time Machine* a concern with geological time, although they treat such a time in a very different manner: by seeking to tell a continuous historical story, they promise to humanize geological time. Imposing a scheme of meaning over geological time was important for Wells's political aims: he wished to provide his readers with a sense of their common origin in the past that would unsettle narrow national affiliations and support his proposals for a cosmopolitan World State. In doing so, his deep histories articulate conceptions of historical and political agency that complement his project of Huxleyan ethical evolution. When seen in the longer perspectives of history, humans are shown to have powers that imperil their own existence, and yet could also be controlled to secure their survival and open up a new phase of human history.

By telling the story of life across geological time, Wells's histories bring together two sorts of history that have, as Dipesh Chakrabarty points out, usually been taken to be distinct: human history and natural history. According to the first of Chakrabarty's influential theses on the climate of history, recent anthropogenic explanations of climate change spell the collapse of the distinction between these

[96] As Wells put it in his essay 'Zoological Retrogression' (1891), 'man's [...] activities and increase cause the conditions of his existence to fluctuate far more widely than those of any animal have ever done' (*Early Writings*, 168).
[97] Chakrabarty, 'Anthropocene Time', 9.
[98] H. G. Wells, *The Outline of History* (London: Cassell, 1920), v.

two sorts of history. Although the distinction has been largely preserved until recently, he notes that Fernand Braudel's *The Mediterranean* (1949) made 'a breach in the binary of natural/human history', and the rise of environmental history in the late twentieth century made the breach wider.[99] Although Wells was not a professional historian, his universal histories should be recognized as another notable attempt to combine human and natural history. Their account of anthropogenic climate change and human agency resembles some recent accounts of the Anthropocene, and particularly those that seek to realize a 'good Anthropocene'. In part, reading Wells's histories alongside these accounts of the Anthropocene serves as a timely reminder of the political dangers that can accompany attempts to rescale the human. However, I will ultimately suggest that that a more salutary reading of his histories can be generated by attending to their historiographic shortcomings. If their attempt to reconcile human and geological scales and types of time through a continuous historical narrative is read against itself as revealing their disjuncture, then his histories can be seen as posing a challenge that has become increasingly pressing with recent explanations of anthropogenic climate change: the challenge, identified by Chakrabarty, of having to think of human agency 'over multiple and incommensurable scales at once'.[100]

Wells stressed the political urgency of large-scale history, arguing that it was needed to counteract nationalism and avoid war. As he put it in the preface to the *Outline of History*, there is an acute need of 'common historical ideas' to ensure a world peace:

> there can be no common peace and prosperity without common historical ideas. Without such ideas to hold them together in harmonious co-operation, with nothing but narrow, selfish, and conflicting nationalist traditions, races and peoples are bound to drift towards conflict and destruction.[101]

Against the narrow varieties of national history that were taught in schools, he pitted his own version of universal history with its 'sense of history as the common adventure of all mankind'.[102] Such a form of history was needed to prepare readers for their role as cosmopolitan citizens in the coming World State: as he put it elsewhere, '[w]orld federation and the teaching of world history are two correlated and inseparable things'.[103] His championing of universal history thereby forms an important aspect of his cosmopolitan politics. Indeed, driven by what he saw as the failure of the League of Nations in 1919, his universal histories mark

---

[99] Chakrabarty, 'Climate of History', 201, 205.
[100] Chakrabarty, 'Postcolonial', 1.
[101] Wells, *Outline*, v; emphasis removed.
[102] Wells, *Outline*, vi.
[103] H. G. Wells, *After Democracy: Addresses and Papers on the Present World Situation* (London: Watts, 1932), 170.

an important turn in his politics from support of international cooperation to advocacy of forms of cosmopolitan government that would dissolve the nation as a sovereign political entity.[104] In part, the 'sweeping views' of the universal histories help to unsettle nationalism. By placing the modern nation state—which only emerged in the nineteenth century—in the wider perspective of deep history, it is shown to be a comparatively recent phenomenon, and one that is subject to change and supersession by other forms of political association. While Huxley had employed perspectives on geological time to unsettle the idea that 'human nature' is somehow permanent, Wells redeploys a similar perspective to challenge the view that ideas of 'nation' and 'empire' represent something 'fundamental and inalterable in human nature'.[105]

To organize his histories on their vast spatiotemporal scales, Wells drew on two principal historiographical models: biblical history and Immanuel Kant's universal history with a cosmopolitan aim. His histories are teleological, telling the story of 'life and mankind' as one of progress from a common biological origin in the remote geological past towards the *telos* of a coming World State or the political 'federation of all humanity'. '[C]lumsily or smoothly', we are told, 'the world [...] progresses and will progress'.[106] In doing so, he adapted a figural structure from the Judaeo-Christian Bible. For example, in the *Short History*, he holds that the 'new communication and interdependence' of mammalian species in the Cainozoic period 'foreshadows the development of human societies of which we shall soon be telling'.[107] In turn, various human societies are depicted as foreshadowing a lasting peace and unity. For example, in the *Outline*, Alexander the Great is held to be a 'portent of world unity' and his empire is described as 'the first revelation to the human imagination of the oneness of human affairs'.[108] Here, 'revelation' retains a religious connotation: Alexander's empire is the first historical revelation of the 'oneness of human affairs', though the full revelation awaits the coming World State which, like the last days of the Book of Revelation, promises to be a revelation of history's meaning.

Wells found an even more appealing historiographical model for his deep histories in Kant's 'Idea for a Universal History with a Cosmopolitan Aim' (1784). In the introduction to the *Outline*, he attributed to the 'great philosopher Kant' the insight that 'there can be no common peace and prosperity without common historical ideas', and held that his is one of 'the views of history that this *Outline* seeks to realize'.[109] He also praised F. S. Marvin's *The Living Past: A Sketch of Western*

---

[104] See Partington, *Cosmopolis*, 82, 109.

[105] Wells, *Outline*, 528–30.

[106] Wells, *Outline*, 605, 608.

[107] H. G. Wells, *A Short History of the World* (London: Cassell, 1922), 38, 40.

[108] Wells, *Outline*, 195–6.

[109] Wells, *Outline*, v–vi, emphasis removed. Wells refers to Kant's 'tract upon universal peace', which seems to indicate Kant's 'Perpetual Peace: A Philosophical Sketch' (1795). However, as William Ross points out, it is clearly Kant's 'Idea for a Universal History with a Cosmopolitan Aim' (1784) that Wells

Progress (1913), which summarizes Kant's writings on history.[110] Like Marvin, he adapted a progressive scheme of history from Kant and imposed it over what Marvin describes as the 'vast tract of geologic time' that had recently been opened up by scientific geology.[111] Following Kant's proposal, Wells developed a scheme of universal history that has the cosmopolitan aim of a 'perfect Civil Union' for pragmatic reasons: its very idea promotes the actualization of such an end.[112] Notably, Kant's idea provided Wells with a means of moving beyond his earlier cosmic pessimism. He could maintain his long-standing view that humans as a species are liable to biological degeneration and extinction, while optimistically championing their progress towards a cosmopolitan World State.

However, while biblical history and Kant's universal history provided Wells with a shape and structure to his history and suggested a broad narrative organization that could be imposed over the expanses of deep time, his attempt to tell the whole story of life and mankind 'in one continuous narrative' still encounters significant difficulties, particularly in the early chapters which cover the Earth's remote past. One difficulty is that so much of the story is missing. In both histories, he draws attention to the imperfect nature of the geological record, and our consequently partial knowledge of the Earth's remote past. In the *Outline*, he employs a variant of the common metaphor of the legibility of the geological record by describing rocks as 'historical documents', and extends this conceit by holding that these rocks are not like the orderly books and pages of a library, but rather are 'torn, disrupted, interrupted, flung about, defaced, like a carelessly arranged office after it has experienced in succession a bombardment, a hostile military occupation, looting, an earthquake, riots, and a fire'.[113] Nevertheless, he is keen not to let incomplete knowledge of the geological past disrupt the continuity of his story. For example, at the end of the seventh chapter of the *Short History*, he points to a gap in our knowledge of perhaps 'several million years':

> [t]here comes a break in the Record of the Rocks that may represent several million years. There is a veil here still, over even the outline of the history of life. When it lifts again, the Age of Reptiles is at an end [...] we find now a new scene, a new and hardier flora and a new and hardier fauna in possession of the world.[114]

This break in the geological record is reflected typographically on the page, with the use of ellipses at the end of the previous paragraph, and the atypical use of a

has in mind (*H. G. Wells's World Reborn: 'The Outline of History' and Its Companions* (Selinsgrove: Susquehanna University Press, 2002), 37).

[110] Wells, *Outline*, vi.

[111] F. S. Marvin, *The Living Past: A Sketch of Western Progress* (Oxford: Clarendon Press, 1913), 11–12.

[112] Immanuel Kant, *Kant's Principles of Politics, Including his Essay on Perpetual Peace: A Contribution to Political Science*, ed. and trans. W. Hastie (Edinburgh: T. & T. Clark, 1891), 25.

[113] Wells, *Outline*, 7.

[114] Wells, *Short History*, 35.

line break between paragraphs. Yet this break is not otherwise allowed to disrupt the continuity of the story, and within the same paragraph he moves on to the next 'scene' of history. Narrative continuity is facilitated here by the ambiguity that attaches to the word 'scene', which refers both to a geological era and to a narrative scene. This second meaning is reinforced by the fact that the 'scene' forms the topic of the next chapter, which covers the Cainozoic era. The transition between narrative scenes and chapters in the story invites the reader to make a similarly smooth imaginative transition between geological eras. In this sense, the metaphor of the 'veil' is telling: it suggests that a stretch of geological history is unclear or obscured from view, but further intimates that this break is being concealed or hidden. Wells becomes like a magician using a narrative trick to rush his readers past an inconvenient break in history, triumphantly lifting the veil to reveal a new scene.

Wells's histories encounter further difficulties that arise from their attempt to condense vast stretches of time into short passages. These difficulties stem from what Timothy Clark calls 'scale effects', which are similar to those faced by geologists in their attempts to narrate the history of the Earth.[115] In the *Principles of Geology*, to illustrate the errors of the catastrophists which arise from assuming too short a timescale in which the geological events of the past are supposed to have occurred, Lyell asks us to imagine that:

> the annals of the civil and military transactions of a great nation [...] be perused under the impression that they occurred in a period of one hundred instead of two thousand years. Such a portion of history would immediately assume the air of a romance; the events would seem devoid of credibility, and inconsistent with the present course of human affairs. A crowd of incidents would follow each other in thick succession. Armies and fleets would appear to be assembled only to be destroyed, and cities built merely to fall in ruins.[116]

By compressing a two-thousand-year history into a one-hundred-year timescale, a narrative account would read like an event-crowded romance, rather than a history. Olaf Stapledon's novel *Last and First Men* (1930), the plot of which turns on a Wellsian conception of history, raises a similar problem in explicitly narrative terms. The novel's principal narrator is a historian from the distant future who tells the story of humankind in a (fictional) deep history of the universe. In the introduction, the narrator, who lives 'aeons' away in the future, invites the reader to

> contemplate for a few moments the mere magnitudes of cosmical events. For, compressed as it must necessarily be, the narrative that I have to tell may seem

[115] Timothy Clark, 'Scale', in *Telemorphosis: Theory in the Era of Climate Change, Vol. 1*, ed. Tom Cohen (Michigan: Open Humanities Press, 2012), 148–66.
[116] Lyell, *Principles*, I, 29.

to present a sequence of adventures and disasters crowded together [...] in fact, man's career has been less like a mountain torrent hurtling from rock to rock, than a great sluggish river, broken seldom by rapids [...]. [E]ven [the] few seemingly rapid events themselves were in fact often long-drawn-out and tedious. They acquire a mere illusion of speed from the speed of the narrative.[117]

The narrative compression in which 'adventures and disasters' appear 'crowded together' is much like that of Lyell's imagined compressed history, in which a 'crowd of incidents would follow each other in thick succession'. The 'illusion of speed' which Stapledon's narrator diagnoses as arising from 'the speed of the narrative' can be glossed through the distinction between story time and discourse time: if vast stretches of story time are narrated in brief stretches of discourse time, then the story appears to be more eventful than it actually was.

In part, Wells's histories negotiate the formal difficulty that Stapledon's narrator diagnoses by telling the story of the prehuman past as one that is supposedly devoid of events. While its introduction stresses that the *Outline* is 'one continuous narrative', Wells also claims in the early chapters to be 'telling of a history without events'. The first 'event' does not occur until the eleventh chapter, entitled 'Neolithic Man'. This 'event of primary importance' is 'the breaking in of the Atlantic waters to the great Mediterranean valley'. It is narrated with the intensity and drama of an adventure story: '[s]uddenly the ocean waters began to break through over the westward hills and to pour in upon [the] primitive people'.[118] Before this point, Wells employs a variety of strategies to maintain a narrative thread through a prehuman past that is devoid of events: he sketches a series of static scenes conjoined by summary and drastic ellipsis, employs rising action and anti-climax to achieve a novelistic rhythm, and uses an imaginative conceit of time travel.

To tell the story of the remote past, Wells's narrative proceeds by sketching a series of static, eventless scenes. Martin Rudwick and Ralph O'Connor have drawn attention to the importance of a tradition of pictorial representation of the primaeval world for the imagination of deep time.[119] Wells's histories contain many such 'scenes from deep time', which help the reader to visualize the successive geological ages being described. For example, the *Outline* contains the 'Diagram of Life in the Later Palæozoic Age', which is reproduced in Figure 1.4, and the *Short History* contains pictures with titles such as 'Landscape Before Life', 'Marine Life in the Cambrian Period', 'Sharks and Ganoids of the Devonian Period', and 'A

[117] W. Olaf Stapledon, *Last and First Men: A Story of the Near and Far Future* (London: Methuen, 1930), 2, emphasis removed.
[118] Wells, *Outline*, 59–60.
[119] Martin Rudwick, *Scenes from Deep Time: Early Pictorial Representations of the Prehistoric World* (Chicago: University of Chicago Press, 1992); O'Connor, *Earth*, 263–324.

Figure 1.4 'Diagram of Life in the Later Palæozoic Age'

Reproduced from Wells, H. G. (1920). *The Outline of History.* London: Cassell.

Carboniferous Swamp'.[120] The narrative of the early chapters functions in a manner similar to the accompanying pictures: it unfolds as a series of static verbal sketches of different geological ages. In his review of the *Outline*, E. M. Forster conveyed this narrative quality when he compared Wells's history to a lecture that is given with the aid of slides that are projected onto a sheet by a lantern.[121] In the *Short History*, a metaphor of sketching pictures explicitly encourages us to think of the narrative in a visual way: '[i]n a few paragraphs a picture of the lush vegetation and swarming reptiles of that first great summer of life, the Mesozoic Period, has been sketched'. Such sketches—which in the *Outline* can be correlated with a time diagram reproduced in Figure 1.5 that sets out some of the main divisions in geological time—become the basic narrative unit in Wells's story of the prehuman past. They are often connected together by means of striking narrative ellipses, through

[120] Wells, *Short History*, 9, 11, 18, 21. In the *Outline*, Wells cautions his readers against the historical inaccuracy of the 'fantastic pictures' of E. T. Reed's *Prehistoric Peeps* (1894) but recommends other works that provide vivid illustrations of the geological past, such as Henry Knipe's *Nebula to Man* (1905) and *Evolution in the Past* (1912), which are 'full of admirable illustrations of extinct monsters' (24).

[121] E. M. Forster, 'A Great History', *Athenaeum*, 2 July 1920, 8.

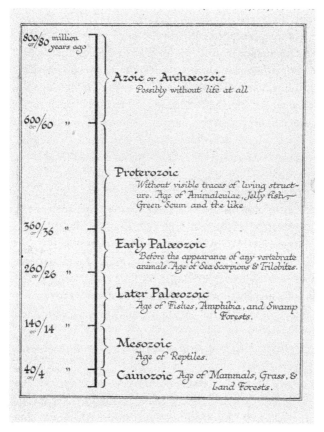

Figure 1.5 'Diagram Giving Some of the Main Divisions in Geological Time'

Reproduced from Wells, H. G. (1920). *The Outline of History*. London: Cassell.

which huge portions of story time are elided: '[t]he Earth aged. One million years followed another.'[122] By advancing a series of static verbal sketches connected by such ellipses, Wells tells the story of the geological past without recourse to any events; the rhythm of his histories consists in the movement between such scenes.

Despite being devoid of events, the early chapters of Wells's histories take on a familiar novelistic rhythm, complete with rising action and anti-climax. The preface to the *Short History* encourages its readers to read the work 'straight-forwardly almost as a novel is read'. A similar approach to the *Outline* was encouraged by its marketing campaign, and the advertisements which highlighted Wells's success

---

[122] Wells, *Short History*, 30, 9.

as a novelist and portrayed him as a 'Master Story-Teller'.[123] Indeed, the histories display many features associated with novelistic narratives. For example, far from resulting in a fragmentary narrative, the break in the geological record at the end of the Mesozoic period discussed above is made to form part of the narrative rhythm of the history. In the *Short History*, we learn that 'the Mesozoic period rose to its climax', a 'climax' which refers most immediately to the climax of a geological age, but also suggests that there will be a narrative climax. However, such an expectation is disappointed, and we never find out what happened.[124] The parallel episode in the *Outline* is marked by a similar cadence of rising action and anti-climax: this 'great period of Mesozoic life, this second volume of the book of life, is indeed an amazing story of reptilian life proliferating and developing. But the most striking thing of all the story remains to be told'. Again, the promise of a 'striking' event in the story proves to be a false one, and we learn anti-climactically that: '[t]hen the record is broken [...]. When next we find abundant traces of the land plants and the land animals of the earth, this great multitude of reptile species had gone'. What must have been an 'abrupt ending', a 'striking revolution' and a 'catastrophic alteration' is speculated about only retrospectively and fails to constitute a narrative event, a failure which only serves to highlight the absence of events from the early chapters of the history.[125]

Employing strategies that Wells had developed in *The Time Machine*, the *Short History* uses the conceit of time travel to tell the story of the deep past. In *The Time Machine*, the device allows the Traveller to traverse millions of years and observe the infinitesimally slow changes of geology and astronomy. The second chapter of the *Short History*, entitled 'The World in Time', employs a similar conceit:

> [i]f we could go back through that infinitude of time and see the earth in this earlier stage of its history, we should behold a scene more like the interior of a blast furnace.[126]

The journey is not a literal one with the aid of a time machine, but an imaginative one, expressed by the hypothetical clause: '*[i]f* we could go back [...] we *should* behold a scene'. The history proceeds to imagine a voyage through time in a passage which, other than being written in the subjunctive mood, closely resembles the Traveller's descriptions of his voyages:

> [a]cross a sky of fiery clouds the glare of the hurrying sun and moon would sweep swiftly like hot breaths of flame. Slowly by degrees as one million of years

---

[123] See Matthew Skelton, 'The Paratext of Everything: Constructing and Marketing H. G. Wells's *The Outline of History*', *Book History*, 4 (2001), 237–75, 247.
[124] Wells, *Short History*, 27, 35.
[125] Wells, *Outline*, 22–3.
[126] Wells, *Short History*, 5.

followed another, this fiery scene would lose its eruptive incandescence [...]. The sun and moon growing now each more distant and each smaller, would rush with diminishing swiftness across the heavens.[127]

This imaginative conceit allows vast stretches of story time to be covered in an extremely short discourse time. As in *The Time Machine*, the conceit of time travel provides a visual way of imagining the Earth's changes through deep time.

Although the *Short History* makes use of some of the resources offered by the earlier scientific romance, the histories otherwise differ markedly in their depiction of deep time. Rather than dwelling on the poverty of our knowledge of the past, as the frame narrator of *The Time Machine* was made painfully aware of his 'vast ignorance' of the future, Wells offers the *Short History* to his reader as an aid to 'refresh and repair his faded or fragmentary conceptions of the great adventure of mankind'.[128] Whereas the fragmentary narrative of *The Time Machine* intimates a vast and inhuman geological time, the continuous narrative of Wells's histories humanizes geological time. In Ricoeur's terms, the narrative structure of the histories allows a poetic resolution between phenomenological and cosmological types of time: through the continuous narrative of the deep histories, lived time is reinscribed on geological time in the form of historical time.[129] Correlatively, the sublime aesthetic, which had been deployed in *The Time Machine* to mediate the encounter with a vast and inhuman geological time that defies comprehension, is largely abandoned in the histories. Although the past depicted therein is immense, it is not a source of sublime terror. For example, in the *Short History*, Wells writes that:

> [t]he Age of Reptiles lasted, it is now guessed, eighty million years. Had any quasi-human intelligence been watching the world through that inconceivable length of time, how safe and eternal the sunshine and abundance must have seemed, how assured the wallowing prosperity of the Dinosaurs and the flapping abundance of the flying lizards![130]

This safe land of eternal sunshine is a far cry from the hostile future world the Traveller visits, or the frame-narrator's speculations about his fate in the deep past among the 'blood-drinking, hairy savages', or among the 'grotesque saurians, the huge reptilian brutes of the Jurassic times' (91). If there are vestiges of the sublime aesthetic in the histories' portrayal of geological time, it functions not to highlight humanity's insignificant position in a hostile universe, but rather to augment the wonder of humanity's progress through deep history towards a cosmopolitan

[127] Wells, *Short History*, 6–8, my emphasis.
[128] Wells, *Short History*, v.
[129] Ricoeur, *Time and Narrative*, III, 4, 99.
[130] Wells, *Short History*, 33.

society: '[a]ge by age through gulfs of time at which imagination reels, life has been growing from a mere stirring in the intertidal slime towards freedom, power, and consciousness'.[131]

Wells's recentring of humans in the universal histories allowed him to articulate new conceptions of historical and political agency at the level of the species. In telling the story of how humans have become more powerful over the centuries, he makes clear that they cause changes to the world's climate, to which all life must then adapt:

> with the appearance of human communities, came what is perhaps the most powerful of all living influences upon climate. By fire and plough and axe man alters his world. By destroying forests and by irrigation man has already affected the climate of great regions of the world's surface. The destruction of forests makes the seasons more extreme; this has happened, for instance, in the north-eastern states of the United States of America [...]. By irrigation, on the other hand, man restores the desert to life and mitigates climate [...]. In the future, by making such operations world-wide and systematic, man may be able to control climate to an extent at which as yet we can only guess.[132]

While this account of anthropogenic climate change suggests that humans have long been one of 'the forces that change climate and the conditions of terrestrial life', Wells stresses that they have become vastly more powerful in recent centuries: in the nineteenth century there 'swept across the world a wave of universal change in human power'.[133] This change has resulted in an increased capacity for waste and destruction—illustrated by the Great War—yet also brings promise for humans if they could coordinate their efforts by forming a World State. As he puts it in the *Short History*, 'the scientific method of fearless thought, exhaustively lucid statement, and exhaustively criticised planning, which has given [man] [...] as yet uncontrollable powers, gives him also the hope of controlling these powers'.[134] Indeed, the final chapters of the histories speculate on the feats that humans could achieve if they were to control their powers. Among the predictions made is that:

> Men will turn again with renewed interest to the animal world. In these disordered days a stupid, uncontrollable massacre of animal species goes on—from certain angles of vision it is a thing almost more tragic than human miseries; in the nineteenth century dozens of animal species, and some of them very interesting

---

[131] Wells, *Short History*, 15.

[132] Wells, *Outline*, 18. In the *Short History*, it is held that 'we do not know sufficient of the causes of climatic change at present to forecast the possible fluctuations of climatic conditions that lie before us. We may be moving towards increasing sunshine or lapsing towards another glacial age; [...] we do not know; we lack sufficient science' (36).

[133] Wells, *Outline*, 18, 505.

[134] Wells, *Short History*, 403.

species, were exterminated; but one of the first fruits of an effective world state would be the better protection of what are now wild beasts.[135]

Just as he raised the possibility that humans could 'control climate' through world-wide and systematic operations, so he holds that they could protect the animal species that they are otherwise destroying. Reiterating the need for 'a new telling and interpretation [...] of history' as a basis for world-cooperation, the *Outline* ends with a note of utopian optimism for humans on Earth and beyond, conveyed by its closing image of life stretching 'out its realm amidst the stars'.[136]

In certain respects, Wells's visions of human agency anticipate recent accounts of the Anthropocene. By identifying humans as one of 'the forces that change climate and the conditions of terrestrial life', he anticipates accounts of the Anthropocene as an epoch in which humans have become a 'geological force'. More specifically, his confidence that humans could control their powers through collective action anticipates optimistic accounts of a 'good Anthropocene', such as those of the 'ecomodernists' who write 'with the conviction that knowledge and technology, applied with wisdom, might allow for a good, or even great, Anthropocene'.[137] As a historical project, his attempt to integrate human and natural history over vast spatiotemporal scales resembles recent popular approaches to history that make use of the concept of the Anthropocene, such as the projects of 'big history' associated with David Christian, and 'deep history' associated with Daniel Lord Smail.[138] Or, by seeking to grant world history a world-historical role, Wells perhaps most closely resembles William H. McNeill, whom Chakrabarty describes as the 'patron saint for [the] vision of a world-historical future for humanity in which humans take collective responsibility for their physical impact on the planet'.[139]

Wells's universal histories might serve as a warning about certain grand narratives of the Anthropocene, and proposals for an elite group of scientific technocrats to assume responsibility for the future of humanity.[140] While Wells advertised the benefits of his histories for securing world peace, others were critical of their

---

[135] Wells, *Outline*, 607.

[136] Wells, *Outline*, 603, 608, emphasis removed.

[137] John Asafu-Adjaye et al., *An Ecomodernist Manifesto* (2015), 6. <https://www.ecomodernism.org/manifesto-english> [last accessed 25 January 2023].

[138] See, for example, David Christian, *Maps of Time: An Introduction to Big History*, 2nd edn (Berkeley: University of California Press, 2011); Fred Spier, *Big History and the Future of Humanity*, 2nd edn (Chichester: Wiley Blackwell, 2015); and Andrew Shyrock, and others, *Deep History: The Architecture of Past and Present* (Berkeley: University of California Press, 2011). Cole argues that Wells's *Outline* can 'justifiably be named a pioneer in the field recently named "Big History"' (*Inventing Tomorrow*, 38, 224–5).

[139] Chakrabarty, 'Anthropocene Time', 14.

[140] Of the grand narratives of the Anthropocene that Christophe Bonneuil and Jean-Baptiste Fressoz distinguish, Wells's histories most closely resemble that which places scientists 'at the command post of a dishevelled planet and its errant humanity': '[s]cientists would then hold a monopoly position both in defining what is happening to us and in prescribing what needs to be done' (*The Shock of the Anthropocene: The Earth, History and Us*, trans. David Fernbach (London: Verso, 2017), 80).

politics. Christopher Caudwell objected to the *Outline* from a Marxist perspective, arguing that it contains 'no classes' and fails to recognize class conflict as the driving force of history, making it the perfect 'bourgeois history'.[141] As well as eliding the issue of class, Wells's biological approach to history involves dividing the human species into racial types, some of which are granted a peripheral role in world history. Claude McKay reports that he took a 'violent prejudice' against the *Outline of History*: 'I did not like Mr. Wells's attitude toward colored people in general and Africa and Negroes in particular'. He was 'shocked by the plan of his large tome outlining world history' because 'it appears there as if Africa and Africans have not been of enormous importance in world history'.[142] And George Orwell criticized Wells's general confidence in progress and his advocacy of a World State. To Wells's manifest displeasure, he suggested that these ideas were best realized in Nazi Germany.[143] He was also particularly unimpressed with his 'by now familiar idea that mankind must either develop a World State or perish', comparing Wells to a nursemaid scolding a naughty child: '"Now, you'll take your nice medicine or the bogey-man'll come and eat you up". Homo sapiens must do what he is told or he will become extinct'.[144]

It is important to acknowledge the force of these objections. The final chapter of this book explores how Jean Rhys's fiction conveys an alternative conception of history that does accord Africa and Africans an enormous importance in world history, and thereby unsettles Wells's universal histories, and some more recent accounts of the Anthropocene that they resemble. However, it is also possible to generate a counter-reading of Wells's histories by attending to their failures. Such a reading follows Cole's suggestion that although Wells's attempt to write the history of all parts and peoples of the world is in some ways unsuccessful and betrays his own Eurocentric biases, its significance lies in the power of its provocation, which has 'goaded historians to respond, in most cases with umbrage'.[145] We might add that in the early chapters, the narrative sleights of hand, faltering passages devoid of events, and drastic ellipses all point to the failures of his attempts to scale up human history. By trying to tell the story of life on geological timescales, Wells's histories do not resolve but rather bring to light an aporia between what Ricoeur characterizes as two distinct and irreconcilable conceptions of time: phenomenological and cosmological. By bringing these two sorts of time into collision, the histories

---

[141] Christopher Caudwell, *Studies in a Dying Culture* (London: John Lane, 1938), 86.

[142] Claude McKay, *A Long Way from Home* (New York: Lee Furman, 1937), 121–2.

[143] George Orwell, 'Wells, Hitler and the World State' (1941), in *The Complete Works of George Orwell*, ed. Peter Davison, 20 vols (London: Secker & Warburg, 1998), XII, 536–41, 538–9. As Davison notes, Wells and Orwell had a 'God-awful row' about this essay at a dinner party held by Inez Holden in 1941 (*Complete Works*, XIII, 250). Following another of his incendiary essays, Orwell recorded receiving an '[a]busive letter from H. G. Wells, who addresses me as "You shit", among other things' (diary entry for 27 March 1942, in *Complete Works*, XIII, 249).

[144] George Orwell, 'Review of '42 to '44: A Contemporary Memoir upon Human Behaviour During the Crisis of the World Revolution by H. G. Wells' (1944), in Complete Works, XVI, 197–9, 197–8.

[145] Cole, *Inventing Tomorrow*, 39.

disclose what Chakrabarty describes as a limit to the time of historicality, and mark a conceptual-temporal place where the 'meaning-making' of human history—the tension between the horizon of expectation and the space of experience—ceases to work.[146] In doing so, the histories betray their own efforts to reposition humans at the centre of history and the universe: the ludicrousness of their attempt to scale up a humanist scheme of history points to an incipient inhumanism, and the need for alternative conceptions of human and non-human agency.[147]

Although Wells's histories ultimately disclose an aporia between incompatible conceptions of time and demonstrate a failure of historical understanding, they do so in a productive way. By reframing history on geological and planetary scales, they signal a collapse in the humanist distinction between human history and natural history, and provide a form in which large-scale phenomena such as climate change and species extinctions—which are normally confined to the realms of natural history—start to become visible. This reframing also starts to show how humans have devastated the environment on a planetary scale. Yet what is ultimately more compelling is the way that the breakdown of his historical scheme intimates types of destructive agency that escape the histories' representational capacities and elude humanist historical understanding. His universal histories thereby expose some of the concealments of histories that are set on smaller scales. Indeed, he drew attention to some of these occlusions in his 1939 talk 'The Poison Called History', in which he argued that the national history that is widely taught in schools has failed to combat unprecedented environmental destruction just as much as it has failed to prevent war:

> In the past hundred years you have seen great regions of the United States turned to sandy desert, you have seen Australia swept by fires, ring-barking and rabbits, you have seen a slaughter of scores of useful animal species, you have seen a monstrous destruction of animal resources, and your old history teaching does nothing [...] to awaken the minds of the coming generation to the supreme gravity of this process.[148]

Regretting that 'history teaches us no better', he suggests that a 'map of the world showing the devastated regions, where devastation is due to mankind, would amaze most people', and calls for a 'history of the devastation of the world, due

---

[146] Chakrabarty, 'Anthropocene Time', 23.

[147] Chakrabarty suggests that the concept of the Anthropocene calls for a rethinking of history at the level of the species, although Derek Woods argues that it demands accounts of agency that displace the concept of the human: 'the "*anthropos*" of "Anthropocene" and "anthropogenic" needs to be divided among scale domains, the tributaries of which fail to converge at "species"' ('Scale Critique for the Anthropocene', *the minnesota review*, 83 (2014), 133–42, 138). While Chakrabarty's challenge has been taken up in a range of disciplines, it is a contention of this book that modernism provides a number of models for such a rethinking of human and non-human agency.

[148] H. G. Wells, *Travels of a Republican Radical in Search of Hot Water* (Harmondsworth: Penguin, 1939), 111.

to planless exploitation, uncontrolled competition and conflict, leading to the hypertrophied war of today'.[149]

Of course, Wells's universal histories were not his only attempt to rethink human agency, and to explore the opportunities for humans if they could control their powers. They function alongside his utopias as components of an overarching cosmopolitan political project, which might retrospectively be described as an 'eco-cosmopolitanism'. While the histories aim to provide common historical ideas capable of fostering a World State, the utopias explore the ways that such a State might be organized. The utopias are not directly concerned with geological time, and they turn their attention from the past to the future, yet they complement the histories in the way that they reshape historical time. Whereas the histories refigure historical time by attempting to reinscribe lived time onto cosmic time in a manner that facilitates a cosmopolitan form of historical consciousness, the utopias disclose the ecological risks that lie within the historical present, and provide a means of envisaging cosmopolitan countermeasures on a planetary scale.

Utopia and ecological risk

Recent fiction that portrays future climate-changed worlds might be seen as the foremost cultural expression of what the sociologist Ulrich Beck calls the 'speculative age'. For Beck, such an age began as 'risk society' emerged with recognition of the unprecedented dangers that modernity brought about as well as its benefits; this reflexive phase of modernity is characterized by a transition of concern from the production and distribution of wealth, to the production and distribution of risks.[150] Certainly, much recent speculative fiction bears a striking resemblance to the future scenarios that are widely used to articulate environmental risks, such as the climate change scenarios that the Intergovernmental Panel on Climate Change (IPCC) has employed in its reports since 1990. For example, the special report *Global Warming of 1.5°C* (2018) develops four model pathways (displayed in Figures 1.6 and 1.7), which use storylines backed up by quantitative models to represent how global warming could be limited to 1.5°C above pre-industrial levels by the year 2100.[151] Supporting Beck's theory of the turn to a risk society, such projections play an increasingly important role in assessing environmental risks and generating policy for action.

It might seem that modernism has little to do with such a speculative age. After all, Beck contends that risk society emerged only in the second half of the twentieth century. And undoubtedly, many of the works that are now considered to be

[149] Wells, *Travels*, 110–11.
[150] Ulrich Beck, *Risk Society: Towards a New Modernity*, trans. Mark Ritter (London: Sage, 1992).
[151] IPCC, *Global Warming of 1.5°C*, ed. Valérie Masson-Delmotte and others (2018), 13–14. <https://www.ipcc.ch/sr15/> [last accessed 25 January 2023].

Global emissions pathway characteristics

General characteristics of the evolution of anthropogenic net emissions of CO_2 and total emissions of methane, black carbon, and nitrous oxide in model pathways that limit global warming to 1.5°C with no or limited overshoot. Net emissions are defined as anthropogenic emissions reduced by anthropogenic removals. Reductions in net emissions can be achieved through different portfolios of mitigation measures illustrated in Figure SPM.3b.

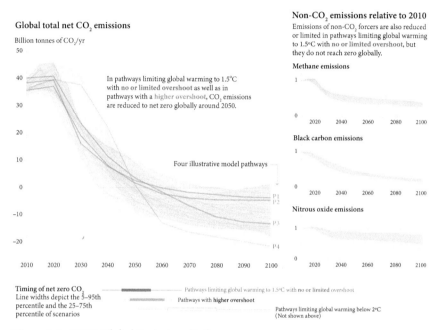

Figure 1.6 IPCC Global Emissions Pathways

Reproduced from IPCC (2018). *Global Warming of 1.5°C*. Figure SPM.1.

modernist preceded the growing concerns about nuclear war, pesticides, and climate change that drove mainstream environmentalist movements from the 1960s onwards. However, Wells's utopias already registered the unprecedented dangers of modernity, and helped initiate the speculative age. Hinting at the role literature plays in how we understand risk, Beck emphasizes that risks are 'particularly open to social definition and construction': they can be 'changed, magnified, dramatized or minimized within knowledge'.[152] Wells's utopias participate in such a construction: combining his interests in biology and ecology with an aesthetic form capable of mediating complex systems on a planetary scale, they produce knowledge of ecological risk. Notably, they produce knowledge about the ecological risks of global pandemics—such as the influenza pandemic of 1918 and the coronavirus pandemic of 2019—and species extinctions, such as those which are now deemed to constitute the sixth mass extinction.

---

[152] Beck, *Risk Society*, 23; emphasis removed.

Characteristics of four illustrative model pathways

Different mitigation strategies can achieve the net emissions reductions that would be required to follow a pathway that limits global warming to 1.5°C with no or limited overshoot. All pathways use Carbon Dioxide Removal (CDR), but the amount varies across pathways, as do the relative contributions of Bioenergy with Carbon Capture and Storage (BECCS) and removals in the Agriculture, Forestry and Other Land Use (AFOLU) sector. This has implications for emissions and several other pathway characteristics.

Breakdown of contributions to global net CO_2 emissions in four illustrative model pathways

● Fossil fuel and industry   ● AFOLU   ● BECCS

P1: A scenario in which social, business and technological innovations result in lower energy demand up to 2050 while living standards rise, especially in the global South. A downsized energy system enables rapid decarbonization of energy supply. Afforestation is the only CDR option considered; neither fossil fuels with CCS nor BECCS are used.	P2: A scenario with a broad focus on sustainability including energy intensity, human development, economic convergence and international cooperation, as well as shifts towards sustainable and healthy consumption patterns, low-carbon technology innovation, and well-managed land systems with limited societal acceptability for BECCS.	P3: A middle-of-the-road scenario in which societal as well as technological development follows historical patterns. Emissions reductions are mainly achieved by changing the way in which energy and products are produced, and to a lesser degree by reductions in demand.	P4: A resource-and energy-intensive scenario in which economic growth and globalization lead to widespread adoption of greenhouse-gas-intensive lifestyles, including high demand for transportation fuels and livestock products. Emissions reductions are mainly achieved through technological means, making strong use of CDR through the deployment of BECCS.

Figure 1.7 IPCC Breakdown of Four Model Pathways
Reproduced from IPCC (2018). *Global Warming of 1.5°C.* Figure SPM.3a.

By producing knowledge of environmental risk, Wells's utopias refigure historical time. Darko Suvin and Fredric Jameson famously argue that literary utopias and science fiction allow the apprehension of the present as history through estrangement and defamiliarization: for Jameson, they function to 'defamiliarize and restructure our experience of our own present'.[153] However, Wells's utopias restructure our experience not simply by disclosing our entrapment in the ideological prison-house of the present, but by producing knowledge about risk.[154] Playing on contemplative and anticipatory senses of speculation, Beck portrays risk society as marking the dawn of a 'speculative age' in which, through anticipation of future hazards, people's experience of the present is changed. Through a 'double gaze' it becomes possible to view the 'second reality' or 'shadow kingdom' of risk that lies concealed behind the visible world.[155] The revelation of this second reality is what Wells's utopias—and the feigned futures of speculative fiction more generally—bring about. If this revelation can be described as an estrangement or

---

[153] Fredric Jameson, *Archaeologies of the Future: The Desire Called Utopia and Other Science Fictions* (London: Verso, 2005), 286; emphasis removed. For Suvin, science fiction achieves cognitive estrangement by imagining alternative futures that force us to historicize the now as 'the determinate past of something yet to come' (*Metamorphoses of Science Fiction: On the Poetics and History of a Literary Genre* (New Haven: Yale University Press, 1979), 7–8).

[154] Jameson suggests that 'at best Utopia can serve the negative purpose of making us more aware of our mental and ideological imprisonment' (*Archaeologies*, xiii).

[155] Beck, *Risk Society*, 72–3.

defamiliarization of the present, it is one that operates by distending the present in anticipation of future harms: by shaping what Reinhart Koselleck calls the 'horizon of expectation', it inflects the historical time of modernity.[156] Although Wells's utopias provide a form in which the ecological risks of modernity start to become visible, it is their failure to imagine convincing mega-hazards and their solutions that most effectively defamiliarizes the historical present of modernity, revealing it to be one saturated with unknown and incalculable ecological risk.

****

Wells was abidingly concerned with species extinctions, from his early essays and scientific romances to his later political writings, in which he repeatedly used the threat of human extinction to motivate his cosmopolitan political projects. In three of his utopias, *A Modern Utopia* (1905), *Men Like Gods* (1923), and *The Shape of Things to Come* (1933), Wells imagines societies in which humans overcome the threat of extinction to form a socialist World State that achieves efficient control over other species and the planet's natural resources. In doing so, he mirrors the anthropocentrism and human exceptionalism of early ecological science, and anticipates some recent optimistic accounts of the Anthropocene.

In his early utopias, Wells drew on the biological training that influenced him so profoundly when he attended T. H. Huxley's class at the Normal School of Science, recasting Huxley's hope that humans might achieve ethical evolution by combating the crude 'struggle for existence'.[157] In his later utopias, as scholars such as Peder Anker, Christina Alt, and Caroline Hovanec have shown, Wells took inspiration from ecology, exploring the possibilities of ecological management.[158] In retrospect, it might seem that Wells could have used his utopias to depict systems in which humans have been decentred or displaced—perhaps systems that resemble the 'mesh' of interconnected beings described by Timothy Morton.[159] However, in practice this was not the case. Wells recentres humans at the level of the species, and increasingly explores the possibility that they could master their environment in a manner that reflects early ecology, which, as Alt points out, displayed 'a new confidence—even arrogance—in humanity's ability to exert control over the natural world.[160]

[156] Reinhart Koselleck, *Futures Past: On the Semantics of Historical Time*, trans. Keith Tribe (Cambridge: MIT Press, 1985), 259–61.

[157] Huxley, *Evolution*, 83.

[158] See Peder Anker, *Imperial Ecology: Environmental Order in the British Empire, 1895–1945* (Cambridge, MA: Harvard University Press, 2001); Christina Alt, 'Extinction, Extermination, and the Ecological Optimism of H. G. Wells', in *Green Planets: Ecology and Science Fiction*, ed. Gerry Canavan and Kim Stanley Robinson (Middletown: Wesleyan University Press, 2014), 25–39; and Caroline Hovanec, *Animal Subjects: Literature, Zoology, and British Modernism* (Cambridge: Cambridge University Press, 2018).

[159] Timothy Morton, *The Ecological Thought* (Cambridge: Harvard University Press, 2010), 28–50.

[160] Alt, 'Extinction', 25.

Wells imagines utopias in which humans have gained control over other species, protecting some and deliberately exterminating others. In *Men Like Gods*, Mr Freddy Mush—an aesthete with a sentimental regard for what he calls the 'balance of nature'—objects that there were 'no swallows to be seen in Utopia because there were no gnats nor midges'. It transpires that 'the attention of the Utopian community had been given to the long-cherished idea of a systematic extermination of tiresome and mischievous species'.[161] This scenario develops that of *The Time Machine*, in which 'the air was free from gnats', and diseases have apparently been stamped out. In this early romance, the eradication is ambiguous: the Traveller is not able to reconstruct the full story of what has happened, partly because he 'had no convenient cicerone in the pattern of the Utopian books' (33, 48). It is unclear whether the attempt to control the environment has benefited the future society or contributed to its demise. However, in *Men Like Gods* there *are* cicerones in the form of the Utopians, and the issue is discussed at length. Mr Barnstaple is able to establish, for instance, that certain species have been conserved and modified: large animals have been turned into 'pets and ornaments', and the 'almost extinct elephant had increased again and Utopia had saved her giraffes' (87). Both of these scenarios explore Huxley's recommendation that humans 'subdue nature' in order to evolve ethically, which he illustrates with the example of a garden in which 'hygienic precautions' would check or remove the natural causes of disease, and 'every plant and every lower animal should be adapted to human wants'.[162] Indeed, Wells echoes Huxley's conceit of the garden in *The Time Machine* with his depiction of the future world as a 'long-neglected and yet weedless garden', and in *Men Like Gods* with his description of the 'weeding and cultivation of the kingdoms of nature by mankind' (27, 87). Huxley's ideal of ethical evolution is underpinned by an assumption that is replicated most clearly in *Men Like Gods*: that humans hold the greatest value, and all other species should be subordinated to their needs.

Wells's engagement with early ecology gave new impetus to his vision of controlling the environment. Anker has drawn attention to this engagement, and to the significant role that Wells played in popularizing ecology through the co-authored textbook *The Science of Life* (1929–30).[163] For example, Julian Huxley, the grandson of T. H. Huxley and himself a prominent figure in the Oxford school of ecology, reviewed *Men Like Gods* enthusiastically as an ecological utopia and praised its depiction of the 'purging of the organic world'.[164] Later, Wells invited Huxley to collaborate with him on *The Science of Life*. Wells edited the chapters on ecology that Huxley wrote, which conclude with a section that considers the

[161] H. G. Wells, *Men Like Gods* (London: Cassell, 1923), 84–5.
[162] Huxley, *Evolution*, 83, 19–20.
[163] Anker, *Ecology*, 110–16.
[164] Julian Huxley, 'Biology in Utopia', *Nature*, 111 (1923), 591–4, 592.

promise and dangers of 'applied biology'.[165] Although Wells had long been exploring the possibility of controlling the environment as part of a project influenced by
T. H. Huxley's ethical evolution, the science of ecology inspired him further, and
he went on to explore the possibilities of ecological management in *The Shape of
Things to Come* (1933).

The Shape of Things to Come draws explicitly on ecology in its depiction of a
modern state that has gained control of life. In telling the history of the world until
the year 2106, Dr Philip Raven identifies the start of a new Age of the Modern State
in 2059:

> [f]rom the point of view of the ecologist the establishment of the Modern State
> marks an epoch in biological history. It has been an adaptation, none too soon,
> of our species to changing conditions that must otherwise have destroyed it.[166]

This new epoch was made possible by 'applied biology' and a 'spate of biological
invention' that led to the creation of new flora and fauna:

> [w]e may have new and wonderful forests; we may have new plants; we may
> replace the weedy and scanty greensward of the past by a subtler and livelier tex-
> ture. Undreamt-of fruits and blossoms may be summoned out of non-existence.
> (398)

In addition to the creation of new species, existing ones are kept in Major Parks
that have been established as reserves for 'various specially interesting faunas and
floras' to 'flourish without human interference' (395).[167] Advances in mineralogy
and meteorology have led to other major changes: the former enabled the extraction of mineral substances that previously lay hidden deep in the earth, while the
latter made possible 'alterations in the composition and movements of the atmosphere', complementing a drive to clean up '[i]ndustrial enterprises that formerly
befouled the world with smoke, refuse and cinder heaps' (397, 399). 'Geogonic'
plans to remodel the contours of the Earth have been drawn up, with the ambition
of increasing the number of desirable habitats on the planet by a 'redistribution of
rainfall, a change in the fall of the surface waters, protection from winds' (400).
Although these plans have not yet been implemented because of their danger, the
planet already looks markedly different from the air. In contrast to the 'Age of

---

[165] H. G. Wells, Julian S. Huxley, and G. P. Wells, *The Science of Life: A Summary of Contemporary
Knowledge about Life and Its Possibilities* (London: Amalgamated Press, 1929), III, 641–90.
[166] H. G. Wells, *The Shape of Things to Come: The Ultimate Revolution* (London: Hutchinson, 1933),
428.
[167] This combination of applied biology and preservation reflects the approach of Oxford ecologists who, according to Anker, 'endorsed both romantic environmental preservation and hard-core
ecological management' (*Ecology*, 110)

Frustration', in which the earth was scarred and disfigured by long wars, it has since been enriched with vegetation and turned into a 'world garden' (389–90).

Throughout his utopias, Wells advertises the great opportunities for humans if they could channel their agency through a cosmopolitan World State. In *The Shape of Things to Come*, he portrays the formation of a socialist World State as necessary to control the 'mercenary enterprise' that is blamed for the disasters of war and disease which threatened humans with extinction in the twentieth century (397). Similarly, in his late non-fiction writing, Wells becomes increasingly critical of the environmental damage wrought by private enterprise. For example, in *The New World Order* (1940), he decries the fact that the 'institution of the private appropriation of land and natural resources, and of private enterprise for profit [...] have been expanded to a monstrous destructiveness':

> [t]he new power organizations are destroying the forests of the world at headlong
> speed, ploughing great grazing areas into deserts, exhausting mineral resources,
> killing off whales, seals and a multitude of rare and beautiful species [...] and
> devastating the planet.[168]

The alternative to such destruction, he argues, is the collective control of economic and biological life by a socialist World State. Such a socialism—which Wells distinguishes sharply from Marxism, to which he was abidingly hostile—would employ new sciences such as ecology to achieve the more efficient management of the planet and its resources. Wells's use of the threat of human extinction to motivate a cosmopolitan World State parallels Beck's contention that the unprecedented risks of modernity create new global 'risk communities', and thereby open new possibilities for political organization and action that undermine the borders of traditional nation states. The 'potential for self-endangering developed by civilization in the modernization process', Beck contends, 'makes the utopia of a world society a little more real or at least more urgent'.[169]

Wells's visions of human agency resemble some recent accounts of the Anthropocene. In *The Fate of Homo Sapiens* (1939), he anticipates Anthropocene discourse by drawing attention to the traces that humans will leave in the geological record through their destructive agency. Returning to his favoured theme of the extinctions that are registered in the geological record, he points out that:

> to-day we are, from the geological point of view, living in a phase of exceptional
> climatic instability, in a series of glacial and interglacial ages, and witnessing
> another destruction of animal and plant species on an almost unparalleled scale.
> The list of species extinguished in the past hundred years is a long one; the list
> of species threatened with extinction to-day is still longer [...]. [T]his time the

---

[168] H. G. Wells, *The New World Order* (London: Secker and Warburg, 1940), 35.
[169] Beck, *Risk Society*, 47.

biologist notes a swifter and stranger agent of change than any phase of the fossil past can show—*man*, who will leave nothing undisturbed from the ocean bottom to the stratosphere, and who bids fair to extinguish himself in the process.[170]

Wells's view of 'man' as a destructive 'agent of change' finds its counterpart in the agency that he accords to humans—following Huxley's conception of ethical evolution and later reinforced by the confidence of early ecology—to control their environment and secure their evolutionary progression rather than extinction. Such a confidence is similar to that of certain optimistic narratives of the Anthropocene. Indeed, Edward Howell draws astute parallels between Wells's utopias and the discourse of 'ecomodernists', who see in human agency the potential for a 'good Anthropocene' to be realized through technology. He shows that both are subject to similar criticisms: both tend to assign blame for environmental damage to the entire species rather than specific groups of humans; both allocate the task of correcting the species' course to an elite group of (male) scientific technocrats; and both advocate dangerous and hubristic geoengineering projects.[171] In this manner, Wells's optimistic visions of human agency might be held as a warning about some recent strains of environmentalism. However, the value of Wells's utopias lies less in their proposed solutions, than in the ability of their aesthetic form to produce knowledge about ecological risk.

****

The ability of Wells's utopias to dramatize ecological risk is an affordance of their literary form. Benjamin Morgan argues that in the late nineteenth century, writers such as Samuel Butler and William Morris shaped the utopia into a literary form that is capable of mediating totality by its use of spatial closure to represent complex interlocking systems that must be conceived at multiple scales simultaneously.[172] In line with the formal expectations of the genre, Wells's utopias rely on spatial closure. *A Modern Utopia* involves the transition to a similar planet far away in the deeps of space, and *Men Like Gods* employs a slightly more elaborate mixture of Einstein and multiple dimensions to allow Mr Barnstaple and a motley collection of Earthlings to be transported to a planet in a parallel universe.[173] The

---

[170] H. G. Wells, *The Fate of Homo Sapiens* (London: Secker and Warburg, 1939), 29–30.
[171] Edward H. Howell, 'Modernism, Ecology, and the Anthropocene' (unpublished doctoral dissertation, Temple University, 2017), 204–6, 236–8. One difference is that while ecomodernists advocate the 'aggressive participation of private sector entrepreneurs' to accelerate the technological change that is supposedly needed to make a 'great Anthropocene', Wells highlights the destructive impact of private enterprise and argues for its regulation by a socialist World State (Asafu-Adjaye and others, *Ecomodernist Manifesto*, 30. <https://www.ecomodernism.org/manifesto-english>).
[172] Benjamin Morgan, 'How We Might Live: Utopian Ecology in William Morris and Samuel Butler', in *Ecological Form: System and Aesthetics in the Age of Empire*, ed. Nathan K. Hensley and Philip Steer (New York: Fordham University Press, 2019), 139–60.
[173] The discussion of multiple dimensions is both an example of 'an ingenious use of scientific patter' to introduce the 'impossible hypothesis' that Wells flagged as his innovation in writing fantastic stories,

thresholds that must be crossed to reach the utopian planets function like the deep channel that separates Thomas More's island of Utopia from the mainland, with the difference that Wells's boundaries allow the depiction of systems that operate on planetary scales. As Wells stresses in *A Modern Utopia*, while previous utopias were content to use a mountain valley or an island to achieve sufficient isolation, '[n]o less than a planet will serve the purpose of a modern Utopia'.[174] This use of spatial closure activates what Morgan describes as the 'ecological possibilities of utopian form'.[175]

While the use of spatial closure enables the representation of complex systems as a whole, Wells was keen to make these systems reflect biological change. Complementing his view that any post-Darwinian utopia 'must be not static but kinetic', the narrator of *A Modern Utopia* flags that he will portray a society that constantly needs to adapt to changing conditions: '[w]e are to shape our state in a world of uncertain seasons, sudden catastrophes, antagonistic diseases, and inimical beasts and vermin' (5, 7). Indeed, having flagged the threat of epidemics that refuse to respect the 'boundary lines' of states in *A Modern Utopia*, Wells depicts such hazards in his later utopias (11). An epidemic unexpectedly breaks out in *Men Like Gods* when the visitors introduce 'measles' and 'a long suppressed influenza' to which the Utopians have no immunity (153). Again, the narrator of *The Shape of Things to Come* records how waves of influenza, cholera, bubonic plague, and maculated fever—collectively known as 'the great pestilence'—struck in the 1950s in the aftermath of a world war, and halved the population of the world (219–22).

Wells's use of utopian form to depict complex systems on a planetary scale parallels the ambition of early ecologists to map ecological systems—whether conceived of as 'life-communities' or 'ecosystems'—on similar scales.[176] In this respect, they resemble the examples discussed in *The Science of Life* of mapping life-communities on 'the grand or planetary scale': 'with sufficient knowledge and patience, we could make a map of the whole world showing the distribution of life-communities as it was at a particular instant'. Or, given that Wells's utopias are kinetic, they more closely resemble the mapping of ecological systems through time that is imagined in *The Science of Life* with the fanciful example of an ecologist who stays aloft in a balloon for hundreds of years, and observes changes in life-communities.[177]

and marks a threshold or boundary that allows Wells to construct his utopia as a totality (*Literary Criticism*, 241–2).

[174] H. G. Wells, *A Modern Utopia* (London: Chapman & Hall, 1905), 11.

[175] Morgan, 'Ecology', 141.

[176] The term 'life-community' is used in *The Science of Life* (III, 645); Arthur Tansley coined the term 'ecosystem' in 1935 (see Anker, *Ecology*, 154).

[177] Wells, Huxley, and Wells, *Science of Life*, III, 659–61. In *The Science of Life*, it is stressed that 'it is not enough to think of life-communities in [a] fixed and static way, for they are constantly changing' (III, 660). More sophisticated techniques are now used to model ecological systems through time. See E. M. Wolkovich and others, 'Temporal Ecology in the Anthropocene', *Ecology Letters*, 17 (2014), 1365–79.

Literature and science both thereby provide the means of representing ecological transformations on a planetary scale, yet being set in the future makes Wells's later utopias particularly effective at dramatizing ecological risk. Beck emphasizes that the 'center of risk consciousness lies not in the present, but *in the future*', and so risk society is one in which 'the past loses the power to determine the present' and its 'place is taken by the future'. He hints at the role that literature can play in such a society when he characterizes this future as something 'non-existent, invented, fictive', and suggests that we must project threats 'in order to determine and organize our present actions'.[178] Wells's utopias are notable literary attempts to project ecological threats in this manner: by anticipating future hazards such as pandemics, they facilitate the 'risk consciousness' that characterizes Beck's risk society. Whereas *A Modern Utopia* depicts a utopia set on a distant planet, *Men Like Gods* portrays a utopian society in a parallel universe that is about 3000 years ahead, and *The Shape of Things to Come* traces future events up until the year 2106. The later utopias thereby constitute part of Wells's 'discovery of the future', which began with his *Anticipations* (1901). Reflecting back on his career, Wells placed his new concern with the future at the forefront of 'an almost complete reorientation [...] of our minds with regard to time'. Until 'the later-Victorian period', he contends, people had been predominantly preoccupied with the past, whereas now '[e]verything we do is becoming preparatory and anticipatory. To-day has vanished almost completely in our enormous preoccupation with to-morrow'.[179] Although happening at an earlier date, this shift of temporal orientation parallels that which Beck sees as happening in risk society.

Beyond anticipating future hazards such as pandemics, Wells's utopias envisage ways in which such risks might be managed. For example, when the epidemic breaks out in *Men Like Gods*, the utopian society responds quickly. Unlike the disease that destroys the Martians in *The War of the Worlds* (1897) and the influenza pandemic of 1918, the epidemic is efficiently suppressed by 'the science and organization of Utopia': the visitors are quarantined, and a cure is swiftly found (234). In *The Shape of Things to Come*, the account of a society in the form of a 'Short History of the Future' similarly allows the portrayal of ecological risks and their management (14). After the great pestilence leads to disastrous consequences for a 'disunited humanity' in the Age of Frustration, the unified World State successfully mitigates ecological risks in the new age which begins in 2059 (218). The narrator reports how, after the nineteenth and twentieth centuries which 'show us mankind scrambling on the verge of irreparable disaster', the threatened species 'did not fall back into [the] abyss of extinction', but 'clambered past its supreme danger phase' to reach a level of safety that 'no living substance has ever attained before' (428).

---

[178] Beck, *Risk Society*, 34.
[179] Wells, *Homo Sapiens*, 82–4.

By speculating on things to come, Wells's utopias reveal ecological risks that would otherwise remain invisible. Amitav Ghosh faults the realist novel for focusing on detailed descriptions of everyday life while banishing improbable events, such as the storms, floods, and unusual weather events that are occurring more frequently during the current climate crisis. 'Here, then, is the irony of the "realist" novel', Ghosh writes: 'the very gestures with which it conjures up reality are actually a concealment of the real'.[180] By endeavouring to imagine the future, Wells's utopias depart from the realist novel—and indeed from other modernist novels, insofar as they turn from the materialism of realist novels to plumb the depths of consciousness. Yet by doing so, Wells's narratives develop the faculty of risk perception—one that allows readers to see behind the visible surfaces of the realist novel—and reveal what Beck calls the 'second reality' of risk that lies concealed behind the visible world.

Paradoxically, however, it is the representational failures of Wells's utopias that best convey the unprecedented ecological risks of modernity. The utopias bend and buckle under the representational demands that are placed upon them, and their totalizing drive soon brings them up against their representational limits. Indeed, *A Modern Utopia* explicitly draws attention to its 'conflicting form', in which the two squabbling travellers at times distract from the utopia that is 'too great for their sustained comprehension': the effect is like watching a 'rather defective' cinematograph lantern, which 'sometimes jams and sometimes gets out of focus'.[181] These difficulties are compounded when the utopia is set in the future. Wells held that 'the best sort of futurist story should be one that sets out to give you the illusion of reality', but acknowledged that this illusion is difficult to sustain. Unlike the historical romancer who 'has a whole mass of history, ruins, old costumes, museum pieces, to work upon and confirm him', the 'futurist writer has at most the bare germs of things to come'.[182] The epidemics in *The Shape of Things to Come* are a case in point. They produce an illusion of reality—they generate what might be called an 'ecological reality effect'—although this illusion quickly falters. Notably, the text's account of maculated fever flags its own deficiencies. Unlike the diseases that preceded it, the narrator suggests that this fever is poorly understood: it seems to have been transmitted from captive baboons to humans, possibly with an intermediary, although '[w]e are still quite in the dark upon these points because at that time there were no doctors or biologists with the leisure to record observations'. A host of tentative hypotheses are advanced, but due to the 'dearth of detailed description' the disease remains 'obscure' and a 'riddle for pathologists': it 'swept the whole world and vanished as enigmatically as it came' (169).

---

[180] Amitav Ghosh, *The Great Derangement: Climate Change and the Unthinkable* (Chicago: University of Chicago Press, 2016), 23.
[181] Wells, *Modern Utopia*, 373, 3; emphasis removed.
[182] Wells, *Literary Criticism*, 247.

The failure to portray a convincing pandemic is even more pronounced in the 1936 film adaptation *Things to Come*. Wells himself comments on the shortcomings of the adaptation, noting that it goes from scenes of 'intense realism' to scenes of 'the intensest detailed improbability'. Although he suggests that 'the final and conclusive defeat of futuristic imagination' lies in 'the small material details' such as those of costume, hair, and furniture in the year 2035, this defeat was already apparent in the earlier epidemic scenes.[183] The film lurches into a melodramatic or expressionist horror mode more reminiscent of some of the films that the producer Alexander Korda made in Berlin in the 1920s, as infected people (such as the woman depicted in Figure 1.8) roam around like zombies during 'The Wandering Sickness'. This generic discontinuity, combined with the resort to an intertitle that announces that the sickness has killed more than half the human race, inadvertently achieves a similar result to that which Wells notes when he compares his earlier utopia to a moving picture projected by a defective cinematograph lantern.

When the utopias fail to be convincing—without lapsing into the sort of knowing irony that Wells discerns as another approach to fiction of the future—they best convey ecological risk.[184] Here, the form of Wells's utopias cuts against their

Figure 1.8 'The Wandering Sickness'

Reproduced from Menzies, William Cameron (Dir.) (1936). *Things to Come* (United Artists).

[183] Wells, *Literary Criticism*, 249–50.
[184] Wells, *Literary Criticism*, 248.

content: their faltering narratives undermine their visions of ecological management and control. Beck points out that the risks of modernity are unknowable in the sense that they relate to future hazards that have not been directly experienced, and when hazards do occur, they are often on such vast scales that they defy representation: the unintended consequences of modernity now 'endanger *all* forms of life on this planet'.[185] Wells's utopias provide a literary form in which such risks start to become visible, yet it is their representational failures—their failures to imagine convincing mega-hazards—that best intimate the incalculable and uncontainable ecological risks of modernity.

[185] Beck, *Risk Society*, 72, 22.

2

D. H. Lawrence and Nietzsche's Thought of Eternal Recurrence

In *Women in Love* (1920) and *Lady Chatterley's Lover* (1928), D. H. Lawrence fuses the provincial realist novel with philosophical materials to refigure the time of modernity in a way that highlights a mode of labour characterized by mechanical repetition, and the catastrophic environmental damage that is caused by the extraction and burning of fossil fuels. Specifically, he combines Joachim of Fiore's apocalyptic idea of a new historical epoch with Friedrich Nietzsche's thought of eternal recurrence to depict the inauguration of a new historical age. In *Women in Love*, this new age is characterized by Gerald Crich's ruthless subjugation of his workforce though time-discipline and his despoliation of the earth through coal-mining, whereas in *Lady Chatterley's Lover* it raises the hope of a 'revaluation of the earth' through Constance Chatterley's opposition to her husband's destructive mining activities. Drawing attention to the environmental damage that is obscured by many progressive accounts of modernity, Lawrence's coalfield fiction thereby uses apocalyptic and Nietzschean thought to imagine the possibility of alternatives to a society that depends on the exploitation of labour and the extraction of fossil fuels.

Lawrence's deployment of epochal schemes of history creates similarities with recent accounts of the Anthropocene. Certainly, there are notable differences: Lawrence's 'epochs' do not mark units of geological time, and are not informed by Earth System science. Yet his imagination of a new historical age bears affinities to accounts of the Anthropocene that foreground the burning of fossil fuels during the Industrial Revolution. For example, in an influential formulation of the concept, Paul Crutzen suggests that the Anthropocene 'could be said to have started in the latter part of the eighteenth century', a date that 'happens to coincide with James Watt's design of the steam engine in 1784'.[1] Although dissenting from Crutzen's use of the species category, Andreas Malm develops such a suggestion with his account of 'fossil capital', and the transition from water to steam power during the British Industrial Revolution.[2] He also contends that certain works of literature register the 'fossil economy' in different states of development, and

---

[1] Paul J. Crutzen, 'Geology of Mankind', *Nature*, 415 (2002), 23.
[2] Andreas Malm, *Fossil Capital: The Rise of Steam Power and the Roots of Global Warming* (London: Verso, 2016).

British Modernism and the Anthropocene. David Shackleton, Oxford University Press. © David Shackleton (2023).
DOI: 10.1093/oso/9780192857743.003.0003

(evoking Walter Benjamin's dialectical images) can be read in relation to the current climate crisis to awaken the present 'to its real structure'.[3] Stewart Cole takes up Malm's contention in relation to Lawrence's fiction, arguing that *Lady Chatterley's Lover* should be recognized as 'a core text in any emergent corpus of fossil fuel fiction'.[4]

Reading Lawrence's coalfield fiction in relation to Anthropocene discourse helps to elucidate the environmental politics of his work. Dipesh Chakrabarty contends that new forms of Anthropocene historiography should be capable of doing justice to what he calls the 'conjoined histories' of climate and capital.[5] Within the critical reception of Lawrence's work, these two types of history have been largely opposed. Lawrence has long been celebrated as environmental writer, initially by Leavisite critics and then by deep ecologists. However, as Greg Garrard notes, these critics have tended to dissociate Lawrence's 'proto-ecological ideas' from his larger political arguments about labour, nation, and race.[6] Malm's account of fossil capital provides an opportunity to read Lawrence's work against the conjoined histories of climate *and* capital. By using his coalfield fiction to explore the imbrication of environmental destruction and class conflict in the Midlands, Lawrence departs from H. G. Wells's attribution of environmental damage to humans at the level of the species. He also differs from Jean Rhys, whose fiction resituates major environmental changes in relation to plantations in the West Indies, and thereby intimates that environmental crisis should be understood not only in relation to industrialization and the extraction of fossil fuels in Britain, but also in relation to settler colonialism and chattel slavery as key aspects of combined and uneven development in the modern world-system.

In terms of genre, Lawrence's incorporation of philosophical elements into the provincial realist novel makes *Women in Love* and *Lady Chatterley's Lover* particularly adept at exploring themes of environmental destruction and recovery. Elizabeth Miller shows how Lawrence uses the 'provincial realist novel' to negotiate anxieties about the exhaustion of fossil fuels.[7] Extending her approach, this chapter argues that Lawrence combines provincial realism with elements drawn from apocalyptic and philosophical traditions—and particularly from Plato and Nietzsche—to create a distinctive form of the novel that makes heavy use of allegory, riddles, myths, parables, and symbolism. (Lawrence himself believed that

[3] Andreas Malm, '"This is the Hell that I have Heard of": Some Dialectical Images in Fossil Fuel Fiction', *Forum for Modern Language Studies*, 53/2 (2017), 121–41, 127–8.

[4] Stewart Cole, 'Sex in a Warming World: *Lady Chatterley's Lover* as Fossil Fuel Fiction', *Studies in the Novel*, 52/3 (2020), 288–304.

[5] Dipesh Chakrabarty, *The Climate of History in a Planetary Age* (Chicago: University of Chicago Press, 2021), 49.

[6] Greg Garrard, 'Nietzsche *Contra* Lawrence: How to be True to the Earth', *Colloquy*, 12 (2006), 9–27, 9–10, 22–4.

[7] Elizabeth Miller, *Extraction Ecologies and the Literature of the Long Exhaustion* (Princeton: Princeton University Press, 2021).

philosophy could revitalize the novel. He holds that it 'was the greatest pity in the world, when philosophy and fiction got split. They used to be one, right from the days of myth. [...] The two should come together again, in the novel.')[8] Marking a departure from the provincial realism of writers such as George Eliot to whom Lawrence was so heavily indebted, what results are novels that unfold on relatively small spatial scales but that function as parables about much broader environmental transformations and historical transitions. In part, it is this generic hybridity that allows Lawrence's novels to be read as parables or allegories of the Anthropocene.

Ultimately, Lawrence's refiguration of the time of modernity might inspire approaches to modernism that are more attentive to the extraction of fossils fuels and to the imagination of alternative energy systems. In introducing the 'energy humanities', Imre Szeman and Dominic Boyer highlight the difficulties involved in the representation of fossil fuels: '[n]ot only energy in general but also fossil fuels in particular have been surprisingly hard to figure—narratively, visually, conceptually—as a central element of the modern'.[9] Such difficulties became more pronounced with the growing reliance of cheap energy from oil after the mid-twentieth century. Timothy Mitchell explains that the extraction of coal in the early twentieth century was a relatively visible phenomenon that was open to various forms of political contestation including through strikes, but that such opportunities dwindled with the turn to oil.[10] Setting *Women in Love* and *Lady Chatterley's Lover* in the context of industrial disputes in the Midlands, Lawrence uses apocalyptic and philosophical thought to explore fossil fuel energy systems at a time at which Britain still relied predominantly on domestic coal for the production of energy, but was working to secure a future supply of oil overseas, including in the Middle East. More broadly, by deploying cyclical schemes of history that contrast with Wells's desire for historical progress, Lawrence's creative adaptation of Nietzsche's thought of eternal recurrence puts into question conceptions of modernity that are insufficiently attentive to the damage caused by the burning of fossil fuels.[11] That is, by drawing attention to the social and environmental damage that attends mechanical repetition as the temporality of modernity, Lawrence's fiction challenges what Szeman and Boyer describe as 'our dominant narrative of the modern': one that combines 'the expansion of rights and freedoms, the advent of scientific

---

[8] D. H. Lawrence, 'The Future of the Novel', in *Study of Thomas Hardy and Other Essays*, ed. Bruce Steele (Cambridge: Cambridge University Press, 1985), 149–55, 154.

[9] Imre Szeman and Dominic Boyer, 'Introduction: On the Energy Humanities', in *Energy Humanities: An Anthology*, ed. Imre Szeman and Dominic Boyer (Baltimore: John Hopkins University Press, 2017), 1–13, 6.

[10] Timothy Mitchell, *Carbon Democracy: Political Power in the Age of Oil* (London: Verso, 2011).

[11] Lawrence asks sardonically: 'Hadn't somebody better write Mr Wells' History backwards to prove how we've degenerated, in our stupid visionlessness, since the cave-men?' ('Him With His Tail in His Mouth', in *Reflections on the Death of a Porcupine and Other Essays*, ed. Michael Herbert (Cambridge: Cambridge University Press, 1988), 307–17, 317.

insights and technological innovations, and the ballooning of capitalist economies [...] under the sign of "progress"'.[12] Reading Lawrence's fiction can thereby contribute to what they identify as the task of the energy humanities, which is 'nothing less than to reimagine modernity, and in the process to figure ourselves as different kinds of beings than the ones who have built a civilization on the promises, intensities, and fantasies of a particularly dirty, destructive form of energy'.[13]

Women in Love, mechanical repetition, and eternal recurrence

In *Women in Love*, Lawrence depicts a society permeated by mechanical repetition, and imagines Gerald Crich embracing such repetition when renovating his coal mines. Echoing a series of images of circular motion that run throughout the novel, Gerald adopts a 'pure machine-principle' of 'infinitely repeated motion' that is compared to 'the spinning of a wheel'.[14] This depiction resonates with Malm's account of the Anthropocene, and the emphasis he places on James Watt's patenting of a steam engine in 1784. For Malm, Watt's 'earth-shattering exploit' was to connect coal fire to the wheel to produce continuous circular motion: with this, 'the foundations of the fossil economy were laid down'.[15] In his account, the rotative steam engine also figures the circulation of capital, which Karl Marx conveys in his general formula M–C–M', and which Malm updates for the 'fossil economy' with the revised formula M–C (L + MP (F)) ... P ... C'–M'.[16] By extension, the steam engine might also be taken as a figure for the British cycle of capital accumulation that Giovanni Arrighi sets within world history. Arrighi reinterprets Marx's M–C–M' formula beyond the logic of individual capitalist investments to characterize successive Genoese, Dutch, British, and American cycles of history.[17] Within this scheme, the rotative steam engine stands as an emblem of the British cycle, in which the emergence of the fossil economy through the Industrial Revolution accounted for a huge increase in the combustion of coal, and a concomitant rise in carbon dioxide emissions.[18] While Lawrence's images of machines and

---

[12] Szeman and Boyer, 'Energy Humanities', 1.

[13] Szeman and Boyer, 'Energy Humanities', 3.

[14] D. H. Lawrence, *Women in Love*, ed. David Farmer, Lindeth Vasey, and John Worthen (Cambridge: Cambridge University Press, 1987), 228.

[15] Malm, *Fossil Capital*, 16.

[16] Karl Marx, *Capital: A Critique of Political Economy, Volume 1*, trans. Ben Fowkes (London: Penguin, 1990), 257; Malm, *Fossil Capital*, 289. In Malm's formula, 'M' stands for money, 'C' for commodity, 'L' for labour power, 'MP' for means of production, 'F' for fossil fuels, and 'P' for production. He defines the 'fossil economy' as 'an economy of self-sustaining growth predicated on the growing consumption of fossil fuels, and therefore generating a sustained growth in emissions of carbon dioxide' (11).

[17] Giovanni Arrighi, *The Long Twentieth Century: Money, Power, and the Origins of Our Times* (London: Verso, 1994), 6–7.

[18] Malm, *Fossil Capital*, 13, 249–54.

rotary motion in some respects anticipate Malm's account of the Anthropocene, they stem from an engagement with the philosophical discourse of modernity, and specifically with Nietzsche's thought of eternal recurrence. It is by reworking such philosophical materials that *Women in Love* can be read as an allegory of the Anthropocene: one in which Gerald Crich's renovation of his coal mines suggests a new historical epoch characterized by environmental devastation and the technological mastery of the Earth.

In *Women in Love*, Gerald embraces a type of mechanical repetition that is portrayed as a pervasive feature of society. By contrast, Ursula and Gudrun Brangwen recoil from a life made up of such repetition. In 'Sunday Evening', Ursula broods on death, which she thinks preferable to her life of mechanical repetition: 'better die than live mechanically a life that is a repetition of repetitions' (192). And in 'Snowed Up', Gudrun is driven almost to madness by the thought of 'the mechanical succession of day following day, day following day, ad infinitum' (464).[19] These attitudes can be understood in the context of the new forms of temporal experience that arose with modern industry. In his chapter on 'Machinery and Large-Scale Industry' in the first volume of *Capital* (1867), Karl Marx analyses repetition as a key aspect of labour under the capitalist mode of production. He traces the creation of the uniform working day as it was shaped by new modes of production, the employment of machinery, and parliamentary legislation concerning working hours. He notes that in the factory, the 'dependence of the worker on the continuous and uniform motion of the machinery [...] created the strictest disciple'. The Factory Acts contributed to this discipline by increasing the intensity and repetitiveness of labour: the 'shortening of the working day increases to a wonderful degree the regularity, uniformity, order, continuity and energy of labour'.[20] Later, work was made more repetitive and mechanical by the 'principles of scientific management' pioneered by Frederick Taylor with his 'time and motion' studies, and by the assembly-line techniques developed in the factories of Henry Ford.[21]

Ursula and Gudrun's aversion towards mechanical repetition is a response to the new forms of temporal experience that arose with industrial capitalism. Marx charts the emergence of a new type of labour not carried on by fits and starts, but 'repeated day after day with unvarying uniformity'.[22] Because labour consists of the performance of repetitive tasks within the confines of a tightly regulated working day, each hour comes to seem indistinguishable from the others, and is seemingly repeated endlessly within a well-defined pattern of the working week that is itself endlessly repeated. The Brangwen sisters are horrified by such repetition. For example, Ursula thinks of her life as a school teacher as one of

---

[19] Lawrence, *Women in Love*, 192, 464.
[20] Marx, *Capital*, 535.
[21] See Randall Stevenson, *Reading the Times: Temporality and History in Twentieth-Century Fiction* (Edinburgh: Edinburgh University Press, 2018), 53–8.
[22] Marx, *Capital*, 533.

repetitive, mechanical routine. In a chapter in which anadiplosis and other rhetorical schemes are used to reinforce her sense of numbing repetition, she thinks ahead to the next day: '[t]omorrow was Monday. Monday, the beginning of another [...] school-week, mere routine and mechanical activity' (193). Her repetition of the term 'mechanical' and its cognates is apt, given the role that machinery played in shaping the rhythms of the uniform working day. Yet it also suggests the role her school plays in preparing its pupils for the punctuality and regularity required by industry. 'Once within the school gates', E. P. Thompson comments, 'the child entered the new universe of disciplined time'.[23] Ursula works in an environment that prepares pupils for mechanical and repetitive jobs, and herself suffers from the 'barren school-week', recognizing how her life has been reduced to one of 'sordid routine and mechanical nullity' (193).

Later, Gudrun's horror of mechanical repetition manifests itself in a series of nightmarish images of clocks. She thinks of her head ticking 'like a clock, with a very madness of dead mechanical monotony and meaninglessness', and realizes that Gerald will provide her with no escape: 'it was the same ticking, the same twitching across the dial, a horrible, mechanical twitching forward over the face of the hours'. Time suffuses every aspect of his body, motion, and life, until it seems that even 'his kisses, his embraces' reverberate with the 'tick-tack' of time (464). It is as if their bodies have been so thoroughly imbued with the time-discipline of industrial capitalism, that they have been transformed into clocks. These images resonate with other figurations of people as machines in the novel. Gudrun thinks that the miners at Beldover sound 'like strange machines, heavy, oiled'. The depiction of these 'half-automatised colliers' conforms to Marx's analysis of the effects of machinery in modern industry (115–16). Marx flags how workers are subordinated to machines in the factory system, with its intense exploitation of labour-power: the worker typically spends his entire life serving the same machine, and is taught from a young age to 'adapt his own movements to the uniform and unceasing motion of an automaton'. Indeed, he suggests that the worker is thereby transformed 'from his very childhood, into a part of a specialized machine'.[24] A similar change occurs when Gerald renovates his coal mines. Randall Stevenson notes that Gerald's reforms follow Taylorist principles, and reflect those applied by Thomas Barber in modernizing the Barber, Walker & Company collieries around 1905–07.[25] Gerald introduces '[n]ew machinery' and runs everything on 'the most accurate and delicate scientific method', reducing the miners 'to mere mechanical instruments'. They are forced to undertake work that 'was terrible and heartbreaking in its mechanicalness', becoming themselves 'more and more mechanised' in the process (230).

[23] E. P. Thompson, 'Time, Work-Discipline, and Industrial Capitalism', *Past and Present*, 38 (1967), 56–97, 84.
[24] Marx, *Capital*, 546–7.
[25] Stevenson, *Times*, 55–6.

In *Women in Love*, it is not only miners who are transformed into machines by the conditions of labour, but also the industrial masters. Gudrun thinks of 'the Geralds of this world' being turned into 'mechanisms': '[l]et them become instruments, pure machines, pure wills that work like clock-work, in perpetual repetition' (466). Marx portrays machinery as turning the 'instrument of labour' into 'an industrial form of perpetual motion'.[26] Gudrun's conceit is similar, although she imagines the industrial masters becoming the perpetually working machines. She extends her conceit by compiling a mental list of the machines in Gerald's firm, from the wheelbarrow with 'one humble wheel', to the miners with 'a thousand wheels', up to Gerald with 'a million wheels and cogs and axels': 'such a lot of little wheels to his make-up! He was more intricate than a chronometer-watch' (466). Marx holds that by sweeping away 'every moral and natural restriction on the length of the working day', the machine becomes 'the most unfailing means for turning the whole lifetime of the worker and his family into labour-time at capital's disposal'.[27] Gudrun's comparison of Gerald to a watch reflects this way in which machines place the worker's time at the disposal of the capitalist, and intimates the power that Gerald exerts over his workforce through time-discipline. In this latter case, it is fitting that the comparison should be to a 'chronometer-watch', a highly precise and accurate type of watch that would be well suited to the 'scientific' measurement and regulation of tasks.

Indeed, the chronometer-watch stands a symbol of Gerald's power as an industrial magnate. With the rise of industrial capitalism, time became a site of conflict between the ruling and working classes. Marx points out that the 'establishment of a normal working-day is [...] the product of a protracted and more or less concealed civil war between the capitalist class and the working class'.[28] On the one hand, the industrial masters attempted to extract as much labour-time as possible from their workforce in order to increase labour-power and capital; on the other hand, the working class resisted this drive partly by supporting legislation such as the Factory Acts that regulate and place limits on the extent of the working day. As Thompson puts it, the working class came to accept the new time categories of their employers, and 'learned to fight back within them'.[29] Gudrun's comparison intimates this conflict: the 'chronometer-watch' stands as a symbol of time as a site of contestation between Gerald and his workforce.

Both Ursula and Gudrun search—with limited success—for alternatives to lives made up of mechanical repetition. Ursula dwells on death. 'How beautiful, how grand and perfect death was, how good to look forward to', she meditates, and finds consolation in the fact that 'this remained to look forward to, the pure inhuman otherness of death' (193–4). Her turning towards death finds a philosophical

[26] Marx, *Capital*, 526.
[27] Marx, *Capital*, 532.
[28] Marx, *Capital*, 412 13.
[29] Thompson, 'Time', 85–6.

counterpart in the *Zeitlichkeit* of Martin Heidegger's *Being and Time* (1927). Much as she looks forward to death as an elating eventuality that promises to bring purpose to what was otherwise a 'life of barren routine, without inner meaning, without any real significance', so Heidegger counterposes the authentic stance of 'anticipatory resoluteness in the face of death' to the inauthentic temporality of everyday life (193).[30] Gudrun takes a different approach, and in a moment of desperation thinks of escaping her life of mechanical repetition by fleeing with the artist Loerke to live a 'Bohemian life' in Dresden (464). By entertaining such a plan—and indeed by enacting it after Gerald's death—she settles on what Thompson identifies as '[o]ne recurrent form of revolt within Western industrial capitalism': the 'bohemian or beatnik' practice of 'flouting the urgency of respectable time-values'.[31] The Brangwen sisters' attempts to escape lives of repetition differ markedly from Gerald's approach, and his Nietzschean affirmation of such a life.

While Ursula and Gudrun recoil from mechanical repetition, Gerald comes to embrace such repetition as an intensification of the conditions of modern labour. In 'The Industrial Magnate', he throws himself into modernizing his family's mining firm. He comes to realize that:

> [t]here were two opposites, his will and the resistant Matter of the earth. And between these he could establish the very expression of his will, the incarnation of his power, a great and perfect machine, a system, an activity of pure order, pure mechanical repetition, repetition ad infinitum, hence eternal and infinite. He found his eternal and his infinite in the pure machine-principle of perfect coordination into one pure, complex, infinitely repeated motion, like the spinning of a wheel; but a productive spinning, as the revolving of the universe may be called a productive spinning, a productive repetition through eternity, to infinity. (228)

Here, as Carl Krockel points out, Lawrence draws on Nietzsche's notions of eternal recurrence and will-to-power.[32] That Gerald's system of infinite repetition should be 'eternal' suggests that, as with Nietzsche's doctrine of eternal recurrence, eternity is rethought in terms of infinite repetition within time. Notably, Gerald finds his 'eternal and infinite' in a 'machine-principle' of 'infinitely repeated motion', which is compared to 'the revolving of the universe' as 'a productive spinning, a productive repetition through eternity, to infinity'. This description closely echoes some of Nietzsche's cosmological formulations of the doctrine of

---

[30] Martin Heidegger, *Being and Time*, trans. John Macquarrie and Edward Robinson (Oxford: Blackwell Publishing, 2006), 378–9.

[31] Thompson, 'Time', 95.

[32] Carl Krockel, *D. H. Lawrence and Germany: The Politics of Influence* (Amsterdam: Rodopi, 2007), 170.

eternal recurrence, such as the note reproduced in *The Will to Power* (1901–11) that describes the world 'as a circular movement that has already repeated itself infinitely often and plays its game *in infinitum*.'[33] Distinctively though, Lawrence reimagines the doctrine of eternal recurrence in terms of machines and industry. The circular movement of Nietzsche's infinitely repeating world is transposed to a 'machine-principle' likened to the spinning of a wheel, and the infinite repetition of Nietzsche's doctrine is reconstrued as the endless 'mechanical repetition' of Gerald's modern mining system. This mechanical-industrial version of eternal recurrence is fused with the equally-Nietzschean motif of *Wille zur Macht* or 'will-to-power', as Gerald's perfect mining machine is described as the 'expression of his will, the incarnation of his power'.[34] That is, Gerald's affirmation of eternal recurrence is allied with the expression of his 'will-to-power', understood as a desire to control and subjugate the Earth.

By combining mechanical repetition with Nietzsche's thought of eternal recurrence to characterize the temporality of modernity, Lawrence's fiction resembles Walter Benjamin's adaptation of that thought in his unfinished *Arcades Project* (1941). In that work, Benjamin fuses Marx with Nietzsche to reinterpret the thought of eternal recurrence in terms of the temporality of commodity production: each commodity that is produced under modern conditions of labour appears as both the new and as the ever-always-the-same (*das Neue und Immergleiche*).[35] As Peter Osborne notes, such a temporality comes for Benjamin to define modernity, as that of the 'now' that marks out the exact repetition of the new as the ever-same.[36] In his fiction, Lawrence offers a similar characterization of the temporality of modernity, although with the difference that modernity is understood in relation to the embrace of fossil fuels, and the extraction of coal.

In other respects, Lawrence's adaptation of Nietzsche's thought of eternal recurrence more closely resembles Martin Heidegger's portrayal of that thought as the virulent consummation of modernity.[37] Lawrence and Heidegger independently arrived at an interpretation of the thought in terms of machines and modern technology. In his lectures on Nietzsche, Heidegger asks provocatively: '[w]hat is the essence of the modern power-driven machine other than one expression

---

[33] Friedrich Nietzsche, *The Will to Power*, ed. Walter Kaufmann, trans. Walter Kaufmann and R. J. Hollingdale (New York: Vintage Books, 1968), 549.

[34] Elsewhere, Ursula refers to Gerald's forceful control over his horse as a 'lust for bullying—a real Wille zur Macht—so base, so petty' (*Women in Love*, 150).

[35] Walter Benjamin, *The Arcades Project*, ed. Rolf Tiedemann, trans. Howard Eiland and Kevin McLaughlin (Cambridge, MA.: Belknap Press, 2002); see in particular Convolute D, 'Boredom, Eternal Return', 101–19.

[36] Peter Osborne, *The Politics of Time: Modernity and Avant-Garde* (London: Verso, 1995), 137, 143.

[37] Here, my reading builds on Anne Fernihough's argument that Lawrence and Heidegger both 'bring Nietzsche forward into the age of technology [...] whilst seeing him, curiously, as a kind of philosophical technologist himself'. In particular, it complements her suggestion that 'Gerald Crich seems to offer a supreme example of both Heidegger's "technological man" and of the will-to-power' (*D. H. Lawrence: Aesthetics and Ideology* (Oxford: Clarendon Press, 1993), 13, 146).

of the eternal recurrence of the same?'[38] Similarly, Lawrence reinterprets eternal recurrence as Gerald's embrace of a 'machine-principle' which is compared to 'the spinning of a wheel'. The association between eternal recurrence and the rotary motion of machine parts is by no means self-evident. 'When', asks Karl Löwith rhetorically, 'might Nietzsche ever have thought that the essence of modern technology, of the revolving engine, could be an "embodiment of the eternal recurrence of the same"?'[39] Again, Lawrence's interpretation of will-to-power resembles that of Heidegger. Heidegger portrays the *Übermensch* or 'superman' as 'unconditioned will to power' who seeks to achieve 'absolute dominance over the earth'.[40] For such a subject, the 'world changes into object': the 'earth [...] can show itself only as an object of assault [...]. Nature appears everywhere [...] as the object of technology'.[41] In a similar manner, Gerald thinks of 'mankind' as 'contradistinguished against inanimate Matter', and the history of mankind as the 'history of the conquest of the one by the other' (228). He seeks to achieve dominance over the Earth: 'it was his will to subjugate Matter to his own ends[...] What he wanted was the pure fulfilment of his own will in the struggle with the natural conditions. His will was now, to take the coal out of the earth, profitably' (223–4). For both Lawrence and Heidegger, will-to-power is understood in terms of the domination and subjugation of the Earth.

Indeed, Lawrence portrays Gerald as a Nietzschean *Übermensch* who is intent on the ruthless extraction of coal and the technological mastery of the Earth. In the novel, Gudrun and Gerald adopt opposed stances towards the thought of eternal recurrence. Gudrun's horror at mechanical repetition and the 'terrible bondage of [the] tick-tack of time' is a response both to the repetitive temporality of industrial capitalism and to the thought of eternal recurrence (464). In Nietzsche's writings, this thought presents itself—to those who are unable to affirm it—as the 'greatest weight' and the most 'abysmal thought'.[42] If all things recur an infinite number of times, there can never be an escape from time. As a note in the *Will to Power* puts it: '[e]verything becomes and returns eternally—escape is impossible!'[43] Gudrun regards mechanical repetition in similar terms, thinking of the 'eternal repetition of hours and days' as 'too awful to contemplate': 'there was no escape from it, no escape' (464). By contrast, Gerald's embrace of mechanical repetition is that of

---

[38] Martin Heidegger, *Nietzsche*, ed. and trans. David Farrell Krell, 4 vols (New York: Harper Collins, 1991), II, 223, translation modified and italics removed.

[39] Karl Löwith, *Nietzsche's Philosophy of the Eternal Recurrence of the Same*, trans. J. Harvey Lomax (Berkeley: University of California Press, 1997), 226.

[40] Heidegger, *Nietzsche*, IV, 81–2.

[41] Martin Heidegger, 'The Word of Nietzsche: "God Is Dead"', in *The Question Concerning Technology and Other Essays*, trans. William Lovitt (New York: Harper & Row, 1977), 53–112, 100.

[42] Friedrich Nietzsche, *The Gay Science: With a Prelude in Rhymes and an Appendix of Songs*, ed. and trans. Walter Kaufmann (New York: Vintage Books, 1974), 274; and *Thus Spoke Zarathustra: A Book for All and None*, ed. Adrian Del Caro and Robert Pippin, trans. Adrian Del Caro (Cambridge: Cambridge University Press, 2006), 125.

[43] Nietzsche, *Will to Power*, 545.

the Nietzschean *Übermensch* who desires and wills the eternal recurrence of the same, and thereby overcomes nihilism. Indeed, Gudrun thinks of him in explicitly Nietzschean terms as 'superhumanly strong', and as a 'pure, inhuman, almost superhuman instrument' (402, 418).[44] It is as an industrial *Übermensch* that Gerald achieves a revaluation of his father's Christian values, and reforms the family mining firm according to values that lie beyond good and evil.

Gerald's affirmation of eternal recurrence inaugurates a new historical age. Heidegger emphasizes that the thought of eternal recurrence both requires the individual to adopt a particular attitude within lived time, and gives rise to a new historical age.[45] As Nietzsche puts it in a note from the Zarathustra period, '[f]rom the moment when this thought begins to prevail [...] a new history will begin'.[46] In *Women in Love*, such a historical shift is apparent most immediately in Gerald's relationship with his father, and their contrasting attitudes towards the coal mines. As Robert Montgomery remarks, Lawrence uses this relationship to advance a Nietzschean analysis of Christianity: he 'presents the essential traits of the Christian in Gerald's father, the watchwords of whose life—pity, duty, and charity—are the very ideas Nietzsche singles out for his strongest attack'.[47] In the face of increasing class conflict, his father had tried to balance his role as owner of the mining firm with Christian principles, for example by giving away hundreds of pounds in charity when there was a strike.[48] Gerald dispenses with such a paternalistic attitude, rejecting the 'whole Christian attitude of love and self-sacrifice' as 'old hat' (227). He dismisses his father's qualms about exploiting his workers as superfluous sentiment, and instead exerts his power to subordinate the miners to his will. The 'great religion' of his father becomes 'obsolete' and 'superseded in the world' (229). Gerald's renovation of the mining firm is portrayed as making a complete break with the past: there 'was a new world, a new order, strict, terrible, inhuman, but satisfying in its very destructiveness' (231).

Beyond his own firm, Gerald's industrial activities promise to play a wider historical role. Early in the novel, Gerald and Rupert discuss an article in the *Daily Telegraph* that suggests that 'there must arise a man who will give new values to things, give us new truths, a new attitude to life' (54). As Montgomery remarks, although unnamed, 'Nietzsche is clearly present here'.[49] Before his untimely death in the Alps, Gerald's transformation into an industrial *Übermensch* means that he

---

[44] Similarly, Gerald's reorganization of the mines is described in Nietzschean terms as 'the highest that man had produced, the most wonderful and superhuman' (*Women in Love*, 231).

[45] Heidegger, *Nietzsche*, II, 182–3.

[46] Friedrich Nietzsche, 'Eternal Recurrence', in *The Twilight of the Idols*, ed. Oscar Levy, trans. Anthony M. Ludovici (Edinburgh: T. N. Foulis, 1911), 237–56, 252.

[47] Robert E. Montgomery, *The Visionary D. H. Lawrence: Beyond Philosophy and Art* (Cambridge: Cambridge University Press 1994), 126.

[48] This Nietzschean scheme is grafted onto a series of real industrial disputes—including the Midlands mining lockout of 1893—which provide a model for the episode. See Evelyn Cobley, *Modernism and the Culture of Efficiency: Ideology and Fiction* (Toronto: University of Toronto Press, 2009), 205–6.

[49] Montgomery, *Visionary*, 113.

looks set to play the Nietzschean role heralded by the newspaper. Gudrun thinks of 'the revolution he had worked in the mines', and ambitiously envisages him effecting a similar transformation on a greater scale:

> Gerald, with his force of will and his power for comprehending the actual world, should be set to solve the problems of the day, the problem of industrialism in the modern world. She knew he would, in the course of time, effect the changes he desired, he could re-organise the industrial system. (417)

For Gerald to solve 'the problem of industrialism in the modern world' through his forceful 'will' and 'power'—or will-to-power—would be for him to fulfil the newspaper's promise of a coming Nietzschean *Übermensch*. This role would be one of explosive historical significance, as suggested by the earlier images of England going off like a 'powder-magazine' or a 'display of fireworks' (395).[50] Although explosive, such a 'revolution'—a term which again echoes the images of wheels and rotary motion that run throughout the novel—is imagined as a politically conservative one. In her plan for Gerald's future, Gudrun thinks that 'he would go into Parliament in the Conservative interest' in order to 'clear up the great muddle of labour and industry' (417). Rather than overturn the existing class structure and explode the capitalist form of production, this is a conservative revolution that would consolidate the power of industrialists over their workers.

By combining philosophy with the realist novel, *Women in Love* can be read as an allegory of the Anthropocene. Notably, by allying mechanical repetition with Nietzsche's thought of eternal recurrence to portray Gerald Crich as an industrial *Übermensch* who ruthlessly extracts coal and subjugates his workforce, Lawrence's novel bears affinities with Malm's account of the British Industrial Revolution as the origin of the Anthropocene. However, while Lawrence uses Nietzsche's philosophy to create a critical portrayal of industrial capitalism and a 'hot world silted with coal-dust' in *Women in Love*, he returns to the thought of eternal recurrence in more sympathetic fashion in *Lady Chatterley's Lover* (114). By doing so, he might be seen as responding to the dual structure of this thought, and the way that it is presented as the most abysmal manifestation of nihilism and its joyful overcoming. Benjamin exploits this ambiguity in his characterization of the temporality of modernity as the new as the ever-same: on the one hand, this temporality forms part of his projected depiction of 'modernity as Hell', and on the other, it involves hope and the prospect of happiness through a redeemed future. As he puts it, the idea of eternal recurrence 'conjures the speculative idea [...] of happiness from the misery of the times'.[51] Changing his stance on whether the thought of eternal

---

[50] In this chapter, Gudrun is inspired by the Alpine setting to 'feel übermenschlich—more than human', and remarks that it would 'be wonderful, if all England *did* suddenly go off like a display of fireworks' (*Women in Love*, 394–5).

[51] Walter Benjamin, 'Central Park', in *Selected Writings*, ed. Michael W. Jennings et al., trans. Edmund Jephcott et al., 4 vols (Cambridge, Mass.: Belknap Press, 1996–2003), IV, 161–99, 184.

recurrence overcomes nihilism or stands as its consummation, Heidegger went from an interpretation of Zarathustra's thought as heralding the redemption of the Earth, to seeing it as paving the way for the unbridled technological mastery of the planet in the age of modernity.[52] Lawrence's creative adaptations of Nietzsche's thought display a similar range, although the trajectory is reversed. In *Lady Chatterley's Lover*, he adapts Nietzsche's thought in a sympathetic fashion, to imagine an alternative to an age characterized by the extraction of fossil fuels and the technological exploitation of the Earth.

Lady Chatterley and the revaluation of the Earth

Lady Chatterley's Lover is, as everyone knows, a novel about sex. With copies having been seized by British customs officials shortly after its publication in 1928, it was famously put on trial in 1960 to test the Obscene Publications Act of 1959. The novel was declared 'innocent', and for many, its republication encapsulated the new era of sexual freedom of the 1960s.[53] However, there is a sense in which the novel has remained on trial, as its sexual politics received a series of searing attacks from feminist critics. Most famously, Kate Millett argued that the 'celebration of sexual passion for which the book is so renowned is largely a celebration of the penis of Oliver Mellors, gamekeeper and social prophet'.[54] Without ignoring concerns about its controversial sexual politics, Cole argues that it is important to recognize other dimensions of the novel, including the 'foundational presence throughout the narrative of coal' that makes it a key work of fossil fuel fiction.[55] Indeed, Lawrence uses sex as a means of exploring issues surrounding the extraction of coal, including class conflict and environmental destruction.

Most immediately, Connie's relationships with her aristocratic husband and the gamekeeper become a means of exploring class conflict during a time of industrial disputes. Following Raymond Williams, a number of critics have read the novel in the context of the 1926 General Strike, the aftermath of which Lawrence witnessed when he returned to his home town of Eastwood in the Midlands that year.[56] By doing so, they develop an argument made by the defence in the 1960 obscenity trial: that the book 'does not deal simply and solely with sexual relationship; it deals with other matters as well—the industrial state of the country, the hard lives that people are living'.[57] However, drawing attention to the differences between

---

[52] See David Farrell Krell's 'Analysis' in Heidegger, *Nietzsche*, III, 267.
[53] See H. Montgomery Hyde (ed.), *The Lady Chatterley's Lover Trial: Regina v. Penguin Books Limited* (London: Bodley Head, 1990), 1, 43.
[54] Kate Millett, *Sexual Politics* (London: Rupert Hart-Davis, 1971), 238.
[55] Cole, 'Warming World', 290.
[56] See Charles Ferrall and Dougal McNeill, *Writing the 1926 General Strike: Literature, Culture, Politics* (New York: Cambridge University Press, 2015), 83–4.
[57] Hyde (ed.), *Trial*, 315.

the three versions of the novel, several of these critics express their disappoint-
ment with what they see as the novel's retreat from history. Scott Sanders contends
that by the third version of the novel, Connie and Mellors have become 'two iso-
lated souls who have severed all ties with the degraded world and who seek their
own private salvation through passion and flight'.[58] Graham Holderness similarly
argues that the novel underwent a 'process of retreat from history', culminating in
the final version in which '"class" is abolished': '[s]uch a denial of history is the
necessary precondition for the relationship between Connie and Mellors; history
presents no obstacles to its fulfilment, its symbolic reconciliation of real contradictions'.[59] Peter Scheckner concurs, suggesting that the 'rich tapestry of history,
social struggle, and the interdependence of the public and private sectors is greatly
diminished' over the course of the novels, so that by the final version the 'historical
England of the first two versions now becomes largely two people, Wragby woods,
the hut, and a few animals'.[60]

Yet by relying on a theory of the novel derived from György Lukács—in which
the realist novel's political value arises from its success or failure at representing
society and its contradictions at a given moment in time—these readings overlook Lawrence's distinctive incorporation of philosophical elements into the realist
novel.[61] Lawrence's focus on sex and the body might be explicated in terms of
Fredric Jameson's conception of the antinomies of realism. For Jameson, the realist novel is animated by the tension between two opposed impulses: a narrative
impulse, and a scenic impulse towards the realm of affect. He contends that the
antinomy between these impulses arises because narrative is essentially temporal
and historical, whereas the scenic exploration of affect and the body is ahistorical, leading to an issueless 'scenic present'.[62] Lawrence attempts to circumvent this
antinomy by fusing the provincial realist novel with elements drawn from apocalyptic and philosophical traditions. In particular, sex becomes not a means of a
retreat from history and social concerns—a view perhaps surprisingly shared by
Lukácsian critics and the moral crusaders who denigrated Lawrence's fixation on
sex and the body—but the site of an apocalyptic allegory and Nietzschean states
of rapture, both of which are used to explore the possibility of an alternative to an
age of environmental destruction caused by industry and the extraction of fossil
fuels.[63] That is, in *Lady Chatterley's Lover*, the body becomes not the means of

---

[58] Scott Sanders, *D. H. Lawrence: The World of the Five Major Novels* (New York: Viking Press, 1974),
204.
[59] Graham Holderness, *D. H. Lawrence: History, Ideology and Fiction* (Dublin: Gill and Macmillan,
1982), 223, 226.
[60] Peter Scheckner, *Class, Politics, and the Individual: A Study of the Major Works of D. H. Lawrence*
(London: Associated University Presses, 1985), 161.
[61] See Sanders, *Lawrence*, 18, 32; Holderness, *Lawrence*, 7–12, 220; and Scheckner, *Class*, 93, 157.
[62] Fredric Jameson, *The Antinomies of Realism* (London: Verso, 2015), 8, 10–11.
[63] Such a reading complements Ferrall and McNeill's challenge to the earlier critical consensus that
saw Lawrence turning from politics to sex as he rewrote the novel. They argue that the 'revisions of the

escape into an issueless present, but the site of an affective refiguration of history and the rekindling of a historical sense—the sense of the social and environmental damage caused by fossil capitalism, and the (fictional) imagination of alternatives that could constitute a new age.

Specifically, Lawrence uses apocalyptic thought to stage the inauguration of a new historical age in *Lady Chatterley's Lover*. The novel opens with Connie's apocalyptic sense that she lives in a 'tragic age': '[t]he cataclysm has happened, we are among the ruins, we start to build up new little habitats, to have new little hopes. It is rather hard work: there is now no smooth road into the future'. The 'cataclysm' refers most immediately to the Great War, from which Connie's husband Clifford returned 'more or less in bits'.[64] Yet it also suggests other political and environmental upheavals that are explored throughout the novel. Lawrence himself reacted to the 1926 strikes in apocalyptic terms, writing that 'the coal-strike is on, and a general strike threatened, and altogether it feels like the end of the world'.[65] In *England and the Octopus* (1928)—which Lawrence recommends as a 'sincere, honest, even passionate' book about 'the utter and hopeless disfigurement of the English countryside by modern industrial encroachment'—Clough Williams-Ellis depicts England in similar terms.[66] Speculating that future generations 'will view with consternation the wreckage wrought in our delirium', he reflects that the 'ten millions' thrown into the 'present sudden and largely unforeseen state of chaos and unemployment in coal-mining and some of the old heavy industries' must 'for the most part stay where they are and survey the ruins'. Yet he notes that 'where the mines and furnaces and foundries are closed down, there is some hope for regeneration', and a 'new and different future'.[67] Connie's sense of living among the ruins and her tentative hopes for the future resonate with Williams-Ellis's rhetoric, and the 'habitats' that she thinks of rebuilding intimate that the 'cataclysm' is partly one of natural history or ecology.

Having framed history in apocalyptic terms, Connie develops a relationship with Mellors that signals the birth of a new Joachite historical epoch. As critics have shown, Lawrence often made use of an apocalyptic shape of history inspired by Joachim of Fiore.[68] In his textbook *Movements in European History* (1921), he advances an account of two different forms of apocalypticism: the early Christian

novel intensify both the "sex" and the "politics"': politics becomes 'becomes more sexualised but sex also more politicised' (*General Strike*, 84).

[64] D. H. Lawrence, *Lady Chatterley's Lover and A Propos of 'Lady Chatterley's Lover'*, ed. Michael Squires (Cambridge: Cambridge University Press, 1993), 5. Unless otherwise specified, all further references are to this version and edition.

[65] Letter to Ada Clarke, 3 May 1926, in *The Letters of D. H. Lawrence*, ed. James T. Boulton et al., 8 vols (Cambridge: Cambridge University Press, 1979–2000), V, 448.

[66] D. H. Lawrence, 'Review for Vogue', in *Introductions and Reviews*, ed. N. H. Reeve and John Worthen (Cambridge: Cambridge University Press, 2005), 337–43, 341.

[67] Clough Williams-Ellis, *England and the Octopus* (London: Geoffrey Bles, 1928), 106, 43–4.

[68] For example, Peter Fjågesund identifies 'Joachism' as the most important of five types of history that together make up Lawrence's 'apocalyptic-millennial' conception of history (*The Apocalyptic World of D. H. Lawrence* (Oslo: Norwegian University Press, 1991), 8–13).

belief in the Millennium, which signals an end to history, and a Joachite apocalyptic rupture, which signals the inauguration of a new historical epoch.[69] He is hostile to the first type of apocalypticism, which, as T. R. Wright points out, he criticizes by reproducing almost verbatim Nietzschean's argument that the desire for the Millennium is the fantasy of a slave class, avenging itself on the powerful 'by imagining the sudden destruction of the world to be near at hand'.[70] However, Lawrence is far more sympathetic to the second type of apocalypticism. He outlines Joachim of Fiore's interpretation of history, emphasizing how it achieved 'great power over the minds of men':

> In 1254 a book was published called *Introduction to the Everlasting Gospel*, supposed to contain the teaching of a famous seer or prophet, the Abbot Joachim, who had died at Naples in 1202. In this book it said that Judaism was the revelation of the Father: Christianity was the revelation of the Son: now men must prepare for the revelation of the Holy Ghost.[71]

In addition to giving a historical account of the ideas of Joachim, Lawrence's own history takes a Joachite apocalyptic form. As Daniel Schneider observes, his European history 'exhibits the Joachite movement from the revelation of the Father [...] to the revelation of the Son [...] but stops short of the revelation of the Holy Ghost'.[72] Lawrence deploys a similar apocalyptic scheme in *Lady Chatterley's Lover*. In *A Propos of 'Lady Chatterley's Lover'*, he situates the novel within a tripartite scheme of history. Expanding on Connie's sense that she lives in a 'tragic age', he contends that there are three historical epochs—pre-tragic, tragic, and post-tragic—and that we live at the end of the tragic epoch, which has been marked by 'escape from the body' (329–31). In the novel, the various sex scenes between Connie and Mellors correspond to Lawrence's esoteric interpretation of the Book of Revelation in his *Apocalypse* (1931), in which the seven seals describe the stages of a '"secret" ritual of initiation into one of the pagan Mysteries'.[73] For example, her orgasm in the woods—'[s]he was gone, she was not, and she was born'—parallels Lawrence's account of the opening of the seventh seal in Revelation, as 'a death and birth at once' (174).[74] Connie's apocalyptic rebirth also signals the birth of a new

---

[69] D. H. Lawrence, *Movements in European History*, ed. Philip Crumpton (Cambridge: Cambridge University Press, 1989), 31.

[70] T. R. Wright, *D. H. Lawrence and the Bible* (Cambridge: Cambridge University Press, 2002), 48.

[71] Lawrence, *Movements*, 147.

[72] Daniel J. Schneider, 'Psychology in Lawrence's *Movements in European History*', *Rocky Mountain Review of Language and Literature*, 39/2 (1985), 97–106, 103. He notes that with its Joachite structure, *Movements* 'works out in detail many of the ideas that Lawrence had already suggested in "Study of Thomas Hardy" and in *The Rainbow* and *Women in Love*' (103).

[73] See D. H. Lawrence, *Apocalypse and the Writings on Revelation*, ed. Mara Kalnins (Cambridge: Cambridge University Press, 1980), 85; and Frank Kermode, *Lawrence* ([London]: Fontana, 1973), 128–9.

[74] Lawrence, *Apocalypse*, 105.

Joachite historical epoch—that which Lawrence calls 'the post-tragic epoch' (329). Indeed, in the second version of the novel, Connie's rebirth is directly aligned with Joachim's historical scheme. Shortly before her departure for the Continent, Clifford says to her: '[i]f only we were an aeon or two ahead, you'd have no need to go out looking for a Holy Ghost on two legs'.[75] He thereby alludes to Joachim's 'reign of the Holy Ghost', which in *Movements* is promised as the coming historical epoch: there 'still remains the last reign of wisdom, of pure understanding, the reign which we have never seen in the world, but which we must see'.[76]

Complementing his deployment of an apocalyptic scheme, Lawrence uses Nietzsche's thought of eternal recurrence to imagine the inauguration of a new historical age in *Lady Chatterley's Lover*.[77] Whereas he adapts the thought in *Women in Love* to portray Gerald's extraction of coal as the apotheosis of an age of mechanical repetition, he uses it in *Lady Chatterley's Lover* to imagine Connie and Mellors's revaluation of the Earth in response to Clifford's destructive coal-mining activities. The latter novel uses Nietzsche's thought to stage the overcoming of a historical age of Platonism, which is associated with the devaluation of the body and the Earth. Critics have drawn attention to the anti-Platonism of the *Lady Chatterley* novels. Joseph Voelker traces this feature through the three versions of the novel; Dennis Jackson highlights Connie's 'rebellion against Platonism' and her rejection of the *Phaedrus* myth; and Barry Scherr situates the anti-Platonism of the novel within the wider context of Lawrence's 'quarrel with Plato', which dates from at least the time of the First World War.[78] It might be added that the anti-Platonism of *Lady Chatterley's Lover* is deeply Nietzschean. As Heidegger points out, during the last years of his creative life, Nietzsche laboured 'at nothing else than the overturning of Platonism'.[79] That is, Nietzsche interprets the 'collective history of Western philosophy' as Platonism, understood as the belief in the distinction between the true and apparent worlds, and sees this Platonism

[75] D. H. Lawrence, *The First and Second Lady Chatterley Novels*, ed. Dieter Mehl and Christa Jansohn (Cambridge: Cambridge University Press, 1999), 465.

[76] Lawrence, *Movements*, 147, 167.

[77] As well as forming part of a Joachite scheme of history, Connie's idea of a 'tragic age' is Nietzschean. For example, Nietzsche proclaims in the first section of the *Gay Science* that: '[f]or the present, we still live in the age of tragedy, the age of moralities and religions' (74). Similarly, in the *Will to Power*, he describes the historical age of nihilism, during which confidence in 'the "true world"' is lost, as 'the tragic age' (24).

[78] See Joseph C. Voelker, 'The Spirit of No-Place: Elements of the Classical Ironic Utopia in D. H. Lawrence's *Lady Chatterley's Lover*', *Modern Fiction Studies*, 25/2 (1979), 223–39, 226; Dennis Jackson, 'Literary Allusions in *Lady Chatterley's Lover*', in Michael Squires and Dennis Jackson (eds), D. H. Lawrence's *'Lady': A New Look at 'Lady Chatterley's Lover'* (Athens: University of Georgia Press, 1985), 170–96, 174; and Barry J. Scherr, *D. H. Lawrence's Response to Plato: A Bloomian Interpretation* (New York: Peter Lang, 1996), 35.

[79] Heidegger, *Nietzsche*, I, 154. In 'The Word of Nietzsche: "God is Dead"', Heidegger contends that 'Nietzsche understands his own philosophy as the countermovement to metaphysics, and that means for him a movement in opposition to Platonism'. He interprets Nietzsche's pronouncement 'God is dead' to mean that the Platonic suprasensory world (the heaven of the *Phaedrus*) 'is without effective power': '[m]etaphysics, i.e., for Nietzsche Western philosophy understood as Platonism, is at an end' (61).

as determinative of 'the history of Western man'.[80] Such an understanding is particularly evident in the section of the *Twilight of the Idols* (1888) entitled 'How
the "True World" Finally Became a Fable'. As Heidegger comments, the six numbered parts of this section 'can be readily recognized as the most important epochs
of Western thought'.[81] Plato's distinction between the true and apparent words re-
emerges in the Christian distinction between heaven and Earth, Kant's distinction
between the noumenal and phenomenal worlds, and Schopenhauer's distinction
between the world as will and the world as representation. The sixth numbered
part of this section marks the juncture at which the opposition between the true
and apparent worlds is to be overcome:

> The true world is gone: which world is left? The illusory one, perhaps? [...] But
> no! *we got rid of the illusory world along with the true one!* [...] end of longest
> error; high point of humanity; INCIPIT ZARATHUSTRA.[82]

The 'end of [the] longest error' marks the overcoming of Platonism as the history of
philosophy, and the 'high point of humanity' signals the advent of the *Übermensch*
who is to supersede the 'last man'. This overcoming is to be achieved through
the thought of eternal recurrence, which, as Heidegger puts it, aims to overturn and 'twist out of' the Platonic antithesis between the true and false worlds:
'INCIPIT ZARATHUSTRA'.[83] Or in a different (although closely related) idiom,
the thought of eternal recurrence is employed to deconstruct the binary oppositions between the true and apparent worlds, being and becoming, and eternity and
time—oppositions which have underpinned philosophy and metaphysics from
Plato onwards, and which have led to the devaluation of the body and of the Earth.

In *Lady Chatterley's Lover*, Connie rebels against her husband's Platonism, and
the pursuit of Platonic truth and beauty which had characterized the early years
of their marriage. For example, in the second version of the novel, Clifford reads
Plato's *Phaedrus* to Connie, but she 'didn't care about the progress of the soul,
nor for pure Truth nor pure Knowledge, nor the Philosophers' heaven'. She revolts
against Clifford: 'I am sick to death of your philosophy and your immortality! It
deadens everything out of existence. Look at you, how dead you are!'[84] In the third
version of the novel, she gives an account of the death of the body:

> [t]he human body is only just coming to real life. With the Greeks it gave a lovely
> flicker, then Plato and Aristotle killed it, and Jesus finished it off. But now the

---

[80] Heidegger, *Nietzsche*, II, 171.

[81] Heidegger, *Nietzsche*, I, 202.

[82] Nietzsche, *Twilight*, 171.

[83] Heidegger, *Nietzsche*, I, 208. As flagged above, Heidegger ultimately suggests that the thought of
eternal recurrence fails to overcome metaphysics understood as Platonism, and instead stands as its
virulent consummation.

[84] Lawrence, *First and Second*, 298–9.

body is coming really to life [...] And it will be a lovely, lovely life in the lovely universe, the life of the human body. (234–5)

This account resembles those of Lawrence's late writings. Adapting Nietzsche for an age of technology, Lawrence advances grand narratives that portray the history of the world as the history of Platonism. In his essay 'Introduction to These Paintings' (1929), he describes the 'history of our era' as 'the nauseating and repulsive history of the crucifixion of the procreative body', for which Plato was 'arch-priest'.[85] And in *Apocalypse*, he holds that with the 'coming of Socrates [...] the cosmos died', and the next 'two thousand years' constitute a Platonic-Christian epoch characterized by the denial of the body and the triumph of the machine: 'our ideal civilisation has been one long evasion' whose 'only fruit is the machine!'[86] Lawrence depicts such a civilization in *Lady Chatterley's Lover*. In *Twilight of the Idols*, Nietzsche proposes that it 'would not make any sense to fabricate a world "other" than this one unless we had a powerful instinct for libelling, belittling, and casting suspicion on life: in that case, we would be using the phantasmagoria of an "other", a "better" life to *avenge* ourselves on life'.[87] Clifford's obsession with Platonic immortality, which turns life into a 'grisly phantasm', is just such an act of revenge on life.[88] In the second version of the novel, people like Clifford who want 'immortality and eternity' are portrayed as being 'like a huge cold death-worm encircling the earth, and letting nothing live. It was Will, the will of dead things to make everything dead'.[89] Such people exert what Nietzsche calls a 'will to denial of life': through their desire for immortality and eternity, they exert their 'unyielding, insistent human Will, cold, anti-life, and insane'.[90]

Throughout the novel, the effects of Clifford's Platonic devaluation of the body and of the Earth are clearly apparent. Under his Platonist regime at Wragby, Connie's body suffers, and is reduced to a corpse-like state. In the first version, this harm is conveyed in the terms of the *Phaedrus* myth: the 'poor black horse of her body [...] had been lying now for months as if he were dead, with his neck twisted sideways as if it had been broken'.[91] In the third version, the harm is apparent in the scene in which she looks at herself naked in the mirror. She notices that her body was 'a little greyish and sapless', her breasts 'unripe' and 'a little bitter', her belly 'slack', and her thighs were going 'flat, slack, meaningless'. The sight of her withering body makes her depressed and miserable, causing her to hate '[t]he mental

---

[85] D. H. Lawrence, 'Introduction to These Paintings', in *Late Essays and Articles*, ed. James T. Boulton (Cambridge: Cambridge University Press, 2004), 182–217, 203.
[86] Lawrence, *Apocalypse*, 96, 78. In *A Propos*, Lawrence similarly contends that 'the great crusade against sex and the body started in full blast, with Plato' (332).
[87] Nietzsche, *Twilight*, 170.
[88] Lawrence, *First and Second*, 216.
[89] Lawrence, *First and Second*, 300.
[90] Nietzsche, *Will to Power*, 452; Lawrence, *First and Second*, 301.
[91] Lawrence, *First and Second*, 27.

life' (70–1). Similarly, Clifford's Platonist regime drains all value from the Earth. Wragby is described as 'spectral, not really existing', just as for Plato, the world perceived by the senses is one of non-being. And in markedly Platonic terms, Connie thinks of Wragby as like the 'simulacrum of reality' (18).

Clifford's devaluation of the Earth is conveyed by a scene that parodies Plato's *Phaedrus*. In the *Phaedrus*, Socrates advances a myth in which he likens the soul 'to the natural union of a team of winged horses and their charioteer', and describes the 'steep climb' of such souls 'to the high tier at the rim of heaven'.[92] Lawrence parodies this Platonic ascent to heaven as Clifford attempts to ascend a hill in his mechanical chair: he fails, and to his humiliation has to be rescued by the gamekeeper. In his writings on Revelation, Lawrence contends that history since Plato has been 'one long process': the 'triumph of Mind over the cosmos progresses in small spasms: aeroplanes, radio, motor-traffic'.[93] Given this association between Platonism and machines, it is appropriate that Clifford makes his Platonic ascent in a motorized wheelchair. Connie reimagines Plato's conceit by replacing the horses with a 'Ford car', or, as Clifford would have it, a more aristocratic Rolls-Royce: 'Plato never thought we'd go one better than his black steed and his white steed, and have no steeds at all, only an engine!' (179). The scene also intimates the harm that Clifford's Platonism inflicts on the environment. Connie watches his bath-chair 'jolt over the wood-ruff and the bugle', 'squash the little yellow cups of the creeping-jenny', and make a 'wake through the forget-me-nots' (184). His crushing the flowers on his ascent ironically conveys the damage done by his Platonic devaluation of the Earth. Sitting impotently amid the wrecked flowers at the bottom of the hill, Clifford is emblematic of what Lawrence describes as the 'men of mind and spirit' who 'only succeed in spoiling the earth'.[94]

Clifford's devaluation of the Earth reaches it apotheosis in his coal-mining activities. Like Gerald in *Women in Love*, he embarks on an ambitious programme to renovate his mining firm, immersing himself in 'the technicalities of modern coal-mining' (108). Reflecting the damage suggested by the parody of the *Phaedrus* myth, the environmental harm caused by coal-mining is particularly evident in the scene in which Connie is driven through Tevershall. In spite of it being a spring day, 'there was smoke on the rain, and a certain sense of exhaust vapour in the air' (152). The smoke and fly ash emitted from the coal-mines and steel-works have blackened the Midlands landscape. Connie drives past the 'blackened brick dwellings', the 'mud black with coal-dust', the Wesleyan chapel of 'blackened brick' with its 'blackened shrubs', and the church among 'black trees' (152–3). Even the fields have been turned 'dark-green' (153). As she passes Stacks Gate, she observes the 'huge new installations' of a 'really modern mine, chemical works and long

[92] Plato, *Phaedrus*, in *Plato: Complete Works*, ed. John Cooper, trans. G. M. A. Grube et al. (Indianapolis: Hackett, 1997), 506–56, 246a, 247b, 524–5.
[93] Lawrence, *Apocalypse*, 198–9.
[94] Lawrence, *Apocalypse*, 200.

galleries', from which rose 'vast plumes of smoke and vapour' (154). This colliery has made its owner and shareholders rich, but has 'eaten deep into the bodies and souls' of the colliers, turning them into '[e]lemental creatures, weird and distorted' (159–60). In the adjacent town, 'iron clanked with a huge reverberating clank, and huge lorries shook the earth, and whistles screamed' (155). Returning to this part of the world from the Continent in the second version of the novel, Connie finds a 'realm of twilight and the mystery of iron, this disembowelled earth of coal and steel and steam, and the glare of red fire and of shadow'.[95] By figuring the Earth as a body, the metaphor of the disembowelled Earth neatly links the harm inflicted on both the body and the Earth by Platonism. In this version, Clifford's intensification of his mining activities is accompanied by a blunt determination to take vengeance on the world: he 'still was going to make his mark on the environment: even if the mark should only be a scar!'[96]

Connie's drive leads her to think of history, and of historical continuity. Looking at the stately homes that have been abandoned, she becomes aware of a historical transition: '[t]his is history. One England blots out another. The mines had made the halls wealthy. Now they were blotting them out' (156). On the one hand, this transition from an 'agricultural England' to an 'industrial England' is a social and economic one, which threatens the continuity of the aristocratic landowning class (156). Having seen 'great lorries full of steel-workers from Sheffield' looking like 'half-corpses', Connie realizes that 'there can be no fellowship any more' between 'the leaders of men' and their 'fellow men'; her sympathies shift from Clifford towards Mellors, and she shudders with dread at the idea of having 'an heir to Wragby' (153). Yet the transition is also an environmental one, as suggested syntactically by a sentence that begins abruptly with 'But': '[t]he stately homes of England make good photographs, and create the illusion of a connexion with the Elizabethans [...]. But smuts fall and blacken on the drab stucco, that has long ceased to be golden' (156). Here, the smuts stand metonymically for industrial pollution that marks a decisive historical break, much like that registered by Malm's conception of the Anthropocene. Lawrence's depiction of a smoke-blackened landscape also echoes contemporary anxieties about pollution caused by the burning of coal. For example, Williams-Ellis points out that 'in nothing has England suffered more from her position as a pioneer than in her reckless production of smoke', remarking that 'there is a quite definite limit to the pollution of the air and the denial of sunlight below which life itself is not only prejudiced but actually endangered'.[97] And the authors of *Coal: A Challenge to the National Conscience* (1927), which was published by Virginia and Leonard Woolf at the Hogarth Press, write that 'the burning of raw coal creates a smoke pall over our modern cities that interferes

---

[95] Lawrence, *First and Second*, 514.
[96] Lawrence, *First and Second*, 347.
[97] Williams-Ellis, *Octopus*, 37–8.

gravely with the actinic rays of the sun', causing a lowering of vitality in the population. For this reason, they call for 'a policy of conservation': 'there is need of restraint in the raising and consumption of coal'.[98]

More broadly, Lawrence draws attention to environmental damage from coal-mining throughout *Lady Chatterley's Lover*. Noxious gas emissions can be smelled from Wragby Hall:

> Teltershall pit-bank was burning, had been burning for years, and it would cost thousands to put it out. So it had to burn. And when the wind was that way, which was often, the house was full of the stench of this sulphureous combustion of the earth's excrement. But even on windless days, the air always smelled of something under-earth: sulphur, coal, iron, or acid. (13)

From the house can be heard 'the rattle-rattle of the screens at the pit, the puff of the winding-engine, the clink-clink of shunting trucks and the hoarse little whistle of the colliery locomotives', and 'even on the Christmas roses the smuts settled persistently, incredible, like black manna from skies of doom' (13). Clifford's mining activities also obtrude on the woods. Returning from an assignation with Connie, Mellors tries to escape into the 'darkness and seclusion of the wood', but

> knew that the seclusion of the wood was illusory. The industrial noises broke the solitude, the sharp lights, though unseen, mocked it [...]. The fault lay there, out there, in those evil electric lights and diabolical rattlings of engines. There, in the world of the mechanical greedy, greedy mechanism and mechanised greed, sparkling with lights and gushing hot metal and roaring with traffic, there lay the vast evil thing, ready to destroy whatever did not conform. Soon it would destroy the wood, and the bluebells would spring no more. All vulnerable things must perish under the rolling and running of iron. (119)

Reflecting his perspective through free indirect discourse, the repetition in 'mechanical greedy, greedy mechanism and mechanised greed', in which adjectives pile up and modify each other in tautological fashion, conveys the anger that Mellors struggles to articulate. Yet the cyclical repetition of words derived from the same root also intimates the repetitive nature of the processes involved in coal-mining, and the repetitive labour of the colliers. Mellors is a fierce critic of what he calls the 'industrial system', remarking that even from the moon 'you could look back and see the earth, dirty, beastly, unsavoury among all the stars: made foul by men' (223, 220). He declares that if he were able, he would 'wipe the machines off the face of the earth again, and end the industrial epoch absolutely,

---

[98] V. A. Demant et al., *Coal: A Challenge to the National Conscience*, ed. Alan Porter (London: Hogarth Press, 1927), 57.

like a black mistake' (220).[99] Connie similarly resents the intrusion of industry into what would otherwise be her perfect pastoral haven. Staying at Mellors's cottage in the woods, she thinks: '[i]f only there weren't the other ghastly world of smoke and iron!' (212).

Connie rejects Clifford's Platonism in a manner that resembles Zarathustra's attempt to overcome Platonism through the thought of eternal recurrence. In the first version of the novel, Clifford challenges Connie, asking her whether 'Plato's ideas, and heaven, and those things, mean nothing to you?', to which she responds:

> Pictures! They make pictures [...]. No! With heaven and Plato's ideas and all those things, I feel as I do in the National Gallery, or in the Uffizi. I'm looking at something rather lovely, or very lovely, but the world is outside, and my life is in the world.[100]

Here, she implicitly dissents from Socrates' view of art in the tenth book of Plato's *Republic*. Therein, Socrates holds painting to be 'third removed from reality' as the imitation of objects which are made by craftsmen, and he and Glaucon famously resolve to banish painters from their ideal republic.[101] Inverting Socrates' hierarchy, Connie degrades Plato's ideas and heaven to the level of pictures. Claiming that the 'world is outside, and my life is in the world', she values Plato's 'apparent world' over his 'true world'. This inversion corresponds to the fifth stage of the history of philosophy in Nietzsche's 'How the "True World" Finally Became a Fable': '[t]he "true world"—an idea that is of no further use [...] let's get rid of it! [...] Plato blushes in shame'. Whereas the 'true world' in Nietzsche's history becomes first 'unattainable', then an 'obsolete, superfluous idea', so Connie feels distanced from Plato's ideas and heaven: 'I'm an onlooker, I'm not in the picture'.[102]

As with Nietzsche's thought of eternal recurrence, Connie combats Platonism by adopting a new temporal stance.[103] She rebels against Clifford's obsession with a Platonic immortality in which 'your soul, or your self [...] has a life eternal', feeling that she had to 'establish her own sort of immortality, perhaps; not always be commandeered by his'.[104] This task matches that of Zarathustra in Nietzsche's

---

[99] As David Bradshaw shows, some of Mellors's (surprising) recommendations for combating industrialism—such as that men should wear red trousers—were inspired by John Hargrave, founder and leader of the Kindred of the Kibbo Kift ('Red Trousers: *Lady Chatterley's Lover* and John Hargrave', *Essays in Criticism*, 55/4 (2005), 352–73).

[100] Lawrence, *First and Second*, 50.

[101] Plato, *Republic*, in *Plato: Complete Works*, ed. John Cooper, trans. G. M. A. Grube et al. (Indianapolis: Hackett, 1997), 971–1223, 605b, 348.

[102] Nietzsche, *Twilight*, 171; Lawrence, *First and Second*, 50.

[103] Adrian Del Caro points out that a 'solid first step towards opposing or reversing the effects of Platonism', which is to be achieved through the thought of the eternal recurrence, is 'a reorientation toward time, such that time in its transient dimension is not used to cast aspersions on the passing nature of earthly life' (*Grounding the Nietzsche Rhetoric of Earth* (Berlin: De Gruyter, 2004), 82).

[104] Lawrence, *First and Second*, 49–50. A deleted passage in the manuscript makes clear that this 'question of [...] immortality had been dinned in to her by Clifford, during their readings of Plato' (622).

Thus Spoke Zarathustra (1883–85). Zarathustra attains a new type of immortality by willing the infinite repetition of each moment, thereby stamping becoming with the character of being through the thought of eternal recurrence. As Nietzsche puts it in a note from the Zarathustra period:

> [l]et us stamp the impress of eternity upon our lives! This thought contains more than all the religions which taught us to contemn this life as a thing ephemeral, which bade us squint upwards to another and indefinite existence.[105]

Similarly, Connie seeks a sense of immortality in this life: '[i]f I don't feel immortal, now, what's the good of fussing about it later on?' She pursues her sense of immortality through the moment, claiming—to Clifford's chagrin—that Miss Bentley blushing and looking 'like a shy girl for a minute [...] interests me as much as Plato'.[106] Her finding immortality in such a seemingly transitory and ephemeral moment parallels Zarathustra's stamping the moment (the gateway 'Moment') with the character of eternity by wishing its eternal recurrence.[107] Much like Nietzsche's Zarathustra, Connie achieves a transformation of being through time, and discovers what she calls the 'immortality of the flesh'.[108]

Having relinquished Clifford's Platonism, Connie pursues a project of revaluing the body and the Earth. By collapsing the Platonic antithesis between the true and apparent worlds, Nietzsche's thought of eternal recurrence opens the way for a revaluation of values. For Nietzsche, the antithesis between the true and apparent worlds constitutes the '[p]rejudice of prejudices', which must be overcome:

> It is of cardinal importance that one should abolish the *true* world. It is the great inspirer of doubt and devaluator in respect of the world *we are*: it has been our most dangerous attempt yet to assassinate life. War on all presuppositions on the basis of which one has invented a true world.[109]

By overcoming this antithesis, the thought of eternal recurrence invites a revaluation of what had been devalued as the apparent world of becoming. As Heidegger puts it, with 'the abolition of Platonism the way first opens for the affirmation of the sensuous [world]'.[110] The revaluation of values is undertaken by Zarathustra, who iconoclastically 'breaks tablets and old values': he sits with 'old broken tablets around [him] and also new tablets only partially written upon'.[111]

Like Nietzsche's Zarathustra, Connie pursues a revaluation of the body. Lawrence's attention to the body distinguishes his approach to characterization

[105] Nietzsche, 'Eternal Recurrence', 254.
[106] Lawrence, *First and Second*, 50.
[107] Nietzsche, *Zarathustra*, 125–6.
[108] Lawrence, *First and Second*, 50.
[109] Nietzsche, *Will to Power*, 313–14.
[110] Heidegger, *Nietzsche*, I, 209.
[111] Nietzsche, *Zarathustra*, 171, 156.

from that of many contemporary writers, who were more interested in exploring what he calls 'self-consciousness'.[112] In this sense, there is some truth in the prosecutor's description during the obscenity trial of Connie and Mellors as 'little more than bodies, bodies which continually have sexual intercourse with one another'.[113] As well as constituting an apocalyptic rebirth, the gradual coming to life of Connie's body corresponds to a Nietzschean revaluation of the body by means of states of aesthetic rapture. In opposition to states of aesthetic disinterest, Nietzsche champions states of aesthetic rapture which are physiologically grounded in the body. For example, in *Twilight of the Idols*, he identifies 'rapture [Rausch]' as a 'physiological precondition [that] is indispensable for there to be art or any sort of aesthetic action or vision', and singles out 'sexual excitement' as the 'most ancient and original form of rapture'.[114] In the *Lady Chatterley* novels, Lawrence portrays Connie turning away from Clifford's aesthetic disinterest to embrace Nietzschean states of rapture with the gamekeeper. Clifford lives at Wragby,

> cut off from the breathing contact of the living universe. He loved a beautiful landscape, a beautiful flower. Most of all, he loved art, pictures, books. Because here, his mind and his critical appreciation could play freely. He could get real aesthetic pleasure from books and pictures.[115]

That 'art, pictures, books' allow Clifford's mind and critical appreciation to 'play freely' suggests a Kantian account of aesthetic pleasure as arising from the 'free play' of the cognitive faculties in a judgment of taste.[116] In contrast to such states, which only carry Clifford 'further away from any deep bodily interchange', Connie finds beauty through touch and bodily states of rapture.[117] As Mellors touches her, she initially 'wondered a little over the sort of rapture it was to him': she 'did not understand the beauty he found in her, through touch upon her living secret body, almost the ecstasy of beauty' (125). Yet she comes to experience such states herself:

> Suddenly, in the deeps of her body, wonderful rippling thrills broke out, where before there had been nothingness; and rousing strange, like peals of bells ringing of themselves in her body, more and more rapturously.[118]

---

[112] Lawrence, 'Future of the Novel', 152.

[113] Hyde (ed.), *Trial*, 66.

[114] Nietzsche, *Twilight*, 195–6, translation modified.

[115] Lawrence, *First and Second*, 41.

[116] See Immanuel Kant, *Critique of Judgement*, ed. Nicholas Walker, trans. James Creed Meredith (Oxford: Oxford University Press, 2007), 49.

[117] Lawrence, *First and Second*, 41. In an attack on Kant's famous definition of the beautiful as something that gives pleasure 'without interest', Nietzsche writes sardonically: 'let us pay tribute to Kant for expounding the peculiarities of the sense of touch with the naïvety of a country parson!' (*On the Genealogy of Morality*, ed. Keith Ansell-Pearson, trans. Carol Diethe (Cambridge: Cambridge University Press, 2008), 74). Lawrence offers his own genealogical critique of 'aesthetic ecstasy' in 'Introduction to These Paintings'.

[118] Lawrence, *First and Second*, 38.

In the second version of the novel, her discovery of the aptly-named 'immortality of the flesh' precipitates a revaluation of her previously-neglected body, which is brought to life by having sex with the gamekeeper: 'for the first time in her life she had felt the animate beauty of her own thighs and belly and hips'.[119] She discovers a new sense of beauty: no longer 'beauty in the world of art', but 'beauty come alive and dangerous'.[120] Connie's revaluation of the body is like that of Zarathustra, who declares that he will not go the way of the 'despisers of the body' who 'are angry now at life and earth'. In contrast to 'the sick and the dying-out who despised the body and the earth', he values the 'perfect and perpendicular body', for 'it speaks of the meaning of the earth'.[121]

The revivification of Connie's body leads her to desire a similar revaluation of the Earth. Thinking of the gamekeeper, a 'tenderness came over her, for this disfigured countryside, and the disfigured, strange, almost wraith-like populace. To her, there was something grey and spectral about them: and something so inflexibly ugly'.[122] She is particularly struck by the ugliness of the coal-blackened landscape at Tevershall:

> the blackened brick dwellings, the black slate roofs glistening their sharp edges, the mud black with coal-dust, the pavements wet and black. It was as if dismalness had soaked through and through everything [...]. [A]ll went by ugly, ugly, ugly. (152)

Nietzsche holds that '[t]he ugly is the form things assume when we view them with a will to implant a meaning, a new meaning, into what has become meaningless'.[123] In these terms, the people and landscape assume the form of ugliness when Connie views them with a will to implant a new meaning, just as she implants a new meaning in Mrs Bentley by seeing in her the immortality of the flesh. Indeed, Connie wonders whether a 'life with beauty' might arise as 'a pure antithesis to what they had now':

> The future! The far future! Out of the orgy of ugliness and of dismalness and of dreariness, would there, could there ever unfold a flower, a life with beauty in it? [...] After all this that existed at present was gone, smashed and abandoned, repudiated for ever—could the children of miners make a new world, with mystery and sumptuousness in it? [...] She shuddered a little, at the awful necessity for transition.[124]

---

[119] Lawrence, *First and Second*, 336.
[120] Lawrence, *First and Second*, 265, 267.
[121] Nietzsche, *Zarathustra*, 21–4.
[122] Lawrence, *First and Second*, 369.
[123] Nietzsche, *Will to Power*, 224.
[124] Lawrence, *First and Second*, 369.

This beauty is imagined as repeating that of an earlier stage of history—not just of an earlier stage of human history, but of a remote geological past when the coal whose extraction has wrought such damage was not yet created: from 'ugliness incarnate, they would bring forth, perhaps, a luxuriant, uncanny beauty, some of the beauty that must have been in the great ferns and giant mosses of which the coal was made'.[125]

The effects of Connie's revaluation of the Earth start to become apparent. Nietzsche comments about the thought of eternal recurrence: '[f]rom the moment when this thought begins to prevail all colours will change their hue'.[126] That is, with the collapse of the Platonic antithesis between the real and apparent worlds, colour returns to what had previously been the dim and shadowy 'apparent world'. A similar transformation occurs in *Lady Chatterley's Lover*. Under Clifford's Platonist regime, Wragby was rendered 'spectral', and Connie picks 'primroses that were only shadows' (18).[127] However, once she has overturned Clifford's Platonism, the previously murky world becomes suffused with colour. On entering the woods, she notices that in 'the dimness of it all trees glistened naked and dark, as if they had unclothed themselves, and the green things on earth seemed to burn with greenness' (122). Similarly, in an excised passage, Connie having sex in the woods is accompanied by 'a flushing like the birth of colour, strange and suffused': it was 'the sensual birth of the loveliness of colour. Then the brightness came in gushes, gushes of dawn that flashed brilliant at the edges' (419). Here, repetition functions as the stylistic correlate of eternal recurrence. As is well known, Lawrence's prose can be repetitive. In the foreword to *Women in Love*, he acknowledges that '[i]n point of style, fault is often found with the continual, slightly modified repetition'.[128] Yet contrasting with the repetition in the 'Sunday Evening' chapter of *Women in Love* that reinforces Ursula's despairing view of the world as one of 'sordid routine and mechanical nullity', the repetition of 'green' and 'gushes' conveys the revaluation of the Earth that follows Connie's willing the repetition of each moment. These two sorts of repetition in Lawrence's prose correspond to the two aspects of eternal recurrence, as marking the highpoint of nihilism and its overcoming. In the latter case, they conjure the hope of environmental renewal and regeneration from the otherwise hellish mechanical repetition of modernity.

In the *Lady Chatterley* novels, Lawrence combines apocalyptic and Nietzschean thought to imagine hope for environmental renewal and regeneration. In the second version of the novel, in response to the deadening effects of Clifford's

---

[125] Lawrence, *First and Second*, 370.

[126] Nietzsche, 'Eternal Recurrence', 252.

[127] The spectrality of Wragby reflects what Lawrence diagnoses as one effect of Platonism: 'All we know is shadows [...] Shadows of everything, of the whole world, shadows even of ourselves [...]. [O]ur world is a wide tomb full of ghosts, replicas. We are all spectres' ('Introduction to These Paintings', 203).

[128] Lawrence, *Women in Love*, 486.

'anti-life' Platonist concern for immortality and eternity, Connie wishes for the revivification of the Earth:

> The body of men, and the animals, and the earth!—it could all come alive again [...]. there was to be a resurrection, the earth, the animals, and men. She didn't want any more dead things [...] No more engines, no more machines [...] She wanted live things, only live things: grass and trees on the earth, and flowers that looked after themselves; and birds and animals, stoats and rabbits, hawks and linnets, deer and wolves, lambs and foxes. There *must* be life again on earth.[129]

While her idea of a 'resurrection' aligns with Tommy Dukes' prophecy of a 'resurrection of the body', by juxtaposing predators with prey, she also echoes the rhetoric of Isaiah, in which the 'wolf also shall dwell with the lamb, and the leopard shall lie down with the kid'.[130] Her hope for a new Earth thereby takes a biblical prophetic form, and suggests the possibility of a Millennial resurrection. Yet her desire for a new Earth is also Nietzschean, and echoes Zarathustra's rhetoric of Earth. Zarathustra beseeches his brothers: 'remain faithful to the earth and do not believe those who speak to you of extraterrestrial hopes! [...] [T]o desecrate the earth is the most terrible thing'.[131] He exhorts them not to let their virtue 'fly away from earthly things and beat against eternal walls with its wings! [...] Like me, guide the virtue that has flown away back to the earth—yes, back to the body and life'.[132] Connie's hope for there to be 'life again on earth' parallels Zarathustra's message of optimism: 'the earth shall yet become a site of recovery! And already a new fragrance lies about it, salubrious—and a new hope!'[133]

By charting Connie's realization of the ugliness of the industrial Midlands and her growing desire to change it, the novel encourages a similar response in its readers. Staking out a role for art and aesthetics in addressing environmental crisis, the novel becomes a means of revaluing values, and prompting readers to redress the harm caused by the extraction and burning of fossil fuels. In this sense, Lawrence's coalfield fiction conforms to his response to *England and the Octopus*, and its theme of the 'disfigurement of the English countryside by modern industrial encroachment':

> the point is not whether we can do anything about it or not, all in a hurry. The point is, that we should all become acutely conscious of what is happening, and of what has happened; and as soon as we are really awake to this, we can begin to arrange things differently.[134]

[129] Lawrence, *First and Second*, 300.
[130] Lawrence, *First and Second*, 282; Isaiah 11:6.
[131] Nietzsche, *Zarathustra*, 6, italics removed.
[132] Nietzsche, *Zarathustra*, 57.
[133] Nietzsche, *Zarathustra*, 58.
[134] Lawrence, 'Review for Vogue', 341.

By portraying the damage wrought by coal-mining in the Midlands and by holding out hope for environmental recovery, *Lady Chatterley's Lover* promises to inspire readers to revalue the Earth, and to 'begin to arrange things differently'.

Sex, in *Lady Chatterley's Lover*, is not simply sex. Rather, it is freighted with apocalyptic and philosophical meaning, signalling the birth of a new historical epoch and the Nietzschean revaluation of the body and the Earth. Forming part of a wider modernist interrogation of fossil fuel energy systems and their alternatives, Lawrence embeds apocalyptic and philosophical materials into the provincial realist novel. He reworks symbols and myths from these traditions, as well as creating his own, such as the gamekeeper's hut in the woods. What results is a text that has—as he puts it of the Book of Revelation—'several layers: like layers of civilisation as you dig deeper and deeper to excavate an old city'.[135] By extension, *Lady Chatterley's Lover* invites a reading that does not simply attend to its plot in a linear fashion, but also recognizes its symbolic and mythic dimensions. In this respect, it the resembles the sections of Revelation that Lawrence sees as operating with a 'pagan conception of time as moving in cycles' rather than the modern idea of 'time as a continuity in an eternal straight line': using 'the old pagan process of rotary image-thought', every image 'fulfills its own little of cycle of action and meaning, then is superseded by another image'.[136] Correlatively, although Lawrence is often depicted as advocating a (reactionary) retreat from modernity into some 'primitive' mode of existence, the apocalyptic and Nietzschean schemes of *Lady Chatterley's Lover* suggest otherwise. Rather than involving a retreat from politics and history, sex and the body are used to explore intertwined social and environmental crises, and to imagine a transition beyond an industrial system based on the exploitation of workers and the extraction of fossil fuels.

[135] Lawrence, *Apocalypse*, 81.
[136] Lawrence, *Apocalypse*, 97, 95.

3

Olive Moore's Queer Ecology

In Olive Moore's novel *Spleen* (1930), the main character Ruth encounters a 'procession of unemployed' passing through Trafalgar Square: '[t]he men, it seemed, were from the distressed areas of the North; were from the closed steel and iron works; were miners from Wales; were dockers from the Clyde. They had gathered in the North and had come down on foot with their banners and their massed appeal to protest'. She 'turned to the group nearest her on the pavement; warmly dressed, middleclass. The man looked carved: the woman dried: the child bled: the dog inflated'.[1] The juxtaposition of the two groups defamiliarizes the middle-class family: several of the family members appear as inanimate objects, and the colons in the sentence which ostensibly connect them together equally function to separate and estrange them. Yet the contrast also makes strange the relationship between the family and the workers, and thereby brings together the sexual and environmental politics that are intertwined throughout the novel: it is not just the family that is put into question therein, but also the reproduction of the conditions of production of a fossil fuel capitalism.

The imbrication of sexual and environmental politics in *Spleen* make it a key work of 'queer ecology' in Catriona Sandilands's sense of the term as the 'constellation of practices that aim, in different ways, to disrupt prevailing heterosexist discursive and institutional articulations of sexuality and nature'.[2] This broad definition allows the possibility that artworks can be examples of queer ecology, and can further its central task of developing a sexual politics that includes consideration of the natural world and its biosocial constitution, and an environmental politics that is sensitive to the ways in which sexual relations shape the material world of nature and perceptions of that world. Indeed, Sandilands opens the way to a fuller investigation of a specifically modernist queer ecology when she identifies E. M. Forster's *Maurice* (1914/1971) and Radclyffe Hall's *The Well of Loneliness* (1928) as literary works that anticipate the queer ecological scholarship that has emerged since the 1990s.[3] As part of a recent ecocritical turn in modernist studies,

---

[1] Olive Moore, *Spleen* (Normal, IL: Dalkey Archive Press, 1996), 126, 128. All further references are to this edition.

[2] Catriona Sandilands, 'Queer Ecology', in *Keywords for Environmental Studies*, ed. Joni Adamson and others (New York: New York University Press, 2016), 169–71, 169.

[3] See Catriona Mortimer-Sandilands, 'Masculinity, Modernism, and the Ambivalence of Nature: Sexual Inversion as Queer Ecology in *The Well of Loneliness*', *Left History*, 13/1 (2008), 35–58; Catriona Mortimer-Sandilands and Bruce Erickson, 'Introduction: A Genealogy of Queer Ecologies', in

British Modernism and the Anthropocene. David Shackleton, Oxford University Press. © David Shackleton (2023).
DOI: 10.1093/oso/9780192857743.003.0004

scholars have extended such an approach: for example, Kelly Sultzbach and Benjamin Bateman have advanced queer ecological readings of Forster.[4] Such readings recognize that, at a time when various discourses had recently defined sexuality as being 'by nature', modernist writers explore the lives of those whose forms of non-normative gender and sexuality put them at odds with prevailing kinship structures and conceptions of 'nature', and use these lives to imagine the possibility of better organizations of society and better relationships with the environment.[5]

In turn, I argue, works of modernist queer ecology can be placed within a wider field of Anthropocene modernism. The Anthropocene is the name of a proposed geological epoch in which humans have fundamentally changed the Earth System and altered the course of the Earth's geological evolution. Anthropocene modernism is a literary and cultural modernism that registers the environmental transformations such as climate change that are now considered to characterize this epoch, and offers the possibility of rethinking the pressing environmental concerns of the present. By drawing attention to Ruth's cultivation of a queer environmentalism and the novel's climatic impressionism, and situating both in the context of anthropogenic climate change, I suggest that *Spleen* should be recognized as a provocative work of Anthropocene modernism.

In part, to read *Spleen* in these terms provides a revised account of the vexed issue of Moore's feminism. Very little is known about Constance Vaughan, who adopted the pseudonym 'Olive Moore'. She worked as a journalist—initially for *John O'London's Weekly*, the *Sunday Pictorial*, and the *Daily Sketch*, and later for *Scope*, an industry magazine—and was a member of Charles Lahr's Red Lion Street circle, a literary group that congregated around Lahr's anarchist bookshop in Holborn.[6] She published three novels—*Celestial Seraglio* (1929), *Spleen* (1930), and *Fugue* (1932)—and a selection from her writing notebooks, including an essay on D. H. Lawrence (which had previously been published by the Blue Moon Press), as *The Apple Is Bitten Again* (1934). Critics have tended to portray her as a feminist, although any straightforward attempt to recuperate her as a woman writer into male-dominated canons of modernist literature is complicated by the hostility that she herself expressed towards women writers. For example, *The Apple Is Bitten Again* contains a series of seemingly misogynistic statements about such writers. 'Art', it is claimed, 'is a masculine prerogative': '[w]omen are not born with creative souls'. Moore responds scathingly to Virginia Woolf's argument in *A Room of One's Own* (1929) that women have historically been disadvantaged as writers by their

Queer Ecologies: Sex, Nature, Politics, Desire, ed. Catriona Mortimer-Sandilands and Bruce Erickson (Bloomington: Indiana University Press, 2010), 1–47, 5, 22–4; and Sandilands, *Keywords*, 169–70.

[4] See Kelly Sultzbach, *Ecocriticism in the Modernist Imagination: Forster, Woolf and Auden* (Cambridge: Cambridge University Press, 2016), 11–12, 25–81; and Benjamin Bateman, 'Avian, Anal, Outlaw: Queer Ecology in E. M. Forster's *Maurice*', *ISLE*, 28/2 (2021), 622–40.

[5] Michel Foucault, *The Will to Knowledge: The History of Sexuality Volume 1*, trans. Robert Hurley (London: Penguin, 1998), 68.

[6] See Sophie Cavey, 'Olive Moore: A New Biography', *Feminist Modernist Studies*, 5/1 (2022), 1–20.

lack of formal education and material support, contending that the 'matter of [having] a room of one's own' has nothing to do with creative achievement; she is similarly contemptuous of Katherine Mansfield, dismissing her writing as vain 'female twittering'.[7] In particular, although she describes 'lesbianism' as 'most provocative and interesting of the feminine vices', she claims that women have failed to give it satisfactory artistic expression. She is particularly scornful of *The Well of Loneliness*, which she describes as 'rambling, apologetic, and emotional outpouring', and 'proof of the subject's misuse; and of how dull, how sober, how domestic, such a theme becomes in woman's literary hands'. Where lesbianism has been expressed in literature, she claims, it has been better expressed by men, such as by Guy de Maupassant in his short story 'La Femme de Paul' (1881); even John Donne's poem 'Sappho to Philaenis' supposedly surpasses the writing of Sappho herself.[8]

Critics have responded in divergent ways to Moore's surprising hostility towards women writers. Johanna Wagner downplays Moore's apparently sexist comments and argues that Moore's animus is not directed at women themselves but at 'the unfortunate cultural construction of the word "woman"'.[9] Maren Linett takes a contrary approach: she describes how she was originally drawn to a reading of *Spleen* as a feminist novel, but eventually found such a reading unsustainable and claims instead that the novel is 'deeply misogynist'.[10]

Moving beyond these alternatives, I read *Spleen* as a queer feminist text by taking inspiration from the 'antisocial' strand of queer theory that is associated with theorists such as Leo Bersani, Lee Edelman, and Jack Halberstam. Bersani employs a strategy of 'embracing, at least provisionally, a homophobic representation of homosexuality' to develop a theory of the socially disruptive potential of sex as self-shattering; Edelman accepts and embraces the reactionary 'ascription of negativity to the queer' in his call to threaten the social order by rejecting the future; and Halberstam refashions the failure that is often attributed to queers to dismantle the logics of success and failure that structure heteronormative capitalist society.[11] Similarly, I suggest that we should take Moore's pronouncements against women and lesbian writers seriously, and recognize that from these misogynist and homophobic materials she develops a queer feminist aesthetics based on negativity, sterility, and failure. In *Spleen*, this aesthetics finds expression (on the level of content) through Ruth's loneliness and her awareness of her limited ability to combat the pollution and the plight of the unemployed workers that she encounters in

[7] Olive Moore, *The Apple Is Bitten Again*, in *Collected Writings* (Elmwood Park, IL: Dalkey Archive Press, 1992), 335–418, 386–7.

[8] Moore, *The Apple Is Bitten Again*, 390.

[9] Johanna M. Wagner, 'Unwomanly Intellect: Melancholy, Maternity, and Lesbianism in Olive Moore's *Spleen*', *Journal of Language, Literature and Culture*, 64/1 (2017), 42–61, 43.

[10] Maren Tova Linett, *Bodies of Modernism: Physical Disability in Transatlantic Modernist Literature* (Ann Arbor: University of Michigan Press, 2017), 153–4.

[11] Leo Bersani, 'Is the Rectum a Grave?', *October*, 43 (1987), 197–222, 209; Lee Edelman, *No Future: Queer Theory and the Death Drive* (Durham, NC: Duke University Press, 2004), 4; Judith [Jack] Halberstam, *The Queer Art of Failure* (Durham, NC: Duke University Press, 2011), 2–3, 110.

London, and (on the level of form) through the novel's climatic impressionism which fails to provide a totalizing representation of the changing climate. What emerges is a queer feminism that, as it is also a type of environmentalism, anticipates the 'queer ecofeminism' called for by Greta Gaard.[12] Paradoxically, read in light of such an aesthetics, *Spleen*'s failures might turn out to be types of success.

However, while Moore's writing contains a vein of queer feminist negativity, it is not exhausted by such a negativity: like other works of modernist queer ecology, it is also driven by a queer utopianism. Here, José Esteban Muñoz's account of queer futurity, in which 'the negative becomes the resource for a certain mode of queer utopianism', can be adapted to analyse *Spleen* and other works of modernist queer ecology.[13] Such works—which include Sylvia Townsend Warner's *Lolly Willowes* (1926), Virginia Woolf's *Orlando* (1928), and Djuna Barnes's *Nightwood* (1936) alongside those of Moore, Forster, and Hall—tend to be wary of what Edelman characterizes as 'reproductive futurism', or the investment placed in the (ever-deferred) future through the figure of the child.[14] Yet they do not turn away from the future altogether, but rather explore varieties of what Nicole Seymour calls 'queer environmentalism': environmentalism that is rooted in a concept of futurity that is established outside the value set of normative, reproductive heterosexuality.[15] Indeed, the signal (but underappreciated) virtue of modernist queer ecology is that it provides a rich archive of queer time, including the imagination of a range of queer environmental structures of care and concern.[16] Muñoz's utopian hermeneutics can be deployed to recuperate the queer utopianism of these works—their search for better ways of being in the world and better worlds—in the context of the pressing environmental concerns of the present. By offering anticipatory illuminations of a queer environmental politics and activism that is not yet here, these works can reshape the present and inspire new structures of environmental care and concern.

Ruth's queer environmentalism

'Nature', according to Raymond Williams's often-repeated apothegm, is perhaps the most complex word in the language.[17] Certainly, it is one of the most complex

---

[12] Greta Gaard, 'Toward a Queer Ecofeminism', *Hypatia*, 12/1 (1997), 114–37. On queer feminist modernism, see Jana Funke, *Sexological Modernism: Queer Feminism and Sexual Science* (Edinburgh: Edinburgh University Press, 2022).

[13] José Esteban Muñoz, *Cruising Utopia: The Then and There of Queer Futurity* (New York: New York University Press, 2009), 13.

[14] Edelman, *No Future*, 2, 31.

[15] Nicole Seymour, *Strange Natures: Futurity, Empathy, and the Queer Ecological Imagination* (Urbana: University of Illinois Press, 2013), 12.

[16] These structures include modes of what Benjamin Bateman calls 'queer survival' (*The Modernist Art of Queer Survival* (Oxford: Oxford University Press, 2017)).

[17] Raymond Williams, *Keywords: A Vocabulary of Culture and Society* (London: Fontana, 1976), 184.

words in *Spleen*. Critics have shown how Ruth rebels against a conception of nature that dictates that her role as a woman is to be a mother, and that makes her rejection of her child on learning that she is pregnant appear unnatural and even pathological. Indeed, she is diagnosed by her doctor as suffering from 'sustained hysteria during pregnancy' (29). As Jane Garrity has demonstrated, Ruth recasts contemporary discourses of hysteria—a condition traditionally thought to be caused by a misaligned womb—to imagine that she carries her womb in her forehead, and thereby carve out a space for intellectual agency.[18] I will distinguish one more layer of complexity in the word 'nature' in the novel by showing how Ruth's struggle for a new conception of nature is also one for a queer environmentalism. Such an environmentalism includes her attempt to live according to a queer time, and to counteract the pollution she encounters in London.

At the outset, it should be acknowledged that Ruth's attempts to forge a new conception of nature are beset by internal inconsistencies. Although she strenuously resists the rhetoric that casts motherhood as natural in her own case, she idealizes motherhood in the Italian society in which she has exiled herself, at times employing metaphors of rootedness to valorize the connection of Italian children to the earth. For example, she thinks that the young Italian boy Giovanni 'seemed to have grown gravely from the earth he planted himself on so securely and possessively'; given that she has recently contemplated being buried under a tree and achieving a type of perpetuity by being 'reborn each year in its sap', the pun on 'gravely' suggests Giovanni's organic connection to the earth, as the place from which he has grown and to which he will return (77, 70).[19] Alarmingly, this ideal of rootedness appears to exclude her son Richard—whom she thinks of as 'rootless, null, unproductive: therefore not a living being at all'—because of his disability (109).[20] While critics have highlighted Ruth's shocking disregard for her disabled son and her troubling reproduction of gender and race hierarchies in relation to the Italians, it can be added that her metaphors of rootedness are even more alarming when viewed in the context of Italian fascism.[21] Her valorization of 'strongly planted' Italian children is uncomfortably close to Benito Mussolini's ruralism and his campaign for the growing Italian populace to be rooted in the land (*Spleen*, 120).[22] For

[18] Jane Garrity, 'Olive Moore's Headless Woman', *Modern Fiction Studies*, 59/2 (2013), 288–316. See also Wagner, 'Unwomanly Intellect'.
[19] Similarly, in Moore's novel *Fugue* (1932), Lavinia Reed contrasts the English countryside with that of Tuscany, where 'a man's feet are not white and pitiful but are sunk in the warm earth like stalks with roots'. Olive Moore, *Fugue*, in *Collected Writings*, 233–333, 281.
[20] To the dismay of her solicitor (and later critics), Ruth excludes 'mentally defective children' from her charitable scheme at Sharvells, claiming that they were in 'no sense [...] worth saving' (Moore, *Spleen*, 116).
[21] See Garrity, 'Headless', 294–5, 300, 310; Matt Franks, 'Mental Inversion, Modernist Aesthetics, and Disability Exceptionalism in Olive Moore's *Spleen*', *Journal of Modern Literature*, 38/1 (2014), 107–27, 109, 119; and Linett, *Bodies*, 154, 157–61.
[22] See Marco Armiero and Wilko Graf Von Hardenberg, 'Green Rhetoric in Blackshirts: Italian Fascism and the Environment', *Environment and History*, 19 (2013), 283–311, 291–2.

similar reasons, her view of Italian women as 'natural' mothers should be treated with caution. She imagines that such women give birth with 'scarcely any pain at all', and later opines that 'a million mothers can found a nation. The italian woman, as you say, is a born mother' (17, 123). This opinion is deeply suspect given that, at this time, Mussolini (who had previously been mentioned in conversation at Ruth's hotel) was propagating a cult of the woman as mother, and fascists were calling for women to be honoured as reproducers of the nation (122).[23]

Without discounting these inconsistencies, it might be noted that they are typical of Moore's approach to characterization, in which characters tend to display marked psychological contradictions. Uller, for instance, delivers the novel's fiercest polemic against marriage despite—as is wryly observed—being himself 'a much-married man' (87–8). It is plausible to suggest that Ruth has internalized the strong association between motherhood and nature from which she had herself suffered, and then projected it onto the Italians in a manner that continues to upset her. (Even twenty-two years after arriving in Italy, her experience of watching the pregnant Graziella passing through a vineyard is so intense that she finds tears pouring down her cheeks (18)). Be this as it may, Ruth's view of Italian women as natural mothers functions to throw into relief her own queer environmentalism.

In her own case, Ruth rebels against the role that is prescribed her as a woman in a manner that anticipates later ecofeminist theory. She is thrown into turmoil on discovering that she is pregnant and thinks that she does not want her child; her friend Dora tries to comfort her by suggesting that she will love her child when it comes because it 'is nature' for a mother to do so, and describing creation as a 'wonderful thing' (20–1). Dora's alignment of motherhood with nature exemplifies the pervasive rhetoric diagnosed by ecofeminists that associates women with nature.[24] Ruth is sceptical, thinking that 'in her case it did not seem to be nature', yet she goes on to reimagine her relationship to nature as an act of resistance against her husband Stephen and his family (20). Defying their injunctions not to stray far from the house while pregnant, she takes to wandering alone through the woods and lying 'for hours on the earth as though embracing it' (29). This practice, which brings her great spiritual comfort, originated in her childhood: her father had taught her to 'walk barefooted on the grass', telling her that it put her 'in direct contact with the earth, with the generative power which bore mountains, poured

---

[23] See Victoria De Grazia, *How Fascism Ruled Women: Italy, 1922–1945* (Berkeley: University of California Press, 1992), 41–76. In defiance of such a reproductive futurism, Virginia Woolf later suggested in *Three Guineas* (1938) that educated women could help to prevent war by refusing 'to bear children' (*A Room of One's Own; Three Guineas*, ed. Morag Shiach (Oxford: Oxford University Press, 1992), 370).

[24] For example, Victoria Davion attributes to Susan Griffin's *Woman and Nature* (1978) the central ecofeminist insight that 'women have been associated with nature, the material, the emotional, and the particular, while men have been associated with culture, the nonmaterial, the rational, and the abstract' ('Is Ecofeminism Feminist?', in *Ecological Feminism*, ed. Karen Warren (London: Routledge, 1994), 8–28, 9).

streams, moved sap' (36). Garrity suggests that her father's environmentalism can be read as an amalgam of that of 'late nineteenth-century pre-Raphaelite, socialist, and Medievalist reformers' who desired the emancipation of women.[25] It also anticipates that of later ecofeminists who sought to recuperate the identification of women and the natural world as a means of resistance to the male dominance that produces it. Certainly, Ruth's running barefoot on the grass as a child was already mildly subversive, judging by Mrs Grier's shocked reaction (36). Her later imaginative connection with nature is even more radical. For example, she is repulsed by the idea of having 'to bear her child' in a 'canopied tomb of a bed with its [...] boast of [...] loves and births and deaths', and thinks instead that '[o]ne should be born on hills, on clouds, near streams, in woods, on open and pleasant spaces' (45, 46). By refiguring natural (and mythological) spaces as sites of freedom from the family, Moore can be recognized as one of the feminist writers identified by Stacy Alaimo who 'negotiated, contested, and transformed the discourses of nature that surrounded them.'[26]

However, in contrast to later ecofeminists who seek to reappropriate the association of women with fertility, Ruth imaginatively recasts contemporary discourses of sexual inversion to constitute a distinctively queer version of ecofeminism. She attempts to escape from her unwanted pregnancy by formulating a myth of mental pregnancy. 'I think', she says to her husband, 'I carry my womb in my forehead', a contention that she elaborates to Dora: 'Some there are, she quoted to Dora, whose souls are more pregnant than their bodies. No. Socrates. And no one has ever thought of applying it to women' (24). Critics have noted that Ruth is quoting from Diotima's speech about love and immortality in Plato's *Symposium*, although it can be added that the *Symposium* was an important intertext in sexological discourse.[27] For example, in *The Intermediate Sex* (1908), Edward Carpenter both quotes from the *Symposium* and advances a theory of 'homogenic love'—or love between man and man or woman and woman—which deploys a very similar conception of mental pregnancy:

It certainly does not seem impossible to suppose that as the ordinary love has a special function in the propagation of the race, so the other has its special function in social and heroic work, and in the generation—not of bodily children—but of those children of the mind, the philosophical conceptions and ideals which transform our lives and those of society.[28]

[25] Garrity, 'Headless', 297.
[26] Stacy Alaimo, *Undomesticated Ground: Recasting Nature as Feminist Space* (Ithaca, NY: Cornell University Press, 2000), 1.
[27] See Garrity, 'Headless', 299; and Wagner, 'Unwomanly Intellect', 47–8, 59–60.
[28] Edward Carpenter, *The Intermediate Sex: A Study of Some Transitional Types of Men and Women* (London: Swan Sonnenschein, 1908), 70.

That is, by distinguishing 'bodily children' from 'children of the mind', Carpenter carves out an important social and political role for 'sexual inverts' and what he calls 'the non-child-bearing love'.[29] Carpenter's writing, and that of other reformist sexologists such as Havelock Ellis, can be considered part of what Michel Foucault terms a 'reverse discourse' that operated within the scientific, legal, and literary discourses that forged homosexuality as an identity in the nineteenth century, and otherwise allowed greater 'social controls' into this area of 'perversity'. As Foucault puts it, with such a reverse discourse, 'homosexuality began to speak in its own behalf, to demand that its legitimacy or "naturality" be acknowledged, often in the same vocabulary, using the same categories by which it was medically disqualified'.[30] *Spleen* both draws upon such a reverse discourse, and by reworking conceptions of hysteria and sexual inversion in Ruth's conceit of mental pregnancy, itself forms part of that discourse.[31] Much as the idea of mental pregnancy provides alternatives to biological pregnancy in the *Symposium* and in *The Intermediate Sex*, so Ruth's conceit that she carries her womb in her forehead allows her to reimagine a new role for women, beyond that of 'the eternal oven in which to bake the eternal bun' (24). This newfound confidence allows her to correct Dora's statement that childbirth 'is what woman is made for' to '[w]as made for', with the inflection of the tense from present to past optimistically conveying a new space of possibility opened up for women (26).

By appealing to a sexological myth of mental pregnancy to challenge the supposed naturalness of motherhood, Ruth enters what Gaard characterizes as the contradictory discursive space inhabited by queer ecofeminism: one in which women as an oppressed group have tended to be portrayed as 'closer to nature' but in which non-normative sexualities are frequently devalued for being 'against nature'.[32] Indeed, the status of the sexual invert as regards nature—and how that 'nature' was to be understood—was a contested point in both sexual science and modernist queer ecology. Richard von Krafft-Ebing claimed that 'every expression of [the sexual instinct] that does not correspond with the purpose of nature—i.e. propagation—must be regarded as perverse', but reformist sexologists such as Ellis and Carpenter were keen to stress that sexual inversion was natural.[33] Ellis, for example, claimed that sexual inversion was an 'organic' variation that 'we see throughout living nature, in plants and in animals', and Carpenter similarly

---

[29] Carpenter, *Intermediate Sex*, 69.

[30] Foucault, *Knowledge*, 101.

[31] Although useful, Foucault's distinction between 'discourse' and 'reverse discourse' should not encourage a simplification of sexual science which, as Jana Funke has emphasized, was not a monolithic and reductive field of debate: rather, it provided nuanced frameworks to understand the gendered and sexual self. See Jana Funke, 'Intersexions: Dandyism, Cross-Dressing, Transgender', in *Late Victorian into Modern*, ed. Laura Marcus and others (Oxford: Oxford University Press, 2016), 414–27, 416–17.

[32] Gaard, 'Queer Ecofeminism', 119.

[33] R. von Krafft-Ebing, *Psychopathia Sexualis, With Especial Reference to Contrary Sexual Instinct*, trans. Charles Gilbert Chaddock (Philadelphia: F. A. Davis, 1892), 187, 56.

emphasized that the problems faced by the sexual invert were those 'of Nature's own producing'.[34] Ruth's conceit of mental pregnancy forms part of a similar renegotiation of the concept of nature, whose ultimate purpose is no longer conceived to be the propagation of the species.

Ruth's myth of mental pregnancy forms part of her wider attempt to live her life according to a new form of temporality. Questioning Dora's platitudes and the expectation that a woman 'have a maternal sense as she is expected to have other womanly attributes', she has an epiphany: 'A boy is born. Or a girl. A boy. A girl. And you know before hand every possibility of its life, and like a litany the answer is unalterable and as assured. Birth. Adolescence. Marriage. Birth. Old Age. Death' (22). That is, depending on what sex a baby is born, his or her entire life trajectory is predetermined: for a woman, this includes getting married and having children. The trajectory that Ruth plots is very similar to that which Halberstam later characterized as being shaped by 'reproductive temporality': one that dictates that people's futures lie within 'those paradigmatic markers of life experience—namely, birth, marriage, reproduction, and death'.[35] In a moment of insight, Ruth realizes that this trajectory is a construction: that one is expected to accept childbirth blindly 'because it is called nature and because one is told that one must because everyone does' (22). The movement here from an is to an ought—from the fact that 'everyone does' to 'one must'—is typical of the desire to be 'normal', which Michael Warner suggests rests on a confusion between statistical norms and evaluative norms.[36] Ruth questions such a normalcy. Whilst in the woods, she thinks again of a life in which marriage and childbirth form supposedly unalterable stages, pressing her fingers 'in the grass' as she counts: 'Birth. Adolescence. Marriage. Birth. Old Age. Death' (30). Her pressing her fingers in the grass symbolically suggests how closely this cycle has been connected to nature, yet she challenges the cycle: she finds it 'inadequate' and 'humiliating' and wishes to defy 'the dreary inevitable round of years' (30).

Although she comes to accept that her pregnancy cannot be a purely mental one, Ruth goes on to cultivate a new form of temporality by leaving her husband and rejecting the material support that his wealthy family would have provided.[37] Defying the 'hierarchies of property and propriety' that for Lauren Berlant and Warner characterize heteronormativity, Ruth leaves Stephen to live in self-imposed exile with her son on the Italian island of Foria (which is closely modelled on the island

---

[34] Havelock Ellis, *Studies in the Psychology of Sex: Sexual Inversion* (Philadelphia: F. A. Davis, 1901), 186; Carpenter, *Intermediate*, 66–77.

[35] Judith [Jack] Halberstam, *In a Queer Time and Place: Transgender Bodies, Subcultural Lives* (New York: New York University Press, 2005), 4, 2.

[36] Michael Warner, *The Trouble with Normal: Sex, Politics, and the Ethics of Queer Life* (Cambridge, MA: Harvard University Press, 2000), 56.

[37] Lying in the bath one morning, she noticed that the water refused to cover her, and had to admit that 'it was not happening in her forehead at all, but was happening very much where it was meant to happen' (Moore, *Spleen*, 27).

of Ischia, whose main town is Forio).[38] She refuses to accept an allowance from
Stephen's family, and when she later inherits the family home Sharvells following
his death, she decides to turn it into 'the permanent home of a charitable institute',
ignoring her solicitor's advice that it is unwise to 'throw away' both 'profit and
property' (64, 116–17). By doing so, Ruth lives according to a 'queer time' in Halberstam's sense of a time that develops 'in opposition to the institutions of family,
heterosexuality, and reproduction'.[39] More specifically, by giving away Sharvells,
she disrupts that which Halberstam calls 'inheritance time': the 'generational time
within which values, wealth, goods, and morals are passed through family ties from
one generation to the next', and that tends to connect the family to the historical past of the nation and to the future of both familial and national stability (5).
Indeed, not having been brought up with possession or having a mind 'connected
with possession', Ruth is derisive of Stephen's family's attitude towards the past:
'[l]et them strut [...] through the formal pageantry of dead things and dead people,
renewing themselves only in ghostly memories of these ghostly selves, which leaves
them smiling politely down the centuries' (38). Just as she resents being expected
to reproduce Stephen's family features biologically, so she resents his family's polite
attitude towards the historical past and refuses to find it a source of renewal.

As well as disrupting inheritance time, Ruth's decision to give away Sharvells
forms an important part of her environmentalism. When she returns to London
after having lived in Italy for twenty-two years, she thinks of herself as 'lonely as
an invert': '[f]or surely (she thought) it was a form of mental inversion this loneliness of hers among her fellow-creatures; [...] her lack of hope' (125–6). Here,
she explicitly uses the language of sexology to characterize her 'difference' from
others: the term 'mental inversion' is a variant on the more common term 'sexual
inversion' and echoes her earlier conceit of mental pregnancy. Her tentative initial comparison and her use of this language to characterize her loneliness suggests
that she is using the term not to mark a particular gender or sexual identity, but
to register a form of difference that remains indeterminate, without a single and
stable referent; this difference is something that has often 'been held against her'
and which 'she herself had reproached' (125). Yet while her 'mental inversion' sets
her apart from her 'fellow-creatures', it also drives her environmentalism. As will
be discussed at greater length below, she is shocked by the air pollution that she
encounters in London. It is adopting what she thinks of as the masculine trait of
actively acquiring knowledge of the world—illustrated by the motif of stuffing the
moon into one's pocket—that compels Ruth to question the pollution that she sees,
rather than remaining indifferent (26, 119–20). Her decision to turn Sharvells into
the home of a charitable institute is one that would counteract the harm of polluted
urban conditions by providing 'holidays for London's slum children': the children

---

[38] Lauren Berlant and Michael Warner, 'Sex in Public', *Critical Inquiry*, 24/2 (1998), 547–66, 548.
[39] Halberstam, *Queer Time*, 1.

would be at least temporarily removed from the city and allowed to enjoy the countryside, where they would be trained to do 'their own gardening, producing their
own food' (116–17). While disrupting inheritance time, this scheme still displays
a concern for the future and future generations.

Ruth's loneliness makes a striking contrast with the happiness that Forster's
Maurice finds with Alec Scudder, with both disappearing to fuck in the greenwood
for the happily-ever-after. In his 1960 postscript, Forster stressed that a 'happy ending' was 'imperative' for the novel: 'I was determined that in fiction anyway two
men should fall in love and remain in it for the ever and ever that fiction allows,
and in this sense Maurice and Alec still roam the greenwood'.[40] Despite Moore's
antipathy for Hall's novel, Ruth's loneliness is more akin to that of Stephen Gor-
don in *The Well of Loneliness*. While this loneliness is part of *Spleen*'s aesthetics
of negativity and failure, it should be recognized that the novel's environmentalism is registered not solely at the level of its content, but also in its experimental
form—its 'climatic impressionism'—which reflects the damaged materiality of the
Earth.

Climatic impressionism

Spleen tells the story of Ruth with dazzling technical virtuosity, deploying a modernist literary impressionism. Garrity has remarked that the novel employs many
of the stylistic features that have come to be associated with high modernist
experimentation: free indirect discourse, shifting point of view, repetition and
fragmentation, and broken chronological sequence.[41] More specifically, I suggest that these features—combined with those of delayed decoding, limited point
of view and literary montage—form part of a modernist literary impressionism.
While this impressionism has not been commented on by recent critics, it was
apparent to contemporary reviewers: for example, one noted that Moore 'has the
gift of imagining a scene very intensely and of presenting it with great impressionist vigor'.[42] Jesse Oak Taylor argues that by renouncing the realist aim of producing
a totalizing mimetic representation of its subject matter to focus instead on limited
impressions that nevertheless gesture to a broader totality, literary impressionism
emerged as a form well-suited to render the smoke-laden fogs of London. *Spleen*
employs such an impressionism and constitutes an example of what Taylor calls
'climatic modernism'.[43] In part, its narrative form renders a perceptual and mental

[40] E. M. Forster, *Maurice*, ed. P. N. Furbank (London: Penguin, 2005), 220.
[41] Garrity, 'Headless', 292.
[42] Frank Swinnerton, '"Men Hate Women," New Arlen Book for Coming Spring', *Chicago Daily
Tribune*, 3 January 1931, 9.
[43] Jesse Oak Taylor, *The Sky of Our Manufacture: The London Fog in British Fiction from Dickens to
Woolf* (Charlottesville: University of Virginia Press, 2016), 164–87, 189.

'fog' that is an apt response to the changes that the climate was suffering on such a large scale that they defied representation.

Early in the novel, Ruth recalls her arrival on the island of Foria in a scene that is exemplary of the novel's literary impressionism. While the description of Foria as a 'dark-hearted island' alludes to Joseph Conrad's *Heart of Darkness* (1899), the scene employs a narrative technique very similar to that of Conrad's 'delayed decoding' (10).[44] The narrative renders Ruth's raw initial impressions before she was able to explain them: '[a]ll at once a black spot dissolved and blotted out the other detached black spots' (9). This 'black spot' is her 'first and vague impression of Donna Lisetta', with whom she later lives on the island (9–10). Someone speaks to Ruth and 'out of the mouth came the shrill snapping of a thousand twigs about her ears'; what sounds like the snapping of twigs is in fact Italian, of which she at this time was able to understand only a few words. Exhausted, she experiences a sensory and cognitive overload that manifests itself as a type of synaesthesia: she desires the return of the woman with 'the cool green voice', is 'afraid to step on' certain sounds, and worries that the onlookers 'were going to start shouting again and beating her over the face and eyes with shrill crackling twigs' (9–10). With no immediate explanation '[t]he sky fell beneath her feet' and 'the sands passed away beneath her'; it is only when Lisetta calmed her that she was able to realize that 'the sands were passing away under her because the neapolitan was running across them with her in his arms' (9–10). In this scene, delayed decoding is used as Ruth reconstructs and relives her experience in memory: it conveys her original panic as her comprehension of the situation lagged behind her initial impressions, and brings back the experience with great intensity and immediacy. In the preface to *The Nigger of the Narcissus* (1897), which is often taken to be a manifesto of literary impressionism, Conrad famously claimed, '[m]y task which I am trying to achieve is, by the power of the written word, to make you hear, to make you feel—it is, before all, to make you *see*'.[45] Partly through the technique of delayed decoding, the reader of *Spleen* is able to participate imaginatively in Ruth's unfolding experience, and is—to paraphrase Conrad—'made to see'. As one reviewer put it, during the period that Ruth was in Italy, the 'reader sees and feels acutely all that has happened'.[46]

Ruth's confused initial impressions when arriving on Foria are typical of impressions in the novel, which although vivid tend to be blurred and indistinct. Jesse Matz usefully distinguishes between impressionism in art and literature on the

[44] See Ian Watt, *Conrad in the Nineteenth Century* (Berkeley: University of California Press, 1979), 175–79. It is a moot point how imbricated the novel's impressionism is in Ruth's racist representation of the Forians. Both Dickinson and Franks have drawn attention to parallels between *Spleen* and *Heart of Darkness* in their discussions of Ruth's reduction of the Forians to primitive Others. See Renée Dickinson, *Female Embodiment and Subjectivity in the Modernist Novel: The Corporeum of Virginia Woolf and Olive Moore* (New York: Routledge, 2009), 93; and Franks, 'Mental Inversion', 120–1.

[45] Joseph Conrad, preface to *The Nigger of the Narcissus* (New York: Doubleday, 1914), xi–xvi, iv.

[46] 'An Unhappy Life', *New York Times Book Review*, 2 November 1930, 6–7, 6.

grounds that the former attempts to present sensory impressions, whereas the latter strives to render impressions that combine sense and thought.[47] Indeed, Ruth's
impressions when she arrives on the island are both perceptually and cognitively
blurred. As she is driven away from the port in a carriage, she is aware of little
of her journey: '[s]he had seen nothing but the hot powdery road rolling away
beneath her, and that imperfectly and through a mist' (11). The 'mist' that blurs
her vision is a literal one, caused by the 'unaccustomed heat', the 'yellow glare'
and 'the dust' of the road, which 'were as a blanket held gently but persistently
over her face and head' (11). Yet it is also a metaphorical mist—she had earlier
been described looking 'around her helplessly as though making her way through
a fog'—that characterizes her abiding experience of the island (10). Indeed, following her disorienting arrival, she reflects that it is '[s]trange that in twenty-two
years her environment and existence should have become scarcely more real to
her' (13).

Ruth's indistinct impressions are shared by the reader, who experiences a parallel confusion in reading *Spleen*. For example, in the part of the novel set in London,
dialogue is often not demarcated typographically, fragments of conversation are
given without context, and words are rendered phonetically without any explanation (the office boy's 'not tin' for 'not in'; 'was sow' for 'was out'; and 'was sin' for
'was in' (115)). Ruth's train of thought is at various times rudely interrupted ('[a]
tramcar hurtled past like a rocket') and includes a series of vivid mental images of
her son who is never explicitly named (119). As throughout the novel, the extensive use of free indirect discourse creates an ambiguity between the voice of the
extradiegetic narrator and that of the various characters, which results in an inter-
pretative difficulty for the reader. It is not only through such stylistic features that
an effect of vagueness is created, but also through what Adam Parkes identifies as
broader 'structural' strategies of impressionist vagueness, such as achronological
narration, limited point of view, and narrative ellipsis.[48] Together, these stylistic
and structural features contribute to that which Garrity has identified as 'Moore's
greatest innovation': 'her ability to generate a salutary cognitive and affective
confusion in the reader.'[49]

Moore exploits literary impressionism's capacity for vagueness to portray the
hazy climates of Italy and London. Towards the end of the novel, when Ruth
returns to London after having lived in Italy for twenty-two years, she becomes
aware of the changes that have occurred since her departure in 1907, and is particularly shocked by the air pollution. While she 'remembered the tang of horse dung
and the trimly beaten measure of slow-stepping carriage horses', she encounters

[47] Jesse Matz, *Literary Impressionism and Modernist Aesthetics* (Cambridge: Cambridge University Press, 2001), 49–50.
[48] See Adam Parkes, *A Sense of Shock: The Impact of Impressionism on Modern British and Irish Writing* (New York: Oxford University Press, 2011), 19–20.
[49] Garrity, 'Headless', 292.

streets 'smoked out with petrol fumes and alive with motor horns'; she 'found the air thick and unpalatable and hung like a piece of sodden grey cloth above the opening between squares and streets' (120). She experiences not only the sound-scapes of London (which she contrasts with those of Italian cities), but also its smellscapes: she comes on 'rows of damp and stale-smelling alleys', and sees pale children sitting on 'cold evil-smelling pavements' (119). As she walks through the rain, the lexical repetition in an antimetabolically-twisted phrase conveys the dull monotony of the London streets, which she sees only as blocks of grey and black: '[g]rey and black and black and grey [...] She passed through it all as through a cloud, seeing nothing but opaque grey and solid black' (126). The simile suggests that the cloud is a metaphorical one, as she trudges through the city immersed in her thoughts, yet once again her vision is also literally limited, this time by the driving rain and the fumes that hang in the air.

Although *Spleen* deploys a climatic impressionism throughout, there is a pro-nounced difference between the climates of Italy and London. In Italy, the haziness is the result of the intense sunlight, the heat, and the dust in the air. The effect is particularly marked in the early hours of the afternoon, during which 'heavy pow-dery dust' lifts everywhere in clouds 'only to settle more greyly and heavily' (80). Notably, the climate appears not to have changed over time. The islanders wear their bushy hair 'held down by a thread of osier root' to free their eyes of dust; this fashion is supposedly the same as that adopted by 'the youths in the greek statuary', which suggests a continuity of climate between ancient Greece and present-day Italy (80). By contrast, the 'petrol fumes' and 'sooty rain' suggest that the fog that Ruth encounters in London is at least partly anthropogenic and a more recent phenomenon (120, 118). She becomes conscious of the contrast between the two climates, suddenly realizing that she is only aware of the dismalness of London because of her long absence from the city: 'had she lived among it all these years she would have noticed nothing. A blue expanse of sky had done that for her' (126). The contrast is reinforced by the literary montage in which the narrative cuts between the scene in London and Ruth's mental images of her son: '[a]gain she had a sight of him lying in the shade of the rock on the hot yellow sand under a blue outstretched sky' (127). In part, the strong colours of these images—with their 'yellow sand' and 'blue outstretched sky'—throw into relief the greys and blacks of London's colour-drained streets.

The indistinct impressions of *Spleen* point towards wider imperial and climatic totalities that elude representation. Ruth fails to see London as she wishes: 'now she wanted, she tried, to see World-Trade and Hub of the Universe and London's [...] great army of workers, and saw nothing but herded millions rushing to their daily death' (120). Her vision of London workers as herded millions rather than an inspiring army suggests a splenetic perspective. Indeed, she wonders elsewhere: 'what then lies behind the eye of man that can so alter the perspective of his soul as to bring to the one courage and decision and to the next anger and futility?'

(119–20). Yet her failure to 'see World-Trade and Hub of the Universe' also suggests a conceptual crisis, in which she cannot see London as part of a wider network of world trade. In this sense, Ruth's failure is typical of a more general phenomenon that Fredric Jameson diagnoses as animating modernism: the inability to conceive the imperial world-system as a totality.[50] It thereby makes use of an ambiguity at the heart of Conrad's impressionist desire to 'make you *see*'. As Max Saunders points out, this desire is characterized by an ambiguity between seeing with the eye and with the understanding, and further, the mysteries that are supposed to underlie the visible universe ultimately elude rational 'seeing', and remain recalcitrantly bewildering phenomena.[51] Ruth's attempt to 'see World-Trade' involves a similar ambiguity between literal and metaphorical vision, and is also ultimately unsuccessful as she fails to cognitively map the world trade network in which London might appear as a hub.[52] However, world trade is not the only phenomenon that eludes Ruth's cognitive grasp: in *Spleen*, literary impressionism functions as a powerful aesthetic strategy for drawing attention to the novel's failure to represent the elusive phenomenon of climate change.

Exploiting a suggestive analogy between climate change models and the novel, Taylor argues that certain 'climate change novels' successfully attest to climate change because they aggregate discrete atmospheric events into a broader totality of long-term global patterns.[53] Although it is a novel that signals environmental damage, *Spleen* is just as notable for its representational failures as regards climate change. Returning to London, Ruth is unsure whether it is herself or the city that has altered: '[h]ad it always been like this?' (119). The novel is so tightly focalized around her that it affords little independent clarification of these matters; apparent changes are hazed by memory and clouded by disruptions in chronological sequence. *Spleen* is a novel that, in György Lukács's terms, lacks 'perspective': unlike the realist novel, it does not portray events in an objective manner and convey a clear sense of development and change over time.[54] However, rather

---

[50] Fredric Jameson, 'Modernism and Imperialism', in *Nationalism, Colonialism, and Literature*, ed. Terry Eagleton and others (Minneapolis: University of Minnesota Press, 1990), 43–66, 50–1.

[51] Max Saunders, *Self Impression: Life-Writing, Autobiografiction, and the Forms of Modern Literature* (Oxford: Oxford University Press, 2010), 267–8.

[52] Jameson famously argues that Conrad's literary impressionism involves an aestheticization of perception, which functions both as an ideological continuation of and utopian compensation for capitalist rationalization and reification. See Fredric Jameson, *The Political Unconscious* (London: Routledge, 2002), 213–31. However, if we accept Matz's revision of Jameson's position and understand the impression as not just a category of sense but also of intellect, then literary impressionism can be recognized as capable of playing a role in what Jameson elsewhere discerns as the wider modernist failure to represent the unrepresentable totalities of monopoly capitalism (*Impressionism*, 136–7). Indeed, Taylor argues that Conrad's literary impressionism is integral to his invention of 'the fiction of global connection', in which 'readers are conscious of being embedded in global networks such that the very obfuscating dynamics that make vision impossible are also the substance of planetary connection (*Sky*, 167, 173).

[53] Taylor, *Sky*, 10.

[54] Georg Lukács, *The Meaning of Contemporary Realism*, trans. John and Necke Mander (London: Merlin Press, 1963), 33.

than interpreting *Spleen*'s lack of perspective as an ideological failing, it can be understood as revealing wider social and historical problems that are registered in the artwork as problems of form.[55] Specifically, its formally experimental climatic impressionism can be read in relation to the histories of climate and capitalism in early twentieth-century Britain.

Climate change and capitalism

Ruth's queer environmentalism and the novel's climatic impressionism can be situated in the context of the environmental transformations that are now considered to characterize the Anthropocene. To do so is to recognize *Spleen* not just as a work of modernist queer ecology but also of Anthropocene modernism, and to highlight its ability to help rethink the challenges of the troubled present. Its virtue—along with other works of modernist queer ecology—is that it provides an anticipatory illumination of a queer environmental politics and activism that is not yet here.

Most immediately, the fume-filled London to which Ruth returns in the 1920s can be placed in the historical context of the London fog. As Christine Corton informs us, while London has always been susceptible to mist, it suffered a series of fogs from the 1840s onwards that were caused principally by the burning of coal in domestic fires and industry. There were a series of particularly bad fogs through the 1920s, which also saw the passing of the Smoke Abatement Act in 1926. Visible fog effectively disappeared in 1962, following the 1956 Clean Air Act, although London's air remains highly polluted, and today apparently causes more than 9,000 deaths a year.[56] Moore was clearly aware of the harmful effects of London fog. A wry note in *The Apple Is Bitten Again* entitled '*Fog*' suggests that '[t]hey should use the London streets for smoking bacon, hams, and sausages, as they use the sun in Italy', but 'we keep our smoke for our lungs'; she adds that '[a] post-mortem examination on a Londoner reveals his lungs to be not only atrophied but black'.[57] The fogs that beset London were also given extensive coverage in the *Daily Sketch*, the newspaper for which Moore worked as a journalist. For example, the newspaper displayed a front-page photograph of an office building illuminated at midday in early 1929 because 'London was under a pall of black fog that turned day into night'.[58] The issue was addressed by 'Onlooker', who worried that due to suburbanization the 'smoke and din may spread', and therefore advocated the creation of a 'verdant belt' around the city. It is possible, the journalist suggested, that

---

[55] See Theodor Adorno, 'Reconciliation Under Duress', trans. Rodney Livingstone, in *Aesthetics and Politics*, ed. Ronald Taylor (London: Verso, 2007), 151–76, 162–3.
[56] See Christine L. Corton, *London Fog: The Biography* (Cambridge, MA: Harvard University Press, 2015).
[57] Moore, *The Apple Is Bitten Again*, 384.
[58] *Daily Sketch*, 8 January 1929, 1.

'such a provision would have a beneficent effect, not only on the nerves and eyes and lungs of a racked population, but also upon such plagues as fog.'[59] In *Spleen*, the '[w]eeks of sooty rain' that keep Ruth indoors are typical of the coal soot and acid rain that blackened and corroded many of London's buildings (118).[60] Again, the 'petrol fumes'—presumably caused by motor cars which, as Joan points out, were becoming 'less expensive'—are evidence of the rapidly increasing pollution from motor vehicles, which itself was made possible by the expansion of the petroleum industry (120, 126).

More broadly, the fog in *Spleen* can be viewed in the context of what Will Steffen, Paul Crutzen, and John McNeill have called 'stage 1' of the Anthropocene: the period 1800–1945, which preceded the 'Great Acceleration', yet is marked by a vast increase in the use of fossil fuels and a significant rise in atmospheric concentrations of greenhouse gasses such as carbon dioxide, methane, and nitrous oxide.[61] *Spleen* can be aligned with other works of modernism that register these environmental changes, which are registered in the famous 'hockey stick' graphs shown in Figure 3.1. Notably, its concern with air pollution is shared by D. H. Lawrence's *Lady Chatterley's Lover* (1928), which portrays the noxious fumes emitted by the coal and steel industries in the Midlands that become particularly apparent to Constance Chatterley on her drive through Tevershall.[62] Again, the dangers of air pollution were later vividly highlighted by Mary Butts in her pamphlet *Warning to Hikers* (1932). Therein, Butts contends that

in our cities we have done what man has never done before, almost manufactured a weather, a climate, a whole environment, in which there is little amelioration as possible and every curse. For light we have substituted smoke, for blue air or silver or gold or white or dark crystal, a partially solidified brown-grey. For the scent-box of nature, a smell, curiously compounded of burnt carbon, oils and dust.[63]

Like the recent concept of the Anthropocene which conveys the historical uniqueness of the changes that humans have wrought on the Earth system, Butts stresses that the changes in cities are historically unprecedented: while previously there

---

[59] 'Onlooker', 'Why Not Sanctuaries for Us?', *Daily Sketch*, 23 January 1929, 4.

[60] A note in *The Apple Is Bitten Again* similarly evokes miles of 'soot-soaked brick house' in Wandsworth (Moore, *The Apple Is Bitten Again*, 383).

[61] Will Steffen, Paul J. Crutzen, and John R. McNeill, 'The Anthropocene: Are Humans Now Overwhelming the Great Forces of Nature?', *Ambio*, 36/8 (2007), 614–21, 616–17.

[62] D. H. Lawrence, *Lady Chatterley's Lover*, ed. Michael Squires (Cambridge: Cambridge University Press, 1993), 152–60. *Spleen* might be compared with *Lady Chatterley's Lover*, in which Connie pursues a sexually-charged revaluation of the Earth with Mellors the gamekeeper. However, Moore seems to have been unimpressed with the sex in this novel: '[s]exually', she suggests, 'it is an improbable study'. She judges that 'the only convincing scenes of passion in his books are the love scenes between men' (*The Apple Is Bitten Again*, 398, 400).

[63] Mary Butts, *Warning to Hikers* ([London]: Wishart, 1932), 13.

Earth system trends

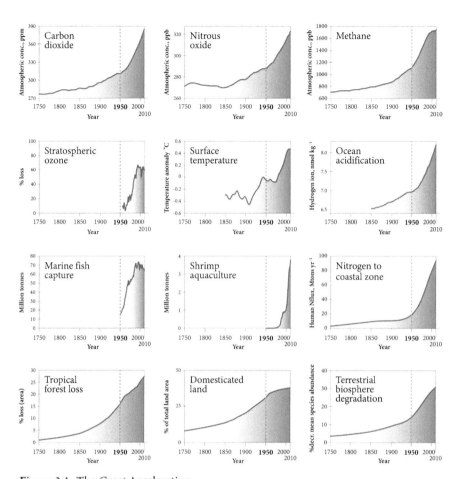

Figure 3.1 The Great Acceleration

Reproduced with permission from Steffen, Will, et al. (2015). 'The Trajectory of the Anthropocene: The Great Acceleration', *The Anthropocene Review*, 2/1, 81–98.

had been slums, 'never before were the works and wealth of man based on coal, and the largest cities were easy to get out of'.[64] However, Butts invokes such an environmental catastrophe for a conservative political purpose. In reaction to environmental movements that were encouraging city dwellers to visit the countryside, she fulminates against hikers and the contemporary 'cult of nature'. In particular, she reviles working class hikers and implies that the preservation of the English

---

[64] Butts, *Warning*, 14.

countryside requires the maintenance of the property rights of the landowning class.[65] Such a rural conservatism, which also finds expression in her novels *Ashe of Rings* (1925) and *Armed with Madness* (1928), forms a stark contrast with the portrayal of environmental damage and social injustice in *Spleen*.

Indeed, Ruth is greatly troubled by the fact that London's polluted air is not suffered equally by rich and poor. Walking across the city, she becomes aware that it is the slums with their 'narrow foetid streets' and 'damp and stale-smelling alleys' that are worst affected (119). She realizes that, by virtue of her wealth and privileged class position, it would be perfectly possible for her to avoid such areas and to stay at her exclusive hotel in Hans Crescent where 'one did not have to walk quickly, consciously using as little breath as possible', or to remain within 'that airy strip between Piccadilly and the few discreet squares of Kensington and Belgravia' (119). Such elegant residential streets literally have a better quality of air, as presumably did the 'great squares' with their 'green trees' and 'sense of spaciousness' that she remembers from the early stages of her marriage (118–19). She dwells on the conditions endured by London's workers, and imagines writing a story about an elderly man who had lived 'all his life underground, in trains to and from work, in badly lit offices, in badly ventilated badly designed houses' (120). The inequality that she witnesses affects her profoundly and motivates her to turn Sharvells into a retreat that would provide holidays for London's slum children. This decision contrasts with Butts's exclusionary attitude towards the countryside; indeed, it has more in common with the environmental movements against which Butts was reacting. Many such movements were driven by a concern with poor air quality and a lack of sunlight in cities: as well as societies that campaigned for smoke abatement, movements such as the Kibbo Kift Kin and the Boy Scout movement stressed the drawbacks of city-living for children and extolled instead the virtues of countryside pursuits. In *England and the Octopus* (1928), Clough Williams-Ellis deplored 'the pollution of the air and the denial of light' in cities, but was dismayed at the ugly suburbanization that was blighting the English countryside, and recommended instead the sort of settlements that had long been advocated by the Garden City movement.[66] On the Continent, Le Corbusier—whom Moore mentioned in *The Apple Is Bitten Again* and whom she later interviewed for *Scope* magazine—inveighed against the lack of sunlight and clean air in towns.[67] Instead, as suggested by Figure 3.2, he conceived his vertically rising Radiant City on principles that would maximize sunlight, space, and greenery.[68]

[65] On Butts's rural conservativism, see Jeffrey Mathes McCarthy, *Green Modernism: Nature and the English Novel, 1900 to 1930* (Basingstoke: Palgrave Macmillan, 2015), 157–98; and Jane Garrity, *Step-Daughters of England: British Women Modernists and the National Imaginary* (Manchester: Manchester University Press, 2003), 188–241.

[66] Clough Williams-Ellis, *England and the Octopus* (London: Geoffrey Bles, 1928), 38.

[67] Moore, *The Apple Is Bitten Again*, 368.

[68] See Olive Moore, 'Man of the Month: Le Corbusier', *Scope*, August 1951, 60–73, 71.

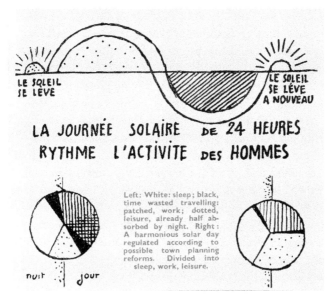

Figure 3.2 Le Corbusier's plan to reform cities to accord with the solar day

Reproduced from Moore, Olive (1951). 'Man of the Month: Le Corbusier', *Scope*, 60–73.

In addition to portraying a polluted London, *Spleen* intimates the suffering of workers in the fossil fuel industries that facilitated the pollution. Ruth's encounter with the 'procession of unemployed' in the culminating scene of the novel can be read in the context of the series of industrial disputes and workers' protests that ran throughout the 1920s, foremost amongst which was the 1926 Lockout and General Strike.[69] More specifically, the protest that Ruth witnesses is likely based on the Second National Hunger March to London, which reached Trafalgar Square on 24 February 1929. This march was organized by the National Unemployed Workers' Movement, and included miners from the South Wales coal pits, as well as a contingent from Scotland led by Wal Hannington that marched for five weeks through bitter winter weather before arriving in London. It was a protest against the Conservative government's attempts to exclude large numbers of unemployed workers from labour exchange benefit during a period of mass unemployment and widespread starvation. Ruth is greatly moved by the plight of the protestors and is painfully aware of their condition of starvation: their faces were 'grey and haggard and emptied of all expression save hunger and weariness'; they shuffle past

---

[69] For an account of literary representations of the 1926 General Strike, see Charles Ferrall and Dougal McNeill, *Writing the 1926 General Strike: Literature, Culture, Politics* (New York: Cambridge University Press, 2015).

'unsubstantial as ghosts' (126–7). She is upset by an altercation in which a police-man threatens to strike a protestor for answering him back: she 'began to tremble' and wishes to cry out: 'It could not be that such a wraith of a man, such a grey hol-low thing, should be struck a blow, a well-fed hearty blow, for a mere interchange of words' (127). The contrast between the starving protestor and the policeman capable of delivering a 'well-fed hearty blow' conveys a deep sense of injustice.

Fittingly, historical contradictions concerning climate and class are never resolved within the fictional world of *Spleen*. For example, Ruth is aware of the limitations of her charitable scheme, asking herself whether 'the gift of Sharvells' was 'merely the gratification of an ill-considered and quixotic impulse'; she further wonders whether it would make a worthwhile difference, and is left 'bitter and dis-couraged' (119). Similarly, although she seems to achieve a resolution regarding her son at the end of the novel, this personal resolution only serves to disclose greater unresolved contradictions on the historical level. The hunger march is portrayed as a failure.[70] In some respects, the portrayal of the 'worn and spirit-less' protestors resembles the politically conservative *Daily Sketch*'s coverage of the hunger march, including its brief report entitled 'Drab Pathos of Demonstration in Trafalgar-square' (127). This report—which was accompanied by the photograph that is reproduced in Figure 3.3—described the arrival of a thousand footsore men 'singing songs pathetically thin in spirit', and contended that 'instead of making history' the marchers found that they 'had made an idler's holiday'.[71] Both depic-tions contrast starkly with Hannington's account of the arrival of the marchers in Trafalgar Square as one of rousing class solidarity, in which thousands of cheering London workers turned out to show their support, and inspiring speeches were punctuated by spontaneous renditions of the 'Red Flag' and the 'International'. However, this is not to say that *Spleen*'s presentation of the march as a failure is itself conservative. On the contrary, its depiction of unresolved class difference is appropriate for a historical situation in which unemployment continued to rise, and the labour movement remained incapacitated by the anti-strike legislation imposed by the government in the aftermath of the General Strike. Even Han-nington acknowledged the hunger marchers' lack of success in obtaining their immediate objectives, illustrated by the Prime Minister Stanley Baldwin's refusal to grant them an audience.[72]

---

[70] Like Charles Baudelaire's leisured flaneurs, Ruth looks on this scene of poverty from a position of wealth and privilege and imbues it with allegorical significance: the procession of unemployed becomes a 'grotesque Calvary' (Moore, *Spleen*, 128). More generally, Ruth's impressions of London are inflected by her privileged class position: for example, the descriptions of the 'promiscuous herded millions' and 'men unfitted for their work' betray degenerationist anxieties about labour (119).

[71] *Daily Sketch*, 25 February 1929, 3. The *Daily Sketch* tended to be hostile to the labour movement: it had, for instance, rejoiced at the failure of the General Strike.

[72] Wal Hannington, *Unemployment Struggles 1919–1936: My Life and Struggles Amongst the Unem-ployed* (London: Lawrence and Wishart, 1936), 194–7, 199.

Figure 3.3 National Hunger March, 1929

Reproduced from *Daily Sketch*, 25 February 1929, 13.

In *Spleen*, Ruth returns to London to find a polluted city and a nation wracked by poverty and unemployment. The novel, tightly focalized around Ruth, does not provide a comprehensive representation of the city's changing climate. Nevertheless, the partial glimpses it affords of fume-filled alleys and bedraggled hunger marchers point towards wider historical transformations: of a fossil fuel industry that led to starvation for many of its workers, and that drove climate change on a global scale. By failing to provide a totalizing representation of climate change, *Spleen* supports Amitav Ghosh's argument that the novel as a literary form has failed to depict global warming adequately and is thereby guilty of mode of 'concealment'.[73] Yet at the same time, its representational limitations—the foggy concealments of its climatic impressionism—contribute to making it such

[73] Amitav Ghosh, *The Great Derangement: Climate Change and the Unthinkable* (Chicago: University of Chicago Press, 2016), 11. For Ghosh, the failure of the novel 'will have to be counted as an aspect of the broader imaginative and cultural failure that lies at the heart of the climate crisis' (8).

a notable work of Anthropocene modernism. In terms of her own theory of the 'creative artist' as a '[p]riestless oracle' whose works serve as prophecies of major social and political changes, Olive Moore might be thought of as a 'Cassandra' figure, and *Spleen* might be considered a prophecy of the environmental damage that has accelerated since the mid-twentieth century. Given that this damage is now deemed irreversible, it may well be that she is a 'Cassandra whose message is read too late'.[74]

However, it is also possible read the novel in a more hopeful way by employing Muñoz's utopian hermeneutics. Although Ruth characterizes her 'mental inversion' by 'loneliness' and 'lack of hope' and the march is depicted as a failure, both function as sites of utopian promise. For Karl Marx, every society must reproduce the conditions of its production, and in a capitalist society production as 'a process of reproduction [...] produces and reproduces the capitalist relation; on the one side the capitalist, on the other the wage-labourer'. In *Spleen*, the strange stasis of the image of the middle-class family juxtaposed with the protesting workers suggests a suspension of the reproduction of social relations within fossil fuel capitalism. It intimates a disruption to the cycle of capital accumulation—including to the 'incessant reproduction' or 'perpetuation of the labourer' that Marx discerned as the 'sine qua non of capitalist production'—and promises the emergence of a new form of queer collectivity.[75]

Notably, the temporal experiments of *Spleen* and other works of modernist queer ecology become newly legible in the context of the current environmental emergency. With growing concern for the environment, many activists have appealed to a reproductive futurism. For example, the ecofeminist activism at Greenham Common in England began in the 1980s when 'Women for Life on Earth' pressured the Royal Air Force to cease operating and testing nuclear cruise missiles, announcing their 'fear for the future of all our children and for the future of the living world which is the basis of all life'.[76] More recently, Extinction Rebellion launched their 'International Rebellion' in 2019 to protest governments' failures to take appropriate action to minimize the risk of human extinction and ecological collapse, advertising their rebellion as one '[f]or the planet. For our children's childrens's futures'.[77] Works of modernist queer ecology provide models for cultivating queerer structures of environmental care and concern, including queerer forms of activism. By defamiliarizing the conditions of production of a fossil fuel capitalism—with the endless production of the division between rich and poor—*Spleen* further implicitly critiques ascendant forms of environmental

---

[74] Moore, *The Apple Is Bitten Again*, 358.

[75] Karl Marx, *Capital: A Critique of Political Economy, Volume 1*, ed. Frederick Engels, trans. Samuel Moore and Edward Aveling (Chicago: Charles H. Kerr, 1906), 633, 625.

[76] Quoted in Greta Gaard, 'Ecofeminism Revisited: Rejecting Essentialism and Re-Placing Species in a Material Feminist Environmentalism', *Feminist Formations*, 23/2 (2011), 26–53, 29.

[77] Extinction Rebellion, *Rebel Starter Pack*, 14 March 2019, 3.

politics whose strategies of sustainability and resilience are designed to achieve economic growth and make the future safe for the market.

It is important to acknowledge the negativity of works of modernist queer ecology, and the awkward relationship that some of them have to other texts and canons of modernism. Yet attending to the utopian aspects of these texts— including the points at which loneliness anticipates forms of collectivity and resistance to reproductive futurism opens up new structures of environmental care and concern—shows their potential to inflect the environmental concerns of the present. Indeed, works of modernist queer ecology can inspire us to dream and enact what Muñoz calls 'new and better pleasures, other ways of being in the world, and ultimately new worlds'.[78]

---

[78] Muñoz, *Cruising Utopia*, 1.

4

Virginia Woolf and the Pageant of History

In Virginia Woolf's *The Waves* (1931), the characters imagine a vertiginous shift in scale while visiting Hampton Court. Bernard reflects that 'the earth is only a pebble flicked off accidentally from the face of the sun', and Louis hears 'the world moving through abysses of infinite space': '[i]t roars; the lighted strip of history is past and our Kings and Queens'. The imagination of vast spans of cosmic time and space defamiliarizes a sense of history made up of kings and queens ('Our English past—one inch of light'). In such a perspective, the king turns into an absurd figure and loses his authority: 'how strange', muses Bernard, 'to set against the whirling abysses of infinite space a little figure with a golden teapot on his head'. The experience is a momentary one, and the everyday scene quickly re-establishes itself, with the greasy knifes on the table and the cars hooting in the background: 'the world has hailed us back to it'. Yet even so, a conventional conception of history with individuals and events remains disturbed: Bernard struggles to recover belief in what people 'put on their heads', and Neville suspects that it is 'ridiculous' to think that 'all depends on the battle of Blenheim'.[1] The characters' meditations in this scene are similar to those invited by Woolf's prose: they suggest a way of responding to the disorienting shifts in scale that Woolf undertakes throughout her fiction.

In turn, Woolf's experiments with scale provide a means of addressing issues of scale in the Anthropocene. Dipesh Chakrabarty argues that anthropogenic explanations of climate change spell the collapse of the distinction between human history and natural history, and require us to 'scale up our imagination of the human': it 'leaves us with the challenge of having to think of human agency over multiple and incommensurable scales at once'.[2] However, Derek Woods suggests that sufficient attention to scale variation would displace 'the human' as the subject of the Anthropocene. Indeed, he argues that 'scale critique' is needed to show that 'the subject of the Anthropocene is not the human species but modern terraforming assemblages'.[3] Woolf's fiction operates in a similar manner to achieve what might be called a 'feminist scale critique': as suggested by the vertiginous experience of the characters in *The Waves*, her narrative experiments with scale

---

[1] Virginia Woolf, *The Waves*, ed. Michael Herbert and Susan Sellars (Cambridge: Cambridge University Press, 2011), 180–2.

[2] Dipesh Chakrabarty, *The Climate of History in a Planetary Age* (Chicago: University of Chicago Press, 2021), 31; 'Postcolonial Studies and the Challenge of Climate Change', *New Literary History*, 43/1 (2012), 1–18, 1.

[3] Derek Woods, 'Scale Critique for the Anthropocene', *the minnesota review*, 83 (2014), 133–42, 138.

British Modernism and the Anthropocene. David Shackleton, Oxford University Press. © David Shackleton (2023).
DOI: 10.1093/oso/9780192857743.003.0005

unsettle familiar conceptions of human agency, and displace 'great men' from the centre of history and fiction. In part, they do so by drawing attention to what Timothy Clark calls 'scale effects': 'phenomena that are invisible at normal levels of perception but only emerge if one changes the spatial and temporal scale at which issues are framed'.[4] Woolf's fiction thereby provides a model for rethinking agency in the Anthropocene: rather than aggrandizing humans and their agency, her experiments with scale tend to decentre humans, and register the agency of the non-human world.

Woolf's feminist scale critique might be redeployed to counteract masculinist strains of Anthropocene discourse. Stacy Alaimo urges caution against Chakrabarty's contention that the concept of the Anthropocene demands a rethinking of history at the level of the species, arguing that such a universalism threatens to elide meaningful differences between various human groups, histories, and practices, and to reinstall 'man' in all-too-familiar positions of power.[5] Certainly, many have taken the term to imply an aggrandizement of humans and human agency, and move seamlessly between the idea of humans as a geophysical force to the idea of humans as political agents capable of redressing environmental catastrophes through managerial and technological approaches, including geoengineering projects.[6] Recognizing the need to offer alternatives to the 'too often unquestioned masculinist and technonormative approach to the Anthropocene', Alaimo joins others in calling for an 'anthropocene feminism'.[7] Woolf's fiction might contribute to this project.

In order to address Woolf's experiments with scale, this chapter starts by comparing *To the Lighthouse* (1927) and the Annalistes' experimental historiography. Woolf and the Annalistes shared a distaste for 'great men' conceptions of history, and both turned to different scales and types of time to displace emphasis from individuals and events. Yet whereas the Annalistes rejected narrative as unsuitable for history on medium and long timescales, Woolf experimented with quasi-plots to convey a sense of history as composed of multiple processes unfolding at different speeds and on different scales. The chapter then turns to Woolf's last novel, *Between the Acts* (1940), in which Miss La Trobe stages a historical pageant. By drawing attention to Woolf's engagement with Mutabilitie's pageant in *The Faerie Queene*, I show how Woolf borrowed from Edmund Spenser the idea of different orders of temporal duration, and the fiction of a changeless nature. While such a

---

[4] Timothy Clark, *Ecocriticism on the Edge: The Anthropocene as a Threshold Concept* (London: Bloomsbury, 2015), 22.
[5] Stacy Alaimo, 'Your Shell on Acid: Material Immersion, Anthropocene Dissolves', in *Anthropocene Feminism*, ed. Richard Grusin (Minneapolis: University of Minnesota Press, 2017), 89–120.
[6] See Eileen Crist, 'On the Poverty of Our Nomenclature', *Environmental Humanities*, 3 (2013), 129–47.
[7] See Richard Grusin, 'Introduction. Anthropocene Feminism: An Experiment in Collaborative Theorizing', in *Anthropocene Feminism*, vii–xix, x.

fiction provides comfort to Lucy Swithin in a moment of historical crisis, it operates in a more ambivalent manner to expose some of the ways in which nature and history have been intertwined: how the idea of 'nature' has been evoked to sustain gender difference and legitimate violence in patriarchal society, while conversely nature has been transformed through the imposition of plantations in Ireland which led to famine and forced migration.

Although approaching Woolf's fiction by means of her interest in the way that history is written, this chapter joins an established tradition of ecocritical approaches to Woolf. Notably, for example, Christina Alt and Caroline Hovanec historicize Woolf's representations of the natural world, placing them in the context of a broader shift within the natural sciences from evolutionary biology to ethology and ecology; Bonnie Kime Scott pioneers an ecocritical approach to Woolf that engages the feminist new materialisms; Kelly Sultzbach draws on Maurice Merleau-Ponty to inform her eco-phenomenological assessment of Woolf's environmental consciousness; and Jemma Deer offers a brilliant analysis of Woolf's 'radical animism'.[8] Here, I address Woolf's fiction in relation to her interest in historiography, and show how her experiments with scales and types of time offer valuable resources for rethinking issues of agency in the Anthropocene. Specifically, I trace how Woolf employs shifts between scales, switches of focalization to adopt seemingly non-human perspectives, quasi-plots with quasi-characters, and narrative fragmentation to register the agency of the non-human world, and convey a sense of history as made up of a multiplicity of interconnected human and non-human processes unfolding at different speeds on different scales.

Despite both being Anthropocene modernists, Woolf's representations of agency contrast markedly with those of H. G. Wells. Whereas Wells follows early ecology in his visions of humans gaining mastery over other species and the environment, Woolf's narrative experiments unsettle anthropocentrism and human exceptionalism, and critique masculinist conceptions of agency. On a formal level, the difference is registered in Wells's use of a continuous narrative to tell the story of humans across geological timescales in his universal histories, as opposed to Woolf's use of disorienting shifts of scale to displace humans from a position of mastery. The shift of scale in the 'Time Passes' section of *To the Lighthouse* is exemplary: rather than permitting a smooth scaling-up of the human subject, it functions like Woods's scale critique to emphasize 'scale variance', or jumps and discontinuities in the way that systems operate at different scales.[9] While Wells

[8] Christina Alt, *Virginia Woolf and the Study of Nature* (Cambridge: Cambridge University Press, 2010); Caroline Hovanec, *Animal Subjects: Literature, Zoology, and British Modernism* (Cambridge: Cambridge University Press, 2018); Bonnie Kime Scott, *In the Hollow of the Wave: Virginia Woolf and the Modernist Uses of Nature* (Charlottesville: University of Virginia Press, 2012); Kelly Sultzbach, *Ecocriticism in the Modernist Imagination: Forster, Woolf and Auden* (Cambridge: Cambridge University Press, 2016); Jemma Deer, *Radical Animism: Reading for the End of the World* (London: Bloomsbury, 2021).
[9] Woods, 'Scale Critique', 133.

scales up humans until they appear like gods, Woolf decentres humans and deflates ideologies of great men as the agents of history.

Great men versions of history

From an early age, Virginia Woolf was a voracious reader of history. Having devoured numerous volumes of history and historical biography that she borrowed from her father Leslie Stephen's library, she formed enthusiastic plans to study history at university and write historical works, and went on to teach history at Morley College.[10] Yet she became increasingly critical of the way that history was written. Most famously, in *A Room of One's Own* (1929), her narrator marks the absence of women from 'the historian's view of the past'—'one often catches a glimpse of them in the lives of the great, whisking away into the background, concealing, I sometimes think, a wink, a laugh, perhaps a tear'—and contemplates suggesting to the students of Newnham and Girton colleges that they 'should re-write history'.[11] Although Woolf never did write the historical works that she planned, she went on to engage critically with the way that history is written in her fiction. Indeed, Angeliki Spiropoulou convincingly argues that, more than her essays on historiography, Woolf's modernist fiction 'allowed for and was even constitutionally grafted on to more radical experiments in historiography'.[12] Extending such an approach, I will compare the way that Woolf subverts great men conceptions of history in *To the Lighthouse* with the experimental historiography of the Annales school. My claim is not that the Annalistes influenced Woolf or Woolf the Annalistes, but rather that they were motivated by a shared dislike of traditional narrative history, and developed similarly innovative forms of history and fiction in response.

The Annales school pioneered a new approach to the study of history. Based around the journal *Annales d'historie economique et sociale* which was founded by Marc Bloc and Lucien Febvre in 1929, its most celebrated work is Fernand Braudel's *The Mediterranean and the Mediterranean World in the Age of Philip II* (1949). Braudel describes his *Mediterranean* as 'an attempt to write a new kind of history' structured around 'three different conceptions of time': the *longue durée* or very long timespan, taken as a parameter of historical study from geography, and around which the first part of the work is based; the conjuncture or medium timespan, borrowed from economics and the social sciences, around which the second part of the work is based; and the short timespan, familiar from traditional narrative history, around which the third part of the work is based. His

---

[10] See Angeliki Spiropoulou, *Virginia Woolf, Modernity and History* (Basingstoke: Palgrave MacMillan, 2010), 42–8.
[11] Virginia Woolf, *A Room of One's Own; Three Guineas*, ed. Morag Shiach (Oxford: Oxford University Press, 1992), 58.
[12] Spiropoulou, *Woolf*, 49.

approach is thereby to 'dissect history into various planes', or to 'divide historical time into geographical time, social time, and individual time'.[13] Reflecting
back on the significance of the Annales school, Braudel held that it was concern
with the *longue durée* that makes a decisive break in historiography: 'it is in relation to these expanses of slow-moving history that the whole of history is to be
rethought'.[14]

The Annalistes' study of history over different timescales has received renewed
attention in relation to the current environmental crisis. Chakrabarty identifies
Braudel's *Mediterranean* as a notable attempt to make 'a breach in the binary of
natural/human history', although he points out that Braudel's emphasis on patterns of constant repetition and ever-recurring cycles in nature is at odds with
recent explanations of anthropogenic climate change.[15] Jason Moore contests the
widespread view that Braudel treats the environment as a static background, and
argues instead that the relationship between conjunctures and long durational
structures in his *Mediterranean* provides rich resources for theorizing world-
ecology and the way that capitalism has produced cheap nature across the *longue
durée*.[16] Even within its own terms, Braudel's description of long durational history as one of constant repetition and ever-recurring cycles is misleading, insofar
as he dedicates a section of the *Mediterranean* to the issue of climate change, and
discusses the possibility that such change might be caused by 'man's intervention'.[17] Other Annalistes took up the topic of climate change at greater length. For
example, Emmanuel Le Roy Ladurie draws on an unusual archive that includes
records of wine harvests and Alpine glaciers in an attempt to reconstruct fluctuations of climate in his *History of Climate Since the Year 1000* (1967). Highlighting
Ladurie's contributions and its long tradition of studying the histories of climate and the environment, the *Annales* journal has recently addressed the issue
of environmental crisis with a special edition devoted to the concept of the
Anthropocene.[18]

Much as the Annalistes contest traditional narrative history, Woolf stages an
engagement with Walter Scott's and Thomas Carlyle's conceptions of history in
To the Lighthouse. Carlyle's version of history, which was inspired by the vivacity
of Scott's historical novels, is one which treats of 'remarkable action', and is the
story of great men. 'History is', as he famously puts it, 'the essence of innumerable

[13] Fernand Braudel, *The Mediterranean and the Mediterranean World in the Age of Philip II*, trans.
Siân Reynolds, 2 vols, rev. edn (London: Collins, 1972–73), 1238, 20–1.

[14] Fernand Braudel, 'History and the Social Sciences: The *Longue Durée*', in *On History*, trans. Sarah
Matthews (London: Weidenfeld and Nicolson, 1980), 25–54, 33.

[15] Chakrabarty, 'Climate', 204–05.

[16] Jason W. Moore, 'Capitalism as World-Ecology: Braudel and Marx on Environmental History',
Organization & Environment, 16/4 (2003), 431–58.

[17] Braudel, *Mediterranean*, 267–75.

[18] See Les Annales, 'Anthropocene', *Annales HSS (English Edition)*, 72/2 (2017), 161–3.

Biographies'.[19] In turn, Carlyle influenced Leslie Stephen. As Marie Laniel points out, although Stephen's loyalties rested with Carlyle's Benthamite opponents, he was at the same time 'deeply inspired by the Victorian prophet', and his work for the Dictionary of National Biography 'implicitly serves as a tribute to Carlyle's view of history'.[20] Carlyle's conception of history and advocacy of 'Hero-Worship' provide a gender ideology that is largely accepted by the characters of To the Lighthouse, and reinforces the gendered relations between them.

Carlyle has a marked presence in To the Lighthouse. Spurred into thought by reading an article in The Times about the number of Americans who visit Shakespeare's house every year, Mr Ramsay ponders the status of great men in terms which are, as Laniel notes, clearly reminiscent of Carlyle's meditations in On Heroes, Hero-Worship and the Heroic in History (1841).[21] 'Does the progress of civilisation depend upon great men?', Mr Ramsay wonders. Thinking ahead to a lecture that he is due to deliver to 'the young men at Cardiff next month', he worries about the inegalitarian implications of Carlyle's view of history, and decides to 'disparage Shakespeare and come to the rescue of the man who stands eternally in the door of the lift'.[22] His qualification of Carlyle is similar to that which Leslie Stephen makes in his essay 'Carlyle's Ethics', which expresses discomfort about Carlyle's disdain for unheroic people, and his open advocacy of slavery.[23] Yet Mr Ramsay implicitly accepts Carlyle's method of valuation, and contemplates his own greatness in similar terms.

Indeed, Mr Ramsay's preoccupation with his posterity is supported by Carlyle's conception of history. For Carlyle, the achievements of great men make up the substance of history: 'Universal History' is 'the history of what man has accomplished in this world'.[24] Mr Ramsay assesses his intellectual accomplishments in similar terms, wondering how he will be remembered:

> his fame lasts how long? It is permissible even for a dying hero to think before he dies how men will speak of him hereafter. His fame lasts perhaps two thousand years. And what are two thousand years? (asked Mr. Ramsay ironically, staring at the hedge). What, indeed, if you look from a mountain top down the long wastes of the ages? The very stone one kicks with one's boot will outlast Shakespeare. (41)

[19] Thomas Carlyle, 'On History', in Critical and Miscellaneous Essays, 5 vols (London: Chapman and Hall, 1904), I, 493–505, 496–7. In Jacob's Room (1922), Jacob is set the essay question: 'Does History consist of the Biographies of Great Men?' (Jacob's Room, ed. Stuart N. Clarke and David Bradshaw (Cambridge: Cambridge University Press, 2020), 60).

[20] Marie Laniel, 'Revisiting a Great Man's House: Virginia Woolf's Carlylean Pilgrimages', Carlyle Studies Annual, 24 (2008), 117–32, 121–2.

[21] Laniel, 'House', 122.

[22] Virginia Woolf, To the Lighthouse, ed. Stella McNichol (London: Penguin, 1992), 48–9.

[23] Leslie Stephen, 'Carlyle's Ethics', in Hours in a Library, new edn, 3 vols (London: Smith, Elder, 1892), III, 271–305, 302–04.

[24] Thomas Carlyle, On Heroes, Hero-Worship & the Heroic in History: Six Lectures (London: J. Fraser, 1841), 239.

Carlyle had used Shakespeare as his preeminent example of the 'Hero as Poet', yet, as he concedes, 'not the noblest Shakespeare [...] can be remembered forever;—a day comes when he too is not'.[25] In styling himself as a dying hero, Mr Ramsay similarly thinks that the 'very stone one kicks with one's boot will outlast Shakespeare': the stone suggests geological timespans which dwarf the longevity of Shakespeare's reputation. He extends his thoughts in melancholy fashion to 'the perishing of stars', which intimates a heat-death of the universe as popularized by William Thomson in the Victorian age or by James Jeans as part of the New Physics; these longer cosmological timespans make Shakespeare's fame appear even more insubstantial. And yet Mr Ramsay's achievement is negligible when compared to that of Shakespeare: he thinks that his 'own little light would shine, not very brightly, for a year or two, and would then be merged in some bigger light, and that in a bigger still' (41).[26] The metaphor of light is congruent with a network of similar metaphors that Carlyle uses to figure great men. For instance, the great man is 'the living light fountain', and the 'light which enlightens, which has enlightened the darkness of the world'.[27] Leslie Stephen extends this imagery when he praises Carlyle's ability to make you feel that 'history is like the short space lighted up by a flickering taper in the midst of infinite glooms and mysteries [...] where the actors are passing in rapid succession—rising from and vanishing into the all-embracing darkness'.[28] Similarly, Mr Ramsay's light would shine 'not very brightly', presumably marking his shortcomings in comparison with truly great men like Shakespeare; he 'looked into the darkness', much like the 'all-embracing darkness' into which Carlyle's historical actors vanish (41).

In addition to assessing his accomplishments in Carlylean terms, Mr Ramsay comports himself like a great man. As Laniel remarks, his standing 'on a spit of land which the sea is slowly eating away [...] facing the dark of human ignorance' is like Carlyle's hero Teufelsdröckh in *Sartor Resartus* (1836), who 'stands there, on the World-promontory, looking over the infinite Brine'.[29] Mr Ramsay's mind, as he poses as a Carlylean hero, is appropriately filled with the stuff out of which a great man version of history is made: 'the history of that campaign there, the life of this statesman here, [...] with figures too, this thinker, that soldier' (49). He does not forget flesh-and-blood figures, as if he has learnt the lesson from Scott via Carlyle that 'the bygone ages of the world were actually filled by living men, not by protocols, state-papers, controversies and abstractions of men'.[30] His posing as

---

[25] Carlyle, *Heroes*, 315.

[26] Leslie Stephen ruminates in a similar manner in the *Mausoleum Book*: 'putting aside the few very great names [...] even the best thinkers become obsolete in a brief time, and turn out to have been superfluous. Putting my imaginary achievements at the best, they would have made no perceptible difference to the world' (*Sir Leslie Stephen's Mausoleum Book* (Oxford: Clarendon Press, 1977), 96).

[27] Carlyle, *Heroes*, 239.

[28] Stephen, 'Carlyle's Ethics', 282.

[29] Laniel, 'House', 123.

[30] Thomas Carlyle, 'Sir Walter Scott', in *Critical and Miscellaneous Essays* (London: Chapman and Hall, 1904), IV, 135–84, 176–7.

a great man is, to varying degrees, accepted by those around him, who treat him with deference and admiration:

> it was in this guise that he inspired in William Bankes (intermittently) and in Charles Tansley (obsequiously) and in his wife now, when she looked up and saw him standing at the edge of the lawn, profound reverence. (50)

Such 'profound reverence' is akin to that which, according to Carlyle, befits a hero. Carlyle advocated 'Hero-Worship'—or 'transcendent admiration of a Great Man'—and celebrated the fact that it forms the foundation of society:

> All dignities of rank, on which human association rests, are what we may call a Heroarchy (Government of Heroes),—or a Hierarchy, for it is 'sacred' enough withal! [...] Society everywhere is some representation [...] of a graduated Worship of Heroes;—reverence and obedience done to men really great and wise.[31]

Playing on the derivation of 'hierarchy' from the Greek 'hieros', Carlyle suggests that reverence of heroes is 'sacred': social hierarchy rests on such sacred 'reverence and obedience done to men'. Mrs Ramsay's revering attitude towards her husband is one which Carlyle might have approved: '[t]here was nobody she revered more. She was not good enough to tie his shoe strings, she felt' (38). William Bankes, who believes that Carlyle is 'one of the great teachers of mankind', also thinks of Mr Ramsay as a great man: he 'was anxious that Lily Briscoe should not disparage Ramsay (a great man in his own way)' (52, 26). In a less flattering light, he compares Mr Ramsay to Carlyle himself, whose reputation, he regrets, suffers amongst the young: the implication is that Mr Ramsay behaves like Carlyle, a 'crusty old gambler who lost his temper if the porridge was cold' (52).

Mr Ramsay's confidence in his achievements is shaken when it is suggested over dinner that people do not read Scott any more. William Bankes praises Scott's Waverley novels, saying that he reads one every six months, but Charles Tansley denounces them, leading someone to ask, 'how long do you think it'll last?' Mrs Ramsay immediately scents danger for her husband: '[a] question like that would lead, almost certainly, to [...] [remind] him of his own failure. How long would he be read—he would think at once' (115–16). After dinner, Mr Ramsay reads from *The Antiquary* (1816) to assess Scott's literary merit, and to allay his insecurities about his own worth. His assessment is very similar to that of Leslie Stephen in his essay on Scott. Just as Mr Ramsay tries to discern what is 'first-rate' in Scott and what is 'fiddlesticks', so Stephen endeavours to 'sift the wheat from the chaff' (130).[32] In turn, Stephen is guided heavily by Carlyle's essay on Scott. Applying his

---

[31] Carlyle, *Heroes*, 249.
[32] Leslie Stephen, 'Sir Walter Scott', in *Hours in a Library*, new edn (London: Smith, Elder, 1892), I, 137–68, 139.

great man theory, Carlyle attempts to judge whether Scott qualifies as a truly 'great man', or merely a 'noted' and 'notable' man.[33] Stephen accepts Carlyle's terms of debate, as is evident from the opening of his essay: '[t]he question has begun to be asked about Scott which is asked about every great man: whether he is still read'.[34] Stephen painfully acknowledges the obsolescence of many of Scott's historical novels, although he judges *The Antiquary* to be one of those 'which appear to have the best chance of immortality'.[35] Similarly, Mr Ramsay is favourably impressed by *The Antiquary*: '[w]ell, let them improve on that, he thought as he finished the chapter [...] his own position became more secure' (130).

Ironically, a set of Scott's Waverley novels decays in the 'Time Passes' section of *To the Lighthouse*. At the last minute, Mrs McNab and Mrs Bast fetch up 'all the Waverley novels' from oblivion, but before that they had been disintegrating with the passage of time (152). In his essay on Scott, Stephen imagines the decline of Scott's novels in a series of figures of decay: '[w]ill some of his best performances stand out like a cathedral amongst ruined hovels, or will they all sink into the dust together'? Whereas Stephen talks metaphorically of the 'mildew of time [...] stealing over the Waverley Novels', a set of those novels literally becomes mildewed in 'Time Passes': 'black as ravens once', they were 'now white-stained, breeding pale mushrooms and secreting furtive spiders' (152).[36] Stephen draws a conceit in which Scott's novels are likened to the carved cornices at his house at Abbotsford, which look as though they are made out of durable oak, but are in fact composed of insubstantial plaster of Paris. 'The plaster looks as well as the carved oak for a time', writes Stephen,

> but the day speedily comes when the sham crumbles into ashes, and Scott's knights and nobles, like his carved cornices, become dust in the next generation. It is hard to say it, and yet we fear it must be admitted, that many of those historical novels, which once charmed all men, and for which we still have a lingering affection, are rapidly converting themselves into mere débris of plaster of Paris.[37]

Woolf plays on her father's conceit in 'Time Passes'. On a visit to the house, Mrs McNab notices that the books 'were mouldy' and 'needed to be laid out on the grass in the sun; there was plaster fallen in the hall' (147–8). The contiguity in her thought between the moulding books and the fallen plaster echoes Stephen's figurative association between Scott's novels and crumbling plaster of Paris. The decay of the novels in 'Time Passes' suggests that Leslie Stephen's and Mr Ramsay's fears about the decline of Scott's reputation are being realized.

---

[33] Carlyle, 'Scott', 168, 222.
[34] Stephen, 'Scott', 137.
[35] Leslie Stephen, 'Some Words About Sir Walter Scott', in *Hours in a Library* (London: Smith, Elder, 1874), 218–55, 241, 250.
[36] Stephen, 'Scott', 138.
[37] Stephen, 'Scott', 156–7.

Yet more radically, 'Time Passes' intimates the redundancy of Scott's type of historical novel, and Carlyle's great men version of history which they inspired. It is not simply the case that Leslie Stephen's and Mr Ramsay's anxieties about Scott's reputation are confirmed within the framework of a great man conception of history, but rather that this entire framework is put into question. Through a shift of scale that is comparable to those undertaken by the Annalistes, 'Time Passes' subverts the sort of narrative that characterizes Scott's action-packed historical novels and Carlyle's dramatic novelistic histories. Functioning as a feminist scale critique, this shift undermines great men conceptions of history, and the gender ideologies which they support.

'Time Passes'

In 'Time Passes', Woolf breaks with the narrative conventions that underpin great men conceptions of history in a manner that resembles the Annalistes' break with traditional narrative history. Braudel adhered to 'traditional history'—or what he calls *l'histoire événementielle*, the history of events—in the third part of his *Mediterranean*. This is a history that employs narrative and is concerned with individuals and events.[38] Yet he departs from such a conception of history in the first two parts of his work, which are concerned with long and medium timespans. Similarly, 'Time Passes' differs from Scott's historical novels and Carlyle's novelistic histories in being almost devoid of individual characters and events. In both *To the Lighthouse* and the *Mediterranean*, the departure from traditional conceptions of history is marked by a move away from traditional narrative, and a concern with different scales and types of time.

Like the sections of Braudel's *Mediterranean*, the sections of *To the Lighthouse* are based around different timescales. 'The Window' and 'The Lighthouse' both describe what happens over one day, whereas the shorter 'Time Passes' covers the intervening ten-year period. Paul Ricoeur points out that Braudel's conceptualization of multiple times of history is marked by a surprising 'lack of rigor': for example, he not only speaks of short time and long time—that is, of quantitative differences—but also of rapid and slow time.[39] In *To the Lighthouse*, the short timespans of 'The Window' and 'The Lighthouse' most closely resemble those of Braudel's *histoire événementielle*. By contrast, 'Time Passes' stretches (quantitatively) over a period of ten years, which is the typical duration of a conjuncture in Braudel's medium-term history, although the slow movements and processes traversing this interval are qualitatively more like those of the *longue durée*.

[38] Braudel, *Mediterranean*, 21.
[39] Paul Ricoeur, *Time and Narrative*, trans. Kathleen McLaughlin and David Pellauer, 3 vols (Chicago: University of Chicago Press, 1984–8), I, 103–04.

As well as being set over different timescales, the sections of *To the Lighthouse* convey the passing of contrasting sorts of time. 'The Window' and 'The Lighthouse' convey the experience of a lived, phenomenological time. In his celebrated analysis of the brown stocking episode in 'The Window', Erich Auerbach discerns the representation of different 'time strata' as one of Woolf's main narrative innovations: an 'insignificant exterior occurrence releases ideas and chains of ideas which cut loose from the present of the exterior occurrence and range freely through the depths of time'. These time strata represent 'movements within the consciousness of individual personages', and intimate the passing of an 'interior time'.[40] In 'The Window', this lived time is structured principally by expectation. Woolf wrote in an early plan for the first section of the novel that 'there should be a sense of waiting, of expectation: the child waiting to go to the lighthouse: the woman anticipating the return of the couple'.[41] By contrast, and creating a symmetrical pattern, lived time in 'The Lighthouse' is structured more by memory, as Lily and Mr Ramsay remember their previous visits and the losses they have sustained. The narrative conveys a sense of time passing as events held in expectation become present before fading into memory. For example, Mrs Ramsay's expectation of Paul and Minta's return from the beach with possible news of their engagement is fulfilled at dinner, after which the scene fades in memory: 'she waited for a moment longer in a scene which was vanishing even as she looked [...] it had become, she knew, giving it one last look over her shoulder, already the past' (121).

By contrast, 'Time Passes' intimates the passing of a cosmological time, divorced from the lived time of humans. While the phenomenological time of the first and last sections requires a subject to experience it, such a subject is markedly absent from much of 'Time Passes'. There is no one to hear the storms from the upper rooms of the empty house: '[l]istening (had there been anyone to listen) [...] only gigantic chaos streaked with lightning could have been heard' (146–7). The absence of people is made painfully apparent by a pair of shoes, a shooting cap, some faded skirts, and coats in wardrobes that have been shed and left: 'those alone kept the human shape and in the emptiness indicated how once they were filled and animated' (141). Yet time still passes. The cosmos to which this corrupting and decaying cosmological time belongs is portrayed as wild and chaotic, indifferent to humans: winds and waves 'lunged and plunged in the darkness or the daylight (for night and day, month and year ran shapelessly together) in idiot games, until it seemed as if the universe were battling and tumbling, in brute confusion and wanton lust aimlessly by itself' (147). The dissolution of the temporal markers of night and day, month and year, suggests a non-human form of time that threatens the very possibility of narration. Indeed, while 'Time Passes' conveys the

---

[40] Erich Auerbach, *Mimesis: The Representation of Reality in Western Literature*, trans. Willard R. Trask (Princeton: Princeton University Press, 2013), 546, 540, 529.
[41] Virginia Woolf, *To the Lighthouse: The Original Holograph Draft*, ed. Susan Dick (London: Hogarth Press, 1983), 2.

passing of a different sort of time from the other two sections of the novel, it also resembles Braudel's medium- and long-term history in its marginalization of the individual and the event.

'Time Passes' is marked by a disappearance of the novelistic event which parallels the disappearance of the historical event in the first two parts of Braudel's *Mediterranean*. Auerbach notes that one of Woolf's distinctive narrative techniques is to hold to 'minor, unimpressive, random events'.[42] 'The Window' and 'The Lighthouse' are full of such seemingly trivial everyday events: Mrs Ramsay measures a stocking; Lily Briscoe paints her picture; William Bankes is persuaded to dine in company at the house. By contrast, there are almost no events in 'Time Passes': '[n]othing stirred in the drawing-room or in the dining-room or on the staircase' (138). Like the semi-stillness and silent depths of Braudel's eventless history, nothing 'it seemed could [...] disturb the swaying mantle of silence' in the 'empty room' of the deserted house (141). When something does occur, it is so unusual that it highlights the long stretches of time in which nothing happens: '[o]nce only a board sprang on the landing' (142). Similarly,

> once in the middle of the night with a roar, with a rupture, as after centuries of quiescence, a rock rends itself from the mountain and hurtles crashing into the valley, one fold of the shawl loosened and swung to and fro. (142)

The simile evokes slow processes of geological change, such as those that occur over Braudel's *longue durée*. Yet the 'roar' and 'rupture', while perhaps suitable descriptions for the fall of a rock down a mountainside, are absurdly hyperbolic for the fall of the fold of a shawl; once again, they serve to throw into relief the silence and 'centuries of quiescence' against which they make such a contrast. Such eventlessness pushes narrative to its limit. Aristotle defines plot as 'the combination of the incidents, or things done in the story', yet there are almost no incidents to speak of in 'Time Passes'.[43]

The use of square brackets in 'Time Passes' further diminishes the importance of the event. The seven sets of square brackets contain descriptions of what would count as events in a traditional novelistic narrative, ranging from the trivial (Mr Carmichael blows out his candle) to the marriage and deaths of main characters in the novel. Famously, the death of Mrs Ramsay, the principal character of 'The Window', is reported in the subordinate clause of a sentence that is set within square brackets:

> [Mr. Ramsay stumbling along a passage stretched his arms out one dark morning, but, Mrs. Ramsay having died rather suddenly the night before, he stretched his arms out. They remained empty.] (140)

[42] Auerbach, *Mimesis*, 546.
[43] Aristotle, *Poetics*, trans. I. Bywater, in *The Complete Works of Aristotle*, ed. Jonathan Barnes, 2 vols (Princeton: Princeton University Press, 1984), I, 2316–40, 2320.

That such an event is reported in square brackets marks it off from the rest of 'Time Passes', and suggests that it is of less importance, or does not properly belong there. The presentation of Mrs Ramsay's death might be compared to that of Philip II in Braudel's *Mediterranean*. As the climax of the last part of the book, Braudel describes Philip's painful attacks of illness and eventual public death in the Escorial on 13 September 1598, after which news of this event travelled to every corner of the world. However, Braudel concludes his work by pointing out that, although Philip's death features with propriety in a narrative *histoire événementielle*, it is less significant on the other levels of history, and would barely appear in the first two parts of the work:

> the long agony which ended in September, 1598 was not a great event in Mediterranean history; [we should] reflect once more on the distance separating biographical history from the history of structures and even more from the history of geographical areas.[44]

Individuals such as Philip II, who play such an important role in short-term narrative history, largely disappear in medium- and long-term history, dissolved into the anonymous statistical data of conjunctural history, or as passing shadows on the slow-changing geological landscape. Just as the death of Philip II hardly features in the first two parts of the *Mediterranean*, so the death of Mrs Ramsay appears only parenthetically in the almost eventless middle section of *To the Lighthouse*.

Congruent with Woolf's bracketing of events, the First World War appears only obliquely in 'Time Passes'. Early on, war is evoked by the airs which drift through the house asking of objects 'Were they allies? Were they enemies', and by the comparison of autumn trees to the tattered military flags that hang in cathedrals (138–9). Later, and shortly before Andrew Ramsay's being killed by a shell in France is reported in square brackets, there are hints of gunfire:

> there came later in the summer ominous sounds like the measured blows of hammers dulled on felt, which, with their repeated shocks still further loosened the shawl and cracked the tea-cups. (145)

The 'ominous sounds' intimate distant gunfire, yet if there is a battle, it is not narrated as an event that forms part of the story: its presence is registered only indirectly, through the tremors that loosen the shawl and crack the tea-cups. Similarly, a warship appears briefly on the scene, as 'the silent apparition of an ashen-coloured ship [...] come, gone; there was a purplish stain upon the bland surface of the sea as if something had boiled and bled, invisibly, beneath' (146).

---

[44] Braudel, *Mediterranean*, 1237.

The 'purplish stain' suggests that a ship has been sunk, but the story of the naval engagement, if it ever happened, is not told. Woolf's treatment of war resembles that of Braudel. As staples of *histoire événementielle*, battles, campaigns, and wars feature prominently in the third part of the *Mediterranean*. For example, Braudel recounts the defeat of the Turkish fleet in the naval battle at Lepanto on 7 October 1571, which he describes as 'the most spectacular military event in the Mediterranean during the entire sixteenth century'. Yet despite its spectacle, the event had few consequences, and comes to stand as 'a glaring example of the very limitations of "l'histoire événementielle".[45] For Braudel, battles form part of the surface agitation of narrative history, and barely make an impact on the slow moving currents of history that flow beneath.[46] In the eventless passages of Braudel's medium- and long-term history and Woolf's 'Time Passes', battles and wars do not feature as historical or novelistic events, but appear only indirectly, as the fluctuations of an economy, or as the tinkling of glasses in a cabinet.

Woolf's displacement of individuals and events subverts great men conceptions of history and their gender ideologies. James Haule regrets that Woolf excised various references to the war between draft versions of 'Time Passes', and interprets this as a cautious retreat from an antimilitaristic feminism.[47] Yet this is to overlook the fact that the section's ideology is registered more in its form than in its content. Battles and war may provide rich narrative material, but Woolf refuses to be drawn by the lures of what Carlyle calls 'remarkable action'. Instead, by departing from the narrative conventions of Scott's historical novels and Carlyle's novelistic histories, 'Time Passes' challenges the gender roles that are shaped by great men conceptions of history in the other parts of the novel: Mr Ramsay as a hero, and Mrs Ramsay and the other women as what in *A Room of One's Own* are called 'looking-glasses', whose purpose is to reflect the figure of man 'at twice its natural size'.[48] Carlyle celebrates what he portrays as the universality of hero-worship: it may be that the reputation of a particular man falls over time, but the fact of hero-worship is, he claims in his essay on Scott, 'perennial', a 'rock that will endure while man endures'.[49] On the contrary, 'Time Passes' suggests that veneration of great men is susceptible to change and decay over time.

---

[45] Braudel, *Mediterranean*, 1088.

[46] Braudel figures historical events as 'surface disturbances, crests of foam that the tides of history carry on their strong backs' (*Mediterranean*, 21).

[47] James Haule, '*To the Lighthouse* and the Great War: The Evidence of Virginia Woolf's Revisions of "Time Passes"', in *Virginia Woolf and War: Fiction, Reality and Myth*, ed. Mark Hussey (Syracuse: Syracuse University Press, 1991), 164–79, 166.

[48] Woolf, *Room*, 45. Woolf's narrator makes explicit the connection between gender roles in patriarchal society and war, commenting that '[w]hatever may be their use in civilized societies, mirrors are essential to all violent and heroic action. That is why Napoleon and Mussolini both insist so emphatically upon the inferiority of women, for if they were not inferior, they would cease to enlarge' (46).

[49] Carlyle, 'Scott', 168.

In the absence of individuals and events, 'Time Passes' uses quasi-plot to fore-ground other sorts of non-human agency. Here, Woolf's approach to narrative differs from that of the Annalistes. Ricoeur points out that the Annalistes tend to use 'narrative history' and 'history of events' as synonymous expressions, and take it as given that the fate of narrative is sealed at the same time as that of events.[50] By contrast, Woolf experiments with types of narrative that lack events. In this regard, 'Time Passes' is similar to other experiments that Woolf undertook in her fiction: the descriptions of a flower-bed in the short story 'Kew Gardens' (1919); the inter-ludes that fall between the soliloquies in *The Waves*; and (as we shall see) stretches of Miss La Trobe's pageant in *Between the Acts*. These narratives tend to use switches of focalization to adopt seemingly non-human perspectives, and to por-tray scenes in which there are no humans or events. Breaking with the traditional humanistic concerns of fiction, they might be said to contain 'quasi-characters' that participate in 'quasi-plots'. In 'Time Passes', a cast of quasi-characters takes the place of humans in the empty house. Airs, with the ability to look and breathe, drift around the house: 'questioning and wondering', they 'mounted the staircase and nosed round bedroom doors' (138). The seasons are also anthropomorphized: winter 'holds a pack' of nights, and 'deals them equally, evenly, with indefatigable fingers'; later, spring 'threw her cloak about her, veiled her eyes, averted her head' (139, 144). Other quasi-characters are invoked such as divine goodness, imagined sleepers, Nature, and the lighthouse beam. To use Sultzbach's terms, these nar-rative strategies are anthropomorphic but not anthropocentric: indeed, they are used to decentre the human actors in the novel, and resituate them within a wider range of non-human agencies.[51]

In turn, *To the Lighthouse* provides a model for rethinking agency in the Anthropocene. In the *Mediterranean*, Braudel expresses his dissatisfaction with

> the traditional geographical introduction to history that often figures to little pur-pose at the beginning of so many books, with its descriptions of the mineral deposits, types of agriculture, and typical flora, briefly listed and never mentioned again, as if the flowers did not come back every spring.[52]

Like Braudel's turn to long-durational history, the shift to a longer timescale in 'Time Passes' foregrounds the environment, as the house no longer functions as the passive and inert background to the action of the humans in the novel, but is recognized as the site of a range of human and non-human processes and agen-cies. Paradoxically, the impact of humans on their environment is made apparent by their absence, as the house falls into ruin. A thistle 'thrust itself between the tiles in the larder' and 'swallows nested in the drawing-room'; in the garden, poppies

[50] Ricoeur, *Time and Narrative*, I, 101, 111.
[51] Sultzbach, *Ecocriticism*, 83–4.
[52] Braudel, *Mediterranean*, 20.

'sowed themselves among the dahlias' and 'a fringed carnation flowered among the cabbages' (150). The ruin of the house is imagined progressing further, until the traces of humans would be barely evident, and 'some trespasser, losing his way, could have told only by a red-hot poker among the nettles, or a scrap of china in the hemlock, that here once some one had lived; there had been a house' (151). Like the ruins in Wells's *The Time Machine* (1895) and more recent Anthropocene ruins, the decaying house in 'Time Passes' provides a way of imagining the impact of humans over multiple temporal scales. Yet unlike Wells's universal histories and utopias which anticipate recent attempts to bring about a 'good Anthropocene', *To the Lighthouse* provides a fictional model in which attention to differences between scales precludes a suspect scaling-up of familiar conceptions of heroic (masculinist) agency. Much as Braudel emphasizes that his approach to 'total history' aims to 'bring together in all their multiplicity the different measures of time past, to acquaint the reader with their coexistence, their conflicts and contradictions', so Woolf's fiction draws attention to discontinuities across temporal scales.[53] Rather than aggrandizing humans by imagining their godlike ability to master their environment, Woolf decentres humans, and resituates them within a range of human and non-human agencies.

Of course, to claim that Woolf's fiction reconfigures historical agency and the relationship between human and natural history might be surprising, given the long critical tradition that portrays modernist fiction as turning away from history. Georg Lukács famously traces the demise of the historical novel after Scott, and argues that the project of articulating a relationship to history was taken up by realism, rather than modernism.[54] Perry Anderson and Fredric Jameson extend Lukács's account, marking the nadir of the historical novel after the First World War, before its revival in postmodernism as a symptom of an enfeebled historical consciousness.[55] However, as Diana Wallace argues, these accounts obscure the fact that many women wrote historical novels during the interwar period, and even when they turned away from the genre, they developed what might be recognized as modernist historical fiction.[56] *To the Lighthouse* is a case in point: it self-consciously stages its departure from Scott's historical novels, but only to make a different sort of history appear. Woolf continued to write such fiction, including her last novel, *Between the Acts*. Like *To the Lighthouse*, this novel contains eventless passages that convey the agency of the non-human world. Yet Woolf goes beyond her earlier experiment by using the affordances of drama to explore the relationship between human and natural history at a time of historical crisis.

---

[53] Braudel, *Mediterranean*, 1238.

[54] Georg Lukács, *The Historical Novel*, trans. Hannah and Stanley Mitchell (Lincoln: University of Nebraska Press, 1983).

[55] See Perry Anderson, 'From Progress to Catastrophe', *London Review of Books*, 33/15 (2011), 24–8, and Fredric Jameson, 'The Historical Novel Today, Or, Is it Still Possible', in *The Antinomies of Realism* (London: Verso, 2013), 259–313.

[56] See Diana Wallace, *Writing the Past: Modernism and Historical Fiction*, forthcoming.

The pageant of mutabilitie

Set in an English village that is overshadowed by the threat of another World War, *Between the Acts* (1941) is partly a meditation on history. Miss La Trobe stages a historical pageant that is most immediately, as Jed Esty and Ayako Yoshino make clear, a version of the modern pageant-play. This is a genre that was established by Louis Napoleon Parker in 1905, and includes T. S. Eliot's *The Rock* (1934), and E. M. Forster's *Abinger Pageant* (1934) and *England's Pleasant Land* (1938).[57] Esty shows that this genre allowed late modernists the opportunity to explore bounded senses of English national history and tradition at a time of instability for the British Empire.

However, what has not previously been recognized is that Woolf also engages with an older pageant tradition, and specifically with Mutabilitie's pageant in the Mutabilitie Cantos of Edmund Spenser's *The Faerie Queene* (1596, 1609). Woolf borrows from Spenser the concept of the *aevum*, and the fiction of a changeless nature. The *aevum* was, as Frank Kermode informs us, conceived by scholastic philosophers as an order of duration that lies between time and eternity. It 'does not abolish time or spatialize it; it co-exists with time, and is a mode in which things can be perpetual without being eternal'.[58] In the Mutabilitie Cantos, the *aevum* is the state that helps Nature to triumph (somewhat ambiguously) over Mutabilitie, who had claimed that all is susceptible to change and decay. Similarly, in Miss La Trobe's pageant, nature is portrayed as aeviternal, and remains constant throughout the vicissitudes of history. Although its portrayal is ambivalent, aeviternal nature offers a reassuring sense of stability to those at Pointz Hall who are threatened by the disintegration of the British Empire, the rise of fascism, and the prospect of a violent World War.

In some respects, Woolf's engagement with Spenser's pageant complements her depiction of a modern pageant-play. For example, it helps her to portray the villagers in Miss La Trobe's pageant as unchanging over time, in a manner that reinforces what Esty describes as the 'amnesiac logic' of the Edwardian pageant-play: local history is 'performed in order to suggest that history has not really happened in and to this place'.[59] Yet in other respects, Woolf's return to Spenser's pageant allow her to subvert aspects of the Edwardian pageant-play. Rather than collapsing history, it enables her to portray history as one of repeated patriarchal aggression. And rather than celebrating empire, it allows her to draw attention to a history of colonial violence and dispossession in Ireland.

---

[57] See Jed Esty, *A Shrinking Island: Modernism and National Culture in England* (Princeton: Princeton University Press, 2004), 54–61, and Ayako Yoshino, 'Between the Acts and Louis Napoleon Parker—the Creator of the Modern English Pageant', *Critical Survey*, 15 (2003), 49–60.

[58] Frank Kermode, *The Sense of an Ending: Studies in the Theory of Fiction*, new edn (Oxford: Oxford University Press, 2000), 70–2.

[59] Esty, *Shrinking Island*, 81.

Ultimately, the concept of the *aevum* allows Woolf to explore the relationship between natural and human history. While the fiction of a changeless nature provides comfort to Lucy Swithin in a moment of historical crisis, it operates in a more ambivalent manner to expose some of the destructive ways that nature and history have been intertwined, and to highlight the continuing threats being posed to the countryside. Of course, the idea of a changeless nature appears even more suspect in the context of the Anthropocene: it seems increasingly unlikely that seasons will return in a regular and cyclical fashion, that birds will continue to follow their usual migratory routes, and that many species will escape extinction. In this context, Woolf's novel resonates anew. By evoking the idea of a changeless nature in order to unravel it and expose radical threats to historical continuity, *Between the Acts* provides a way of rethinking agency in the Anthropocene. It is the places where Miss La Trobe's pageant breaks down—the scenes in which time passes but nothing happens onstage, or in which rain and cows unexpectedly intervene— that most effectively decentre the human drama, and convey the agency of the non-human world.

******

Although *The Faerie Queene* has not previously been recognized as a significant intertext for *Between the Acts*, Woolf was familiar with Spenser's epic poem. Having read and taken notes on the poem in 1935, she wrote an essay called 'The Faery Queen', which was first published posthumously. Therein, she remarks that Spenser, though 'remote from us in time, in speech, in convention', yet 'seems to be talking about things that are important to us too', and that in his poetry are 'qualities that agitate living people at the moment'.[60] In *Between the Acts*, *The Faerie Queene* is mentioned as one of the books that Isa notices whilst browsing in the Pointz Hall library.[61] Woolf also writes about Spenser in her late unfinished project, which was to be 'a Common History book'; in particular, he features prominently in 'Anon', which was to be the first chapter of this work.[62]

It is certain that Woolf encountered the Mutabilitie Cantos as part of her reading of *The Faerie Queene*. These Cantos stand in a somewhat vexed relationship to the other parts of the poem. They were first published in 1609 under a title that was probably supplied by their printer, Matthew Lownes: *Two Cantos of Mutabilitie: Which, both for Forme and Matter, appeare to be parcell of some following Booke of the Faerie Queene, Under The Legend of Constancie.*[63] They appear under this title,

[60] Virginia Woolf, 'The Faery Queen', in *The Essays of Virginia Woolf*, ed. Andrew McNeillie and Stuart N. Clarke, 6 vols (London: Hogarth Press, 1986–2011), VI, 487–92, 488, 491.

[61] Virginia Woolf, *Between the Acts*, ed. Mark Hussey (Cambridge: Cambridge University Press, 2011), 14.

[62] See Virginia Woolf, '"Anon" and "The Reader": Virginia Woolf's Last Essays', ed. Brenda R. Silver, *Twentieth Century Literature*, 25 (1979), 356–441, 389–92.

[63] See Jane Grogan, 'Introduction', in *Celebrating Mutabilitie: Essays on Edmund Spenser's Mutabilitie Cantos*, ed. Jane Grogan (Manchester: Manchester University Press, 2010), 1–23, 1, 18.

following the first six books of *The Faerie Queene*, in J. Payne Collier's edition of Spenser's *Works* (1862), which is the edition of Spenser that Woolf used.[64] Woolf quotes two lines from the Mutabilitie Cantos in an early version of 'Anon':

> Spenser heard the rhymers and the mummers [...].
> *And after her came jolly june arrayed*
> *All in greene leaves, as he a player were.*
> He had seen the man at the festival, and noted his green leaves
> when the Queen saw the masque at Kenilworth.[65]

As Brenda Silver points out, the two italicized lines are a quotation from VII.vii.35: they describe the allegorical character 'June', who processes as one of the 'Monthes' in Mutabilitie's pageant.[66] Woolf's comment below, following Collier's gloss, suggests that this character was inspired by a masque that Spenser might have seen at Kenilworth in 1575, at which Queen Elizabeth was present.[67] Yet more than simply showing that Woolf knew the Mutabilitie Cantos, these lines invite a broader comparison between Mutabilitie's pageant and that of Miss La Trobe in *Between the Acts*.

In the Mutabilitie Cantos, Mutabilitie challenges Cynthia and Jove, ambitiously claiming dominion over heaven and earth on the grounds that both are subject to change. Jove agrees to meet her challenge, and their dispute is presided over by 'great dame Nature' on Arlo Hill. In response to Mutabilitie's request, Nature calls forth a pageant of the Seasons, the Months, Day and Night, the Hours, and finally Life and Death, all of which process before the gathered assembly. However, Mutabilitie's challenge is ultimately unsuccessful, and Nature asserts her power over her: 'Cease therefore, daughter, further to aspire,/ And thee content thus to be rul'd by me'. In the two stanzas of the 'unperfite' eighth canto, the poet reflects on Nature's verdict, and although he concedes that Mutabilitie was unworthy to rule Heaven, he holds that 'In all things else she bears the greatest sway'.[68]

In these Cantos, the concept of the *aevum* facilitates Nature's (ambiguous) triumph over Mutabilitie.[69] In his *Summa Theologiae* (1274), Thomas Aquinas advanced the concept of the *aevum* as a third order of duration that 'lies somewhere between eternity and time'.[70] It provided him with a rationale for the

[64] *Works of Edmund Spenser*, ed. J. Payne Collier, 5 vols (London: Bell and Daldy, 1862), IV, 241–86, 241. All references are to this edition.
[65] Woolf, 'Anon', 416–7, my italics.
[66] Silver, 'Anon', 417; Spenser, *Faerie*, VII.vii.35, in *Works*, IV, 274.
[67] See Silver, 'Anon', 417.
[68] Spenser, *Faerie*, VII.vii.5, VII.vii.59, VII.viii.1, in *Works*, IV, 263, 284, 285.
[69] See Kermode, *Ending*, 70–81, and Richard A. McCabe, *The Pillars of Eternity: Time and Providence in 'The Faerie Queene'* (Blackrock: Irish Academic Press, 1989), 36–8, 127–30, 132–53.
[70] Thomas Aquinas, *Summa Theologiae: Questions on God*, ed. Brian Davies and Brian Leftow (Cambridge: Cambridge University Press, 2006), 101.

peculiar mode of existence of angels, who are neither eternal nor fully temporal: though immutable as to substance, they are capable of change by acts of will and intellect. The concept of the *aevum* soon acquired political and juristic functions outside the narrow confines of scholastic philosophy, and thereby took on a politics of time. Notably, it was employed in the doctrine of 'the King's Two Bodies'. According to this legal theory, the king's 'natural body' was distinguished from his 'body politic'; while the former was time-bound, the latter was conceived as aeviternally perpetual, giving rise to the idea that the monarch 'never dies'. As Ernst Kantorowicz puts it, the body politic of kingship 'represents, like the angels, the Immutable within Time'.[71] Spenser uses the concept in *The Faerie Queene*. In her verdict on the dispute at Arlo Hill, Nature concedes that all things are subject to change, yet rejects Mutabilitie's arguments by, as Colin McCabe puts it, 'discovering intimations of eternity within the recurrent cycles of generation, decay and death'. Her verdict echoes the presentation of the Garden of Adonis in the third book of *The Faerie Queene* which is, as McCabe points out, Spenser's 'most subtle and imaginative exploration of the *aevum*'.[72] That is, Spenser's Nature inhabits the *aevum*, and is like Adonis in being 'eterne in mutabilitie'.[73]

Spenser's aeviternal Nature finds an analogue in *Between the Acts*. 'Nature' is not personified in Miss La Trobe's pageant, but, as the Rev. Streatfield astutely points out, 'nature takes her part' (138). Notably, to the excitement of the audience, 'real swallows darted across the sheet' during the Victorian picnic scene; they return later in the 'Present Day' scene, dancing '[r]ound and round, in and out they skimmed. Real swallows' (118, 131). Tellingly, when the Rev. Streatfield offers his interpretation that 'nature takes her part', the 'swallows [swept] round him. They seemed cognisant of his meaning' (138). That the same swallows appear in scenes representing different historical ages forges a sense of continuity over time. That is, swallows synecdochically stand for a nature that triumphs over mutability.

Lucy Swithin embraces the sense of continuity that the swallows bring. During one of the pageant's intervals, she watches the swallows swooping from rafter to rafter in the barn, and remarks how they 'come every year [...] the same birds' from Africa, '[a]s they had come, she supposed, when the barn was a swamp' (74–5). She extends her conceit across the whole stretch of geological time about which she has been reading in her Wellsian *Outline of History*:

'Swallows,' said Lucy, holding her cup, looking at the birds. Excited by the company they were flitting from rafter to rafter. Across Africa, across France they had come to nest here. Year after year they came. Before there was a channel, when the earth, upon which the Windsor chair was planted, was a riot of rhododendrons,

[71] See Ernst H. Kantorowicz, *The King's Two Bodies: A Study in Medieval Political Theology* (Princeton: Princeton University Press, 1997), 8, 171.
[72] McCabe, *Pillars*, 208, 138.
[73] Spenser, *Faerie*, III.vi.47, in *Works*, II, 469.

and humming birds quivered at the mouths of scarlet trumpets, as she had read
that morning in her Outline of History, they had come. (79)

By linking the remote geological past to the present day, the swallows provide Lucy
with a reassuring sense of historical continuity. The great changes that the Earth
has undergone in this period, conveyed by Lucy's imaginative juxtaposition of a
riotous primeval forest and the Windsor chair that is currently urbanely planted
on the lawn at Pointz Hall, throw into relief a deeper continuity of nature: that of
swallows migrating year after year from Africa. Her idea that 'the same birds' have
been coming since the remote past is the idea of an aeviternally perpetual nature,
which corresponds to Nature's aeviternal existence in *The Faerie Queene*.

Mrs Manresa is sceptical of Lucy's conceit. She 'smiled benevolently, humour-
ing the old lady's whimsy. It was unlikely, she thought, that the birds were the
same' (74). In one sense, Mrs Manresa is quite correct: it cannot literally be the
same birds that have been coming for thousands of years. Yet in another sense, her
remark overlooks the permanence of birds when they are conceived of as subsisting in the *aevum*. Aeviternal swallows may, like Adonis in his garden, and like the
monarch according to the theory of the king's two bodies, 'never die'. Lucy's conceit
thereby accords subtly with the pageant, and its fiction of an aeviternal nature.

The swallows in *Between the Acts* suggest a continuity and stability within history, which is nevertheless overshadowed by the prospect of a devastating war.
In the 'Present Day' scene of the pageant, the swallows seem to foretell peace and
prosperity:

[t]he swallows—or martins were they?—The temple-haunting martins who
come, have always come [...] Yes, perched on the wall, they seemed to foretell
what after all the *Times* was saying yesterday. Homes will be built. Each flat with
its refrigerator, in the crannied wall. Each of us a free man; plates washed by
machinery; not an aeroplane to vex us; all liberated; made whole. (131)

That the swallows—or martins—'have always come', suggests again the idea of an
aeviternal nature. They promise a continued stability into the future, by seeming to
foretell the previous day's optimistic news stories: that there will not be war ('[e]ach
of us a free man'), but instead economic growth and prosperity ('[h]omes will be
built'). Of course, such optimism is misplaced, given the subsequent outbreak of
war. This irony is intensified by the mention of martins. As Gillian Beer notes, the
'temple-haunting martins' are an allusion to *Macbeth*, and to the 'temple-haunting
martlet', which is interpreted to be a good omen by Banquo, shortly before the
King is murdered.[74] To redouble the irony in *Between the Acts*, while the swallows

---

[74] Gillian Beer, *Virginia Woolf: The Common Ground* (Edinburgh: Edinburgh University Press,
1996), 171; the allusion is to *Macbeth*, 1.vi.4.

or martins seem to foretell that there will be 'not an aeroplane to vex us', this turns out not to be the case. Later in the pageant, twelve 'aeroplanes in perfect formation' interrupt the Rev. Streatfield's speech, and foreshadow war (138).

The combination of aeviternal continuity and a devastating war in *Between the Acts* is fully consonant. As Kermode and McCabe point out, the concept of the *aevum* played an important role in historiography: it was employed to harmonize Aristotelian cycles of recurrent events with linear Church history that was given pattern by an ending—apocalypse.[75] Indeed, this is the shape of history in the Mutabilitie Cantos. Nature both asserts an aeviternal permanence, and points forward to the eschaton.[76] Similarly, in *Between the Acts*, the aeviternal continuity of nature symbolized by the swallows is combined with the prospect of war, which at times assumes apocalyptic proportions. William Dodge speaks bluntly to Isa of '"[t]he doom of sudden death hanging over us [...] There's no retreating and advancing"' (83). More subtly, apocalypse also appears in a darkly comic mode. Through an ambiguity between the discourse time and the story time of the pageant, Giles perhaps inadvertently wishes for there to be no future:

> 'Another interval,' Dodge read out, looking at the programme.
> 'And after that, what?' asked Lucy.
> 'Present time. Ourselves,' he read.
> 'Let's hope to God that's the end,' said Giles gruffly. (126–7)

The same ambiguity between the end of the pageant and the end of the world allows for further comedy:

> [i]t was an awkward moment. How to make an end? [...] Then there was a scuffle behind the bush; a preliminary, premonitory scratching. A needle scraped a disc; chuff, chuff chuff; then having found the rut, there was a roll and a flutter which portended 'God ...' (they all rose to their feet) 'Save the King'. (139–40)

Here, the 'roll and a flutter' herald either the playing of the National Anthem, or, as the sounding of the trumpets of the seven angels, apocalypse. Similarly, the word 'God' is either the first word of the National Anthem, or it refers to God, and thereby suggests the second coming and the end of history.[77] Aeviternal nature thereby offers a picture of constancy which is fully compatible with an end to time in both *The Faerie Queene* and *Between the Acts*.

---

[75] See Kermode, *Ending*, 68, 74, and McCabe, *Pillars*, 36–7.
[76] Spenser, *Faerie*, VII.vii.59, in *Works*, IV, 284.
[77] See Revelation 8:6.

Gender and the politics of a changeless nature

While Miss La Trobe's pageant portrays nature as subsisting in the *aevum*, Woolf was acutely aware of the abusive roles that 'nature', and particularly changeless nature, could be made to play with gender. In *Three Guineas* (1938), she turns a critical eye to the concept of 'Nature', and its deployment in misogynistic arguments, such as those that sought to deny women the right to a university education: 'Nature was called in; Nature it was claimed who is not only omniscient but unchanging, had made the brain of woman of the wrong shape or size'. Even once admitted to the universities, it was claimed that the brain of woman was 'not the creative brain; the brain that can bear responsibility and earn the higher salaries'.[78] Sexual difference is here inscribed in an unchangeable nature, and used as a pretext for keeping women out of the universities and out of the professions.

Sexual difference, supposedly inscribed in nature, took a particularly alarming turn under fascist regimes. Woolf's narrator remarks in a note to *Three Guineas* that:

> [t]he nature of manhood and the nature of womanhood are frequently defined both by Italian and German dictators. Both repeatedly insist that it is the nature of man and indeed the essence of manhood to fight. Hitler, for example, draws a distinction between 'a nation of pacifists and a nation of men'. Both repeatedly insist that it is the nature of womanhood to heal the wounds of the fighter.[79]

The gender roles constructed by fascism, then made out to be 'natural'—man as fighter, and woman as healer—are pernicious, and Woolf's narrator welcomes the contestation by pacifist movements of the supposedly '"natural and eternal law"' that man is a fighter. The narrator is similarly undaunted by Julian Huxley's warning, in his *Essays in Popular Science* (1926), that 'man and woman differ in every cell of their body in regard to the number of their chromosomes [...] [which] have been shown by the last decade's work to be the bearers of heredity', and that 'any considerable alteration of the hereditary constitution is an affair of millennia, not of decades'.[80] Nature here is viewed not as eternal and unchanging, but, through the lens of twentieth-century evolutionary biology, as permitting hereditary change at an extremely slow rate over the course of millennia. Undeterred, Woolf's narrator comments wryly in response that 'as science also assures us that our life on

---

[78] Woolf, *Guineas*, 359–60.
[79] Woolf, *Guineas*, 412.
[80] Woolf, *Guineas*, 412, 410–11, 413; the quotations are from Julian Huxley, *Essays in Popular Science* (London: Chatto & Windus, 1926), 64–5. In context, Huxley is rejecting Mathilde and Mathias Vaerting's view in their *The Dominant Sex: A Study in the Sociology of Sex Differentiation*, tr. Eden and Cedar Paul (London: George Allen and Unwin, 1923), that the 'biological differences between the sexes in man are negligible' (63).

earth is "an affair of millennia, not of decades", some alteration in the hereditary constitution may be worth attempting.'[81]

Throughout, Woolf is acutely critical of conceptions of nature that are used to legitimate gender inequality, or to define the roles of men and women in a bellicose fascist society. Such conceptions of nature are to be challenged. 'And must we not', she writes, 'and do we not change this unalterable nature?'[82] The paradoxical formulation of this defiant call to change the unchangeable invites suspicion concerning formulations of an unchangeable nature: such a 'nature' turns out to be artifice, and moreover, one that can be challenged and rejected.[83]

The aeviternally changeless nature depicted by Miss La Trobe's pageant is similarly problematic. Although Lucy finds the fiction that the same swallows have been visiting since the time when the barn was a swamp a comforting one, swallows also possess more sinister connotations in the novel. As Jane Marcus, Gillian Beer, and Jane de Gay make clear, swallows are associated in the novel with rape, violence, and murder. All of these critics draw attention to the novel's allusions to Algernon Swinburne's poem 'Itylus', which is based on the myth of Procne and Philomena.[84] As Bart leaves the barn where Lucy has been contemplating the swallows, he mutters the first line of 'Itylus'—'"Swallow, my sister, O sister swallow"'—a line that he repeats and modulates when Lucy joins him in his room (80). Likely reflecting Bart's perspective through free indirect discourse, Lucy is figured as a swallow: she 'perched on the edge of a chair like a bird on a telegraph wire before starting for Africa' (84–5). His murmuring the first line of Swinburne's poem encourages the identification of Lucy with Procne, who in the myth was transformed into a swallow after her sister Philomena was raped by Tereus. In turn, as Marcus and de Gay point out, the allusions to 'Itylus' echo the account of the rape of a girl by guardsmen that Isa reads in *The Times*, and which haunts her throughout the day.[85]

The violent associations that surround swallows warrant caution for the aeviternal nature depicted by the pageant. Lucy sees in the swallows a continuity of

---

[81] Woolf, *Guineas*, 413.

[82] Woolf, *Guineas*, 361.

[83] Similarly, on St Paul's use of the 'argument from nature', Woolf's narrator writes: '[t]he argument from nature may seem to us susceptible of amendment; nature, when allied with financial advantage, is seldom of divine origin' (*Guineas*, 392).

[84] Marcus suggests that Woolf rewrote Swinburne's poem in *Between the Acts*, retrieving the myth's 'original claim of the power of sisterhood over the patriarchal family', and turning it into a tale of 'sorority and revenge for rape' (*Virginia Woolf and the Languages of Patriarchy* (Bloomington: Indiana University Press, 1987), 76, 80, 93). Beer draws attention to Swinburne's poem, and points out that the swallows 'who sweep constantly across the barn recall the myth of Procne and Philomela in Ovid's *Metamorphoses*', and thereby allude 'to rape, violation, and murder' (*Common Ground*, 136–41). de Gay considers the allusions to 'Itylus' alongside alternative versions of the Procne and Philomela myth (*Virginia Woolf's Novels and the Literary Past* (Edinburgh: Edinburgh University Press, 2006), 205–7).

[85] See Marcus, *Patriarchy*, 93–4; de Gay, *Literary Past*, 205. As Stuart Clarke has shown, the rape about which Isa reads was a real case, which occurred on 27 April 1938, and was reported in *The Times*: see his 'The Horse with a Green Tail', *Virginia Woolf Miscellany*, 34 (1990), 3–4.

nature, and her own figuration as a swallow places her in this order. However, as Bart's association of Lucy with Procne suggests, this supposedly natural order is one of patriarchal aggression and rape. Just as much as the 'natural and eternal law' that fascists invoke to claim that man is essentially a fighter, the aeviternal continuity of nature in Miss La Trobe's pageant naturalizes the patriarchal order and its incipient violence. Here, Woolf might be thought of as responding to the complex portrayal of nature in the Mutabilitie Cantos. While Nature ostensibly triumphs over Mutabilitie, it is not the case that Spenser was simply a panegyrist of a timeless *aevum*. On the contrary, the inset tale of Faunus and Molanna keeps sexual violence in view, as well as exploring punitive chastity through the figure of Diana. There are parallels between Faunus seeing Diana bathing naked and Woolf's 'brawl in the barrack room when they stripped her naked', and between Diana and Lucy Swithin as vengeful figures 113). Nature is aeviternally constant in the Mutabilitie Cantos and *Between the Acts*, but it is by no means an idealized nature. Rather, in both cases, it is one of incipient sexual violence.

In *Between the Acts*, Isa's circumspect attitude towards the idea of an aeviternal nature creates a further ambivalence towards such a fiction. Unlike Lucy, Isa does not embrace the idea. During one of the pageant's intervals, she wanders through the gardens at Pointz Hall, and picks a rose. In one of her poetic reveries, she thinks of herself wandering where

> there grows nothing for the eye. No rose. To issue where? In some harvestless dim field where no evening lets fall her mantle; nor sun rises. All's equal there. Unblowing, ungrowing are the roses there. Change is not; nor the mutable and lovable. (111–12)

The 'harvestless dim field' that she imagines displays the characteristics of the *aevum*. In language that echoes that of the Mutabilitie Cantos, the field is depicted as one where '[c]hange is not; nor the mutable'. It has a peculiar temporal character, and is seemingly stuck in a state of stasis: 'no evening lets fall her mantle', and no 'sun rises', as if the dim field existed in a state of perpetual dusk. Through its stasis, Isa's field resembles the Garden of Adonis (III.vi) in *The Faerie Queene*. In her reading notes on Spenser's poem, Woolf copied the following lines which describe the Garden: 'There is continual Spring, & harvest there/ Continual', after which she wrote: 'why this beauty?'[86] These lines depict the garden as one in which 'Spring' and 'harvest' never pass, but coexist, both 'meeting at one tyme'. They reflect the garden's aeviternity which, as a state that lies somewhere between time and eternity, permits such a changeless coexistence of different times. Woolf echoes and modulates Spenser's lines. That Isa's field is 'harvestless' suggests a

---

[86] Woolf, 'Notebook XLV', 15. More fully, the lines that Woolf quotes read: 'There is continuall Spring, and harvest there/ Continuall, both meeting at one tyme' (Spenser, *Faerie*, III.vi.42, in *Works*, II, 458–9).

similarly aeviternal state in which the passing of the seasons is suspended, but in contrast to the Garden of Adonis where there is 'harvest [...] Continuall', Isa's field is 'harvestless'. Whereas the Garden of Adonis conveys nature's fertility and generative power, Isa's field is one of sterility. In this respect, her field more closely resembles the Bower of Bliss, which Guyon and Palmer visit in the second book of *The Faerie Queene*, and which stands as the sterile counterpart to the Garden of Adonis.

Whereas the Garden of Adonis celebrates the generative power of nature, and the sexual union of Venus and Adonis, the Bower of Bliss poorly imitates nature, and is a place of destructive and fruitless lust. The rose that Isa picks, and the 'roses' that she imagines in her field, resonate with a song that is sung in the Bower of Bliss, the following lines of which Woolf copied in her reading notes on *The Faerie Queene*:

> So passeth, in the passing of a day,
> Of mortall life the leafe, the bud, the flowre,
> Gather therefore the Rose, whilest yet is prime,
> Gather the Rose of love whilest yet is time,
> Whilest loving thou mayst loved be with equall crime.[87]

In *The Faerie Queene*, this *carpe diem* song is fittingly sung as Acrasia lies in a dishevelled state on a 'bed of Roses', having recently seduced a young knight, Verdant.[88] However, in the wider context of the canto, Acrasia's love, and the Bower of Bliss more generally, are shams through which Guyon sees. Unlike the 'goodly flowres' which 'dame Nature' uses to beautify the Garden of Adonis, flowers in the Bower of Bliss are artificial and gaudy.[89] The 'large and spacious plaine' where the Bower is situated is adorned 'too lavishly' by Art with flowers 'as half in scorne/ Of niggard Nature'; their artifice is conveyed by their description as 'painted flowres'.[90] The 'ungrowing' roses of Isa's field are like the painted, artificial flowers of the Bower of Bliss.

Isa's imagination of a 'harvestless dim field' provides a poetic context for her husband's possible infidelity with Mrs Manresa: their meeting in the greenhouse takes on the qualities of Acrasia's seduction of Verdant in the Bower of Bliss.[91] This context is possibly a comforting one for Isa, insofar as it casts Mrs Manresa in the role of Acrasia the enchantress who uses her 'sorceree/ And witchcraft' to seduce

---

[87] Woolf, 'Notebook XLV', 12; Spenser, *Faerie*, II.xii.75, in *Works*, II, 329–30. Woolf omitted the third, fourth, fifth, and seventh lines of the stanza.

[88] Spenser, *Faerie*, II.xii.77, in *Works*, II, 330.

[89] Spenser, *Faerie*, III.vi.30, in *Works*, II, 454–5.

[90] Spenser, *Faerie*, II.xii.50, II.xii.58, in *Works*, II, 321, 324.

[91] Isa is acutely aware of her husband's possible infidelity: 'Isa was immobile, watching her husband. She could feel the Manresa in his wake. She could hear in the dusk in their bedroom the usual explanation. It made no difference; his infidelity—but hers did' (80).

her 'new Lover' (Giles), who thereby becomes less culpable.[92] Yet the harvestless field also provides an image of aeviternal nature as characterized by destructive lust. Shortly before the door to the greenhouse is 'kicked open' and Giles and Mrs Manresa emerge, Isa in her reverie thinks back to 'the brawl in the barrack room when they stripped her naked' (113). The juxtaposition of Giles and Mrs Manresa in the greenhouse, and the girl being raped in the barrack room, intimates that the two situations might be united by a common violence. Isa's image of the harvestless field, combined with the other associations in the novel between swallows and rape, suggests the dangers of the fiction of an aeviternal nature, and, by extension, the dangers of timelessly naturalized gender roles within a supposedly-changeless patriarchal order. An even deeper ambivalence towards the fiction of an aeviternal nature is created in the novel, as sexual aggression is depicted as intertwined with violent imperialism.

Bother in Ireland

Woolf's engagement with *The Faerie Queene* allows her to critique imperialism, in a manner that subverts some features of the Edwardian pageant-play. Esty argues that *Between the Acts* is one of a number of late modernist works that respond to the instability of the British Empire following the Home Rule Crisis of 1912–16 in Ireland, by seeking to imagine postimperial forms of English national history and tradition.[93] Woolf's return to Spenser helps her to negotiate such forms of history. Yet rather than cutting English history free from its moorings in colonial modernity, this return enables her to draw attention to the devastation wrought by plantations in Ireland.

Woolf would have been aware of the Irish setting of the Mutabilitie Cantos, and Spenser's activities as a New English colonial planter. In contrast to Samuel Taylor Coleridge's earlier view that there is a 'marvellous independence and true imaginative absence of all particular space or time' in *The Faerie Queene*, Collier draws attention to the Irish context of the Mutabilitie Cantos in his note to VII.vi.55, in which Diana decides to leave Ireland: 'Since which, those Woods, and all that goodly Chase,/ Doth to this day with Wolves and Thieves abound:/ Which too-too true that lands in-dwellers since have found'.[94] Collier connects this stanza to Spenser's *A View of the Present State of Ireland* (1596), in which 'the massacres committed upon the people of Munster, in Ireland, after the rebellion' are painted 'in the strongest colours'.[95] In his introductory 'Life of Spenser', on which Woolf

[92] Spenser, *Faerie*, II.xii.72, in *Works*, II, 329.
[93] Esty, *Shrinking Island*, 37, 54–61, 85–107.
[94] *Coleridge's Miscellaneous Criticism*, ed. T. M. Raysor (London: Constable, 1936), 36.
[95] Spenser, *Works*, IV, 261.

took notes, Collier elaborates on the Irish context.[96] He points out that Spenser was appointed Secretary of the Council of Munster in 1588, and that the chief object of this council was 'to repair, as far as possible, the ravages of war and rebellion by repeopling the province with persons, especially natives of England, who were willing to embark capital in the improvement of the soil, and in the promotion of civilization among the inhabitants'. He also notes that Spenser acquired his estate at Kilcolman—where the Mutabilitie Cantos are set—after the Desmond Rebellions had been put down.[97] By the time that Spenser returned to Ireland in 1597, rebellion—this time led by Hugh O'Neill—was once again threatening: 'the rebellion in Munster, in which Spenser lost the whole of his property, was on the eve of breaking out'. In his commentary on *A View*, Collier identifies Spenser with Irenius, and draws attention to their plans of 'extreme severity' by which Ireland was to be 'brought into obedience, and kept under subjection'. He holds that Spenser 'rendered himself obnoxious in Ireland': 'no man living could at that time be more odious than Spenser'.[98]

In the Mutabilitie Cantos, Spenser registers his anxieties about the stability of imperial rule in Ireland partly through his deployment of the concept of the *aevum*. Notably, he conveys his disaffected view of royal policy by his depiction of Cynthia in VII.vii.50 and VII.vi.8. These stanzas operate within the paradigm of the doctrine of the monarch's two bodies, but they do not celebrate the queen's permanent self. Rather, they draw attention to the impermanence of the queen's mortal body, in a manner that reflects anxieties about the possibility of a Catholic successor to the ageing and childless Elizabeth. They complement other unflattering portrayals of Elizabeth in the Mutabilitie Cantos, such as Diana's desertion of Ireland in VII.vi.55, which can be read as a covert criticism of Elizabeth's apparent withdrawal from the country, leaving it unprotected and open to rebellion.[99] Nature's ostensible triumph over Mutabilitie is cast into doubt, and the idea of the monarch's aeviternal permanence is exposed as a fragile one. The intimation, particularly when the Cantos are read alongside *A View*, is that a more aggressive colonial policy is needed to ensure peace and stability for the New English in Ireland.

Like Spenser, Woolf uses her pageant to question imperial power, although she does so in a manner that challenges rather than supports colonial aggression. Esty points out that the Edwardian pageant-play was a genre that channelled patriotic sentiment, and was designed 'to make the local past play an inspirational role for

---

[96] See Brenda Silver, *Virginia Woolf's Reading Notebooks* (Princeton: Princeton University Press, 1983), 132, 187.

[97] J. Payne Collier, 'The Life of Spenser', in Spenser, *Works*, I, ix–clxxviii, li, lvii.

[98] Collier, 'Life', cxxxvii–cxxxviii, cxxvii, cxxx–cxxxi.

[99] See Andrew Hadfield, *Edmund Spenser: A Life* (Oxford: Oxford University Press, 2012), 376. In *A View*, Irenius argues that 'the continuall presence of their King' is needed 'to contain the unrulie people from a thousand evill occasions' (*Works*, V, 308).

[...] colonial action': such pageants would typically end with a round of patriotic speeches, and a celebration of the local town's colonial daughter cities.[100] However, the pageant in *Between the Acts* departs from such a template. Colonel Mayhew is disappointed that the British Army is not suitably celebrated: 'Why leave out the British Army? What's history without the Army, eh?' His wife reassures him, pointing out that 'very likely there would be a Grand Ensemble, round the Union Jack, to end with' (113–14). But her expectations are frustrated, and there is no such finale. Instead, imperialism is satirized in the pageant, most thoroughly in the Victorian scene. Therein, Budge the publican appears in the guise of a Victorian constable, who proclaims the wonders of Empire while directing traffic in London. He comically embodies many of the arguments made in *Three Guineas* about the complicity between patriarchy and imperialism. For example, in a bawdy satire, the eminently masculine Budge directs 'the traffic of 'Er Majesty's Empire', proclaiming that all must 'Obey the Rule of my truncheon'. Further, he draws attention to the need of '[t]he ruler of an Empire' to 'keep his eye on the cot; spy too in the kitchen; drawing-room; library', echoing the argument made in *Three Guineas* that imperialism is sustained by an educative regime that moulds women who consciously desire 'our splendid Empire', and unconsciously desire war (116–17).[101]

The critique of imperialism in *Between the Acts* is reflected in its portrayal of a dangerously aeviternal nature. The novel suggests how imperial violence overseas is upheld by supposedly timeless gender roles in patriarchal society at home. For example, as Esty points out, Mrs Manresa acts as 'a trigger for sexual and aggressive impulses' in the novel. She inspires violence in Giles, and rekindles 'youth and empire' in Bart, stirring memories of his past working as a civil servant in India.[102] In an early draft of the novel, Mrs Manresa is described as making rousing speeches at meetings in the country: '"Our brave boys", she would say; and brought the house down'.[103] Such patriotic rhetoric resembles that which is dissected in *Three Guineas*. Therein, the narrator interrogates the use of the possessive adjective 'our' when used in the emotive phrase 'I am fighting to protect our country', arguing that it occludes the fact that this country has been largely owned by men, and that women have been largely denied property, legal protection, and education throughout the greater part of its history. Mrs Manresa's rhetoric is insensitive to any such distinctions. Rather, it exemplifies the sort of patriotic demonstration that the narrator of *Three Guineas* counsels the members of her Society of Outsiders to spurn.[104]

While British imperialism in general is satirized in the Victorian scene of Miss La Trobe's pageant, there is more narrowly a critique of British imperialism in

---

[100] Esty, *Shrinking Island*, 58–9.
[101] Woolf, *Guineas*, 206–08.
[102] Esty, *Shrinking Island*, 89.
[103] Virginia Woolf, *Pointz Hall: The Earlier and Later Typescripts of Between the Acts*, ed. Mitchell A. Leaska (New York: University Publications, 1983), 65.
[104] Woolf, *Guineas*, 311–14.

Ireland. In his role as a constable, Budge flags the need to address problems over-seas: '[s]ome bother it may be in Ireland; Famine. Fenians. What not' (117). He refers to the 'bother' in Ireland in an offhand way: the logic that joins 'Famine' to 'Fenians' is one that is as much alliterative as one that acknowledges any underly-ing connection between famine and resistance to British rule; the whole matter is dismissively undercut by the qualification 'What not'. Nevertheless, the reference to Ireland is notable. Given the Victorian setting of the scene, Budge's mention of 'Famine' is read most naturally in the context of the Great Irish Famine of the 1840s, during which a million people died, and a further 2 million emigrated.[105] The pageant causes its audience to think back to Victorian times: '[a]nd every-where loaves of bread in the gutter. The Irish you know round Covent Garden' (114). Glossing these lines in their edition of the novel, Susan Dick and Mary Mil-lar point out that many Irish emigrants from the Great Famine settled in London, where under English Poor Law they received relief.[106] However, the 'Famine' that Budge mentions can also be read more obliquely in the context of the famine in Munster in the 1580s that followed the crushing of the second Desmond Rebellion, about which Spenser wrote in *A View*. In this work, Irenius describes in harrowing detail how, during the 'late warres of Mounster', many perished 'by the extremitie of famine', until 'in short space there were none almost left, and a most populous and plentifull countrey suddainely left voyde of man and beast'.[107] In an earlier draft of *Between the Acts*, the plight of the Irish emigrants is conveyed even more vividly: '[t]he Irish you know—they gnawed bones in the street'.[108] In keeping with the novel's theme of the repetition of history, the Irish gnawing 'bones in the street' in Victorian London can be seen as a repetition of the earlier famine in Ireland described by Spenser, in which the Irish, looking like 'anatomies of death', were driven to 'eate the dead carrions, happy where they could find them, yea, and one another soone after, insomuch as the very carcasses they spared not to scrape out of their graves'.[109]

Through the juxtaposition of the pageant and the frame narrative, the novel suggests how a history of imperial violence persists in the present. A criticism that Lucy has evidently made of Giles in the past is filtered through his perspective by means of free indirect discourse at lunch. She was

> always, since he had chosen, after leaving college, to take a job in the city, express-ing her amazement, her amusement, at men who spent their lives, buying and selling—ploughs? glass beads was it? or stocks and shares?—to savages who

[105] See David P. Nally, *Human Encumbrances: Political Violence and the Great Irish Famine* (Notre Dame: University of Notre Dame Press, 2011), 2, 8–15, 132–4.
[106] Virginia Woolf, *Between the Acts*, ed. Susan Dick and Mary S. Millar (Oxford: Blackwell, 2002), 160.
[107] Spenser, *Works*, V, 419.
[108] Woolf, *Pointz Hall*, 147.
[109] Spenser, *Works*, V, 419.

wished most oddly—for were they not beautiful naked?—to dress and live like the English? (34)

Even more explicitly in a draft version of this passage, we read that the various items are sold for the 'savages' to 'dress *or plough* like the English'.[110] Here, a comparison might be drawn with Spenser's role as a planter in Ireland, and the way in which English agricultural methods were exported and used as a means of subduing the colonized populace, in a manner that left them particularly vulnerable to the consequences of agricultural failure and famine. Collier drew attention to the connection between imperialism and capitalism in Ireland, by pointing out that Spenser's role as Secretary of the Council of Munster involved repeopling the province with persons who 'were willing to embark capital in the improvement of the soil'. Lucy's comments evoke such a history, and intimate the continuation of such forms of imperialist domination in the present, through Giles's activities as a stockbroker.

Isa's Irish ancestry in the novel can be interpreted as a further subtle critique of British imperialism in Ireland. Unlike the Olivers, who are English, Isa is of Irish descent: she is the 'niece of the two old ladies at Wimbledon who were so proud, being O'Neils, of their descent from the Kings of Ireland' (12). The two unmarried aunts may be being mocked for their inflated sense of self-importance, but the family connection to the Kings of Ireland is a suggestive one. Not only had various of the Uí Néill ruled as kings of Ireland from the eighth century onwards, but Hugh O'Neill's supporters later vindicated his rebellion against the English—in which Spenser's house was burnt—on the grounds that he was rightful heir to the ancient high kingship.[111] Indeed, according to Irenius in *A View*, the 'arch-rebell' Hugh O'Neill desired to become King of Ireland, setting 'before his eyes the hope of a kingdome'.[112] It is fitting that, as a dissenter from Giles and Bart's patriarchal imperialism, Isa should descend from such a family of rebels.

In *Between the Acts*, the associations between nature, sexual violence, and imperialism suggest that the possibility of a future for England not marred by the repetition of war depends on the rejection of imperial and patriarchal violence. As Esty puts it, the novel makes room for a creative vision of English society redeemed from imperial and warmongering politics: a way 'for the pastoral culture of Lucy Swithin to reassert itself against the imperial and patriarchal politics of Bart Oliver'.[113] Yet even Lucy's pastoralism is portrayed as precarious. Indeed, the novel uses the fiction of a changeless nature to explore anxieties about the

[110] Woolf, *Pointz Hall*, 70, my italics.
[111] See Richard A. McCabe, *Spenser's Monstrous Regiment: Elizabethan Ireland and the Poetics of Difference* (Oxford: Oxford University Press, 2002), 36–8.
[112] Spenser, *Works*, V, 428.
[113] Esty, *Shrinking Island*, 94.

preservation of the English countryside, which were increasingly being articulated by early environmental movements.

Preservation of the countryside

In *Between the Acts*, Woolf uses her historical pageant to explore anxieties about the preservation of the English countryside. By evoking a sense of pastoral tradition which is then shown to be under threat in the present, she follows the example of Forster's pageant-plays. For example, his *Abinger Pageant* ends with an epilogue in which the Woodman proclaims:

> Houses, houses, houses! You came from them and you must go back to them. Houses and bungalows, hotels, restaurants and flats, arterial roads, by-passes, petrol pumps and pylons—are these going to be England? Are these man's final triumph? Or is there another England, green and eternal, which will outlast them?[114]

England's Pleasant Land, which was published in book form by Woolf's Hogarth Press in 1940, mobilizes a similar opposition between a bucolic England and the forces of development that threaten to destroy it. In the closing scene, Jerry the Builder unveils his plans to build a housing estate:

> So cut the trees down and clear the site,
> Bungle the bungalows left and right,
> Pile the pylons as high as you can,
> I'm a practical business man![115]

The epilogue leaves the audience with a stark choice:

> Man made the country as he made the town. He took many years to make it, but he can if he chooses destroy it in a few days. He can do this because in the course of centuries he has become strong. How will he use this strength? To spoil the beauty of his native land or to preserve it?[116]

As Andrew Kalaidjian notes, the pageant is a direct call for environmental protection, which was increasingly being sought by British ecologists and environmental activists.[117] The Recorder exhorts the audience to 'save the countryside' through

---

[114] E. M. Forster, *Abinger Harvest* (London: Edward Arnold, 1936), 351, italics removed.
[115] E. M. Forster, *England's Pleasant Land: A Pageant Play* (London: Hogarth Press, 1940), 78.
[116] Forster, *Land*, 79.
[117] Andrew Kalaidjian, *Exhausted Ecologies: Modernism and Environmental Recovery* (Cambridge: Cambridge University Press, 2020), 17.

'good laws rightly applied, through Parliament, through the nation as a whole', and the audience were helpfully provided with a list of relevant preservation societies.[118]

Woolf's pageant follows those of Forster in evoking a vision of a green England, although in doing so, it also reworks Spenser's conception of a changeless nature. Miss La Trobe's pageant conveys a pastoral tradition through the villagers, who are portrayed as being aeviternally perpetual. A chorus of villagers appears throughout the different historical ages depicted by the pageant, winding in and out of the trees. They first appear in the opening scene, which represents the very earliest days of England's past, and return in the Elizabethan, Restoration, and Victorian scenes (57, 90, 100, 115). The villagers sing of the fall of empires and world orders. At the end of the Restoration comedy, they sing: '[p]alaces tumble adown [...] Babylon, Nineveh, Troy ... And Caesar's great house ... all fallen they lie ... Where the plover nests was the arch ... through which the Romans trod'. The ephemerality of these once-powerful empires is reflected in the fragility and transience of the song, which is only semi-audible: '[t]he words died away. Only a few great names—Babylon, Nineveh, Clytemnestra, Agamemnon, Troy—floated across the open space' (101). The image of the plover nesting in the crumbling arch is one of a nature that persists beyond the rise and fall of civilizations. Its sentiment is similar to that expressed by the sentence of Edgar Quinet, (inaccurately) copied by Léon Metchnikoff, which echoes throughout James Joyce's *Finnegans Wake* (1940):

> *Aujourd'hui comme aux temps de Pline et de Columelle la jacinthe se plaît dans les Gaules, la pervenche en Illyrie, la marguerite sur les ruines de Numance et pendant qu'autour d'elles les villes ont changé de maîtres et de noms, que plusieurs sont entrées dans le néant, que les civilisations se sont choquées et brisées, leurs paisibles générations ont traversé les âges et sont arrivées jusqu'à nous, fraîches et riantes comme aux jours des batailles.*[119]

However, while the villagers sing of the fall of empires, they themselves take on a type of permanence that resists the vicissitudes of history. They sing: '[s]ummer and winter, autumn and spring return ... All passes but we, all changes ... but we remain forever the same' (100). That the same chorus returns throughout the different historical ages reinforces the impression of the villagers' changelessness; this

[118] Forster, *Land*, 79, 11.
[119] James Joyce, *Finnegans Wake*, ed. Finn Fordham (Oxford: Oxford University Press, 2012), 281. In a letter of 22 November 1930 to Harriet Shaw Weaver, Joyce wrote in summary of the 'beautiful sentence from Edgar Quinet': 'E. Q. says that the wild flowers on the ruins of Carthage, Numancia etc have survived the political rises and falls of Empires' (*Letters of James Joyce*, ed. Stuart Gilbert, 3 vols (London, 1957), I, 295). As Inge Landuyt and Geert Lernout have shown, Joyce encountered Quinet's sentence through Léon Metchnikoff's *La civilisation et les grands fleuves historiques* (1889): see their 'Joyce's Sources: *Les grands fleuves historiques*', *Joyce Studies Annual*, 6 (1995), 99–137.

continuity is extended to the present day by the fact that the villagers depicted in the pageant are played by present-day village actors. That is, in Miss La Trobe's pageant, the villagers are assimilated to nature against history, and take on an aeviternal permanence, much like that of Lucy's swallows.

The pageant's portrayal of unchanging villagers is complemented by the countryside which forms the backdrop to the drama. Indeed, the inhabitants of Pointz Hall often remark on how little the 'fine view of the surrounding country' has changed since it was described over a hundred years ago:

> The Guide Book still told the truth. 1833 was true in 1939. No house had been built; no town had sprung up. Hogben's Folly was still eminent; the very flat, field-parcelled land had changed only in this—the tractor had to some extent superseded the plough. The horse had gone; but the cow remained. If Figgis were here now, Figgis would have said the same. (38)

Here, superficial changes such as the tractor superseding the plough serve to reveal a deeper continuity in the landscape. Indicating a confidence that there will not be a significant disruption in the future, Lucy believes that this continuity will persist: '"It'll be there", she nodded at the strip of gauze laid upon the distant fields, "when we're not"' (39).

Like Forster's pageants, Miss La Trobe's pageant summons a vision of a green England in order to draw attention to the threats being posed to the countryside by development and suburbanization. As they are assembling to watch the pageant, one of the audience members remarks: 'That hideous new house at Pyes Corner! What an eyesore! And those bungalows!—have you seen 'em?' (55). At the end of the pageant, the megaphonic, loud-speaking voice comments: 'Mr. M's bungalow. A view spoilt for ever. That's murder' (134). This strident judgement is tempered by the light that falls at the end of the pageant and reveals beauty: the 'searching light of evening that reveals depths in water and makes even the red brick bungalow radiant' (140). Miss La Trobe's pageant thereby satirizes and contains the didactic impulses of Forster's pageants, although it still invites its audience to consider issues of historical change in a similar manner. Waiting for the actors to change costume between scenes, members of the audience comment on the actors' 'dressing up', and are led to discuss the question of 'historical change':

> D'you think people change? Their clothes, of course. ... But I meant our selves ... Clearing out a cupboard, I found my father's old top hat. ... But our selves—do we change? (88)

Lucy's opinion is that people do not change. Watching the pageant, she muses that she does not believe that 'there ever were such people' as '[t]he Victorians': '[o]nly you and me and William dressed differently' (125). Lucy embraces the pageant's portrayal of timeless villagers, much as she embraces its reassuring view of the aeviternal permanence of swallows. However, William responds '[y]ou don't believe in history', intimating that he does not share her unhistorical outlook (125). More directly, Giles is infuriated by Lucy's talk of the unchanging view, and is acutely aware of the imminent threat posed to the landscape around Pointz Hall by war: '[a]t any moment guns would rake that land into furrows; planes splinter Bolney Minster into smithereens and blast the Folly' (39).

Although Woolf uses the affordances of drama to evoke a timeless tradition of English pastoralism that is under threat in the present, it is the places where Miss La Trobe's pageant breaks down that best convey the imbrication of human and natural history. Exploiting the tendency of the modern pageant-play to subordinate character to setting through its outdoor staging, Woolf portrays sections of the pageant in which nothing happens:

> Chuff, chuff, chuff went the machine. Could they talk? Could they move? No, for the play was going on. Yet the stage was empty; only the cows moved in the meadows; only the tick of the gramophone needle was heard. The tick, tick, tick seemed to hold them together, tranced. Nothing whatsoever appeared on the stage. (60)

The ticking of the gramophone needle suggests that time is passing, yet the stage remains empty and nothing happens. As in the 'Time Passes' section of *To the Lighthouse*, the absence of individuals and events draws attention to non-human processes and agents: members of the audience find the experience excruciating, but they turn their attention to the cows moving in the fields. A similar effect is achieved when the pageant threatens to stall, only to be rescued by the intervention of the cows:

> Then suddenly, as the illusion petered out, the cows took up the burden. One had lost her calf. In the very nick of time she lifted her great moon-eyed head and bellowed. [...] The cows annihilated the gap; bridged the distance; filled the emptiness and continued the emotion. (101–02)

Rather than serving as the passive backdrop to the human drama that is portrayed onstage, this inversion conveys the agency of the non-human world. Such inversions anticipate those that Bruno Latour sees as brought about by awareness of global warming: 'through a surprising inversion of background and foreground, it is *human* history that has become frozen and *natural* history that is taking on a frenetic pace'.[120] Indeed, Miss La Trobe's pageant already suggests the importance of weather and climate in history. In his introductory note to *England's Pleasant*

---

[120] Bruno Latour, 'Agency at the Time of the Anthropocene', *New Literary History*, 45/1 (2014), 1–18, 12.

Land, Forster regrets that rain jeopardized the performance of his pageant.[121] Yet in *Between the Acts*, an unexpected shower connects scenes of the pageant when illusion seems to have failed: '"That's done it", sighed Miss La Trobe, wiping away the drops on her cheeks. Nature once more had taken her part. The risk she had run acting in the open air was justified' (130). Finally, her pageant provides a model for resituating human agency within inter-species relationships. Animals play a prominent role in the riotous 'Present Day' scene of the pageant, in which actors reflect the audience's image back to itself:

> Mopping, mowing, whisking, frisking, the looking glasses darted, flashed, exposed. People in the back rows stood up to see the fun. Down they sat, caught themselves ... What an awful show-up! [...] And Lord! the jangle and the din! The very cows joined in. Walloping, tail lashing, the reticence of nature was undone, and the barriers which should divide Man the Master from the Brute were dissolved. Then the dogs joined in. Excited by the uproar, scurrying and worrying, here they came! Look at them! And the hound, the Afghan hound ... look at him! (132)

While previous scenes had achieved an inversion of foreground and background, here the distinction is dissolved as the audience becomes part of the spectacle along with the cows and dogs in a manner that confounds the hierarchy between humans and animals: 'the barriers which should divide Man the Master from the Brute were dissolved'. In all of these cases, the apparent breakdown in the pageant's plot serves to decentre the human drama, undermine human exceptionalism, and draw attention to the agency of the non-human world.

---

[121] Forster, *Land*, 8.

5

Jean Rhys's Plantation Modernism

When writing *Voyage in the Dark* (1934), Jean Rhys was acutely aware that some of her readers found her work depressing. In a letter of 1931, she wrote that 'I am always being told that until my work ceases being "sordid and depressing" I haven't much chance of selling', and adds that 'I used to find this rather stupid but through much repetition I have come half to believe that it must be so'.[1] In another letter, she records the difficulties that she faced getting *Voyage in the Dark* published. Jonathan Cape, the publisher of her previous novel, *After Leaving Mr. Mackenzie* (1931), had apparently 'written and told [her] how grey [she] was, without light or shade', to which she objects: 'really it is not [...] a very grey book'.[2] Some years later, she replied to a reader: 'I'm sorry *Good Morning Midnight* depressed you'—'No I didn't mean it to be hopeless'.[3] By rendering Anna Morgan's melancholic moods in *Voyage in the Dark*, Rhys opened herself to a similar charge of writing depressing novels.

However, reading *Voyage in the Dark* as a work of modernist melancholia suggests that rather than being merely depressing, it is a novel that refuses to forget historical losses that have been suffered in the Caribbean, in a manner that might inspire political counter-moods. As part of a broader affective turn in modernist studies, Jonathan Flatley and Sanja Bahun have argued that instead of being an apolitical affective state associated with withdrawal from society, melancholia can be profoundly political. Flatley contends that modernist literary works can reveal the historicity of affective states in a manner than can galvanize readers into political action, and Bahun shows how modernists make use of melancholic symptoms as a socially-critical way of relating to history through the practice of 'countermourning'.[4] Here, following Flatley's injunction to attend to the historicity of affective states, I will trace how Anna's melancholic states of distraction in

---

[1] Letter to Evelyn Scott, 23 June 1931; *Jean Rhys: Letters, 1931–1966*, ed. Francis Wyndham and Diana Melly (London: André Deutsche, 1984), 21.

[2] Letter to Evelyn Scott, 10 June 1934; *Letters*, 25. Eventually, *Voyage in the Dark* was published by Constable rather than Jonathan Cape.

[3] Letter to Morchard Bishop, 1 June 1939; *Letters*, 34.

[4] Jonathan Flatley, *Affective Mapping: Melancholia and the Politics of Modernism* (Cambridge, MA: Harvard University Press, 2008); Sanja Bahun, *Modernism and Melancholia: Writing as Counter-mourning* (Oxford: Oxford University Press, 2014). On the affective turn within Rhys studies, see Erica L. Johnson and Patricia Moran, 'Introduction: The Haunting of Jean Rhys', in *Jean Rhys: Twenty-First-Century Approaches*, ed. Erica L. Johnson and Patricia Moran (Edinburgh: Edinburgh University Press, 2015), 1–17, 3, 8–9. Cathleen Maslen addresses the topic of Rhys and melancholia in *Ferocious Things: Jean Rhys and the Politics of Women's Melancholia* (Newcastle: Cambridge Scholars Publishing, 2009).

British Modernism and the Anthropocene. David Shackleton, Oxford University Press. © David Shackleton (2023). DOI: 10.1093/oso/9780192857743.003.0006

Voyage in the Dark arose in the context of attempts to mitigate 'wasted time' on Caribbean plantations through the imposition of time-discipline and the introduction of hurricane insurance. In turn, these melancholic states perform a type of countermourning for social and environmental losses suffered in the Caribbean which have been largely unrecognized by traditional forms of historiography.

Indeed, Anna's melancholic states disrupt colonialist modes of historiography. In *The English in the West Indies* (1888), the historian James Anthony Froude notoriously claimed that the West Indies is a place in which '[t]here are no people [...] in the true sense of the word, with a character and purpose of their own'.[5] Similarly, as we saw in Chapter 1, H. G. Wells's universal histories are ones in which Africa and people of African descent barely play a role in world history. They thereby conform to a longer tradition of writing world history, exemplified by G. W. F. Hegel's claim that Africa is an 'unhistorical continent' whose inhabitants live in a state of 'barbarism and savagery', never attaining proper subjectivity.[6] All of these cases exemplify the more general phenomenon by which, as Dipesh Chakrabarty remarks, the sense of history that arose in Europe from the late eighteenth century onwards was used as an ideological weapon in the service of colonial domination.[7] *Voyage in the Dark* is scattered with references to history in the West Indies, yet it uses formal strategies that mimic the symptoms of melancholia to suggest the limitations of the colonial sources that mediate this history, and to draw attention to losses that are not registered therein.

Through its strategies of countermourning, *Voyage in the Dark* can also disrupt more recent accounts of the Anthropocene. Simon Lewis and Mark Maslin argue that this epoch should be understood in relation to the arrival of Europeans in the Caribbean in 1492, and the subsequent colonization of the Americas. This led to a sharp decline in human population, the creation of global trade networks, and the mixing of previously separate biotas known as the 'Columbian Exchange'. More specifically, they propose that the Anthropocene should be considered to start in 1610, as a date when the exchange of plant species between the Old and New Worlds left unique markers in marine and lake sediments, and the death of approximately 50 million indigenous people led to a decline of atmospheric carbon dioxide that is registered in Antarctic ice core records.[8] Aligning their 'Orbis

---

[5] James Anthony Froude, *The English in the West Indies or The Bow of Ulysses* (London: Longmans, Green and Co., 1888), 347. This book is mentioned in Rhys's short story 'The Day They Burned the Books' (*The Collected Short Stories* (London: Penguin, 2017), 147). Peter Hulme notes that one of Rhys's uncles—Acton Don Lockhart—acted as a guide to Froude in Dominica (*Remnants of Conquest: The Island Caribs and their Visitors, 1877–1998* (Oxford: Oxford University Press, 2000), 154, 209–10).

[6] Georg Wilhelm Friedrich Hegel, *Lectures on the Philosophy of World History: Introduction: Reason in History*, ed. Duncan Forbes, trans. H. B. Nisbet (Cambridge: Cambridge University Press, 1984), 190, 174, 176.

[7] Dipesh Chakrabarty, *Provincializing Europe: Postcolonial Thought and Historical Difference* (Princeton: Princeton University Press, 2000), 6–8.

[8] Simon L. Lewis and Mark A. Maslin, 'Defining the Anthropocene', *Nature*, 519 (2015), 171–80, 175.

hypothesis' with Immanuel Wallerstein's account of the beginning of the modern 'world-system', they claim that this time marks the beginning of today's 'globally interconnected economy and ecology'.[9] Lewis and Maslin's account has been criticized by members of the Anthropocene Working Group, who argue that there is an insufficient stratigraphic basis for the 1610 'Orbis spike'. Instead, they favour a mid-twentieth century start date, with an important precursor in the Industrial Revolution which is emblematized by James Watt's refinement of the steam engine.[10] Consequently, the Orbis spike proposal will not be used to formalize the Anthropocene as a geological time unit.

Nevertheless, Lewis and Maslin's proposal has the advantage of foregrounding the role of colonization and slavery in the environmental crisis, as part of what they euphemistically refer to as 'the collision of the Old and New Worlds'.[11] As Kathryn Yusoff remarks, in contrast to other histories of the Anthropocene that 'begin with meditations on the great white men of industry and innovation to reinforce imperial genealogies', the 1610 natal moment ties the 'origin of the Anthropocene to the death of 50 million indigenous people (80 to 95 per cent of the population), systematic violence, and chattel slavery'.[12] It thereby complements other accounts of the environmental crisis such as Françoise Vergès's 'racial Capitalocene', which appeals to a tradition of Black radicalism to reconceptualize climate change and ecological destruction as the result of a long history of colonialism and racial capital, and Malcom Ferdinand's 'Plantationocene', which resituates Caribbean plantations and their colonial modes of inhabitation at the heart of the environment crisis, and identifies the Caribbean as a scene of ecological thinking.[13] Such accounts are particularly valuable at a time when, as Potawatomi scholar-activist Kyle Whyte points out, Anthropocene narratives are being used to signal an impending crisis in a manner that erases the environmental transformations that Indigenous peoples have already endured from colonialism, while simultaneously

---

[9] Lewis and Maslin, 'Anthropocene', 174–5; and Simon L. Lewis and Mark A. Maslin, *The Human Planet: How We Created the Anthropocene* (London: Penguin, 2018), 13, 176.

[10] See Jan Zalasiewicz and others, 'Colonization of the Americas, "Little Ice Age" Climate, and Bomb-Produced Carbon: Their Role in Defining the Anthropocene', *The Anthropocene Review*, 2/2 (2015), 117–27; and Jan Zalasiewicz and others (eds), *The Anthropocene as a Geological Time Unit: A Guide to the Scientific Evidence and Current Debate* (Cambridge: Cambridge University Press, 2019), 250–4, 285–6.

[11] Lewis and Maslin, 'Defining the Anthropocene', 175. Kathryn Yusoff notes that 'the "collision of the Old and New" covers over the friction of a less smooth, more corporeal set of racialized violences': this '"exchange" is the directed colonial violence of forced eviction from land, enslavement on plantations, in rubber factories and mines, and the indirect violence of pathogens through forced contact and rape' (*A Billion Black Anthropocenes or None* (Minneapolis: University of Minnesota Press, 2018), 30).

[12] Yusoff, *Black Anthropocenes*, 15, 32.

[13] See Françoise Vergès, 'Racial Capitalocene', in *Futures of Black Radicalism*, ed. Gaye Theresa Johnson and Alex Lubin (London: Verso, 2017), 72–82; and Malcom Ferdinand, *Decolonial Ecology: Thinking from the Caribbean World*, trans. Anthony Paul Smith (Cambridge: Polity, 2021). Ferdinand adopts the term 'Plantationocene' from Donna Haraway and Anna Tsing (45).

privileging non-Indigenous peoples as their saviours.[14] As Yusoff puts it, with such narratives the colonial assumption of responsibility for the world 'is articulated anew as the white man's burden—a paternalism that is tied to a redemptive narrative of saving the world from harm on account of others while maintaining the protective thick skin of innocence'.[15]

In this final chapter, I will read *Voyage in the Dark* alongside Lewis and Maslin's version of the Anthropocene, and Ferdinand's account of the Plantationocene. Rhys's novel is seldom read from an ecocritical perspective.[16] On the surface, it seems ill-equipped to register major environmental transformations: like *Spleen*, it is tightly focalized around its autodiegetic narrator. Anna, the novel's heroine, has migrated from the Caribbean island of Dominica to England, but has great difficulty articulating her past to other characters, and even struggles to describe how the flora of her island differs from that of England. However, following Mary Lou Emery's suggestion that *Voyage in the Dark* can be read as a novel of the Caribbean plantation, this chapter argues that by rendering Anna's melancholic states of distraction through an innovative narrative form, Rhys's novel opens up a historical counter-narrative in which the Caribbean plantation system and its brutal regimes of labour are seen to have underpinned modernity, and the ecological transformations it has wrought on a planetary scale.[17]

Melancholic states of distraction

Anna, the narrator of *Voyage in the Dark*, is prone to distraction. Indeed, one of the greatest achievements of Rhys's novel is to render these states of distraction through its narrative form. Throughout the novel, ellipses or dashes at the start and end of paragraphs are used to signal Anna's memories, which are typically of Dominica where she grew up before migrating to England after the death of her father. These intrusions also signal narrative ellipses: as the memories are narrated, story time passes. The effect is to convey her drifting into states of reverie or daydream, from which she is occasionally brought back sharply to the present. More generally, many apparently significant events slip through Anna's narrative,

---

[14] See Kyle Whyte, 'Indigenous Science (Fiction) for the Anthropocene: Ancestral Dystopias and Fantasies of Climate Change Crises', *Environment and Planning E: Nature and Space*, 1/1–2 (2018), 224–42.

[15] Yusoff, *Black Anthropocenes*, 27.

[16] By way of exception, Elaine Savory suggests that reading Rhys through the lens of ecocriticism, especially as it relates to the postcolonial, is 'immensely productive', 'Jean Rhys's Environmental Language: Oppositions, Dialogues, and Silences', in *Jean Rhys: Twenty-First-Century Approaches*, 85–106, 87.

[17] See Mary Lou Emery, 'The Poetics of Labor in Jean Rhys's Caribbean Modernism', *Women: A Cultural Review*, 23/4 (2012), 421–44; and 'Caribbean Modernism: Plantation to Planetary', in *The Oxford Handbook of Global Modernisms*, ed. Mark Wollaeger and Matt Eatough (Oxford: Oxford University Press, 2012), 48–77.

and are never directly recounted. The reader is left to infer retrospectively from subsequent events or from other characters' responses that, for example, she engages in increasingly alienated forms of sexual labour as an 'amateur prostitute', and that she used to take quinine as a contraceptive before her abortion.[18]

At various stages during the story, the demarcation between Anna's memories and events occurring in the present becomes blurred. In a letter, Rhys hints that the 'big idea' behind this novel is that time is an 'illusion': 'I mean that the past exists—side by side with the present, not behind it; that what was—is. I tried to do it by making the past (the West Indies) very vivid—the present dreamlike (downward career of girl)'.[19] Certainly, Anna at times remembers her past with great intensity. For example, hearing a church bell ringing on a rainy Sunday afternoon in London leads her to think of Sundays as a child; at the end of her account, the past tenses of her iterative narrative change to the present tense: '[t]he light is gold and when you shut your eyes you see fire-colour' (38). This change of tense conveys the vividness of her memory, as if the sunlit scene still exists; the blurring between times is heightened by the ambiguity of the deictic 'when', which refers both to the past in Dominica (in which case the fire-colour is caused by the sun streaming through eyelids), and to the present of remembering (in which case the fire-colour is imagined behind shut eyes). Past and present were finally to become indistinguishable in the original ending of the novel, in which Anna drifts towards death after haemorrhaging from her abortion. In a letter from 1963, Rhys recalls that this ending was written with 'time and place abolished, past and present the same'. She notes that she went on to develop this technique in her portrayal of Antoinette in *Wide Sargasso Sea* (1966), in which the story, if any, was 'to be implied, *never told straight*'.[20] Although Rhys was forced to rewrite the original ending of *Voyage in the Dark* under editorial pressure, the effect achieved throughout the published version of the novel is to convey time passing in states of distraction, and time slipping away. Anna goes through life in a passive dreamlike state: events seemingly happen to her without her having any agency, in the gaps in which her attention is directed elsewhere. Indeed, she describes not wanting anything more from life except to sleep, or else to lie without moving: '[t]hat's when you can hear time sliding past you, like water running'.[21]

Anna's states of distraction have a marked melancholic dimension. It seems that she was susceptible to melancholia from a young age. She recalls her father saying that the Welsh word for grief is 'hiraeth', and hugging her as a child when she was

---

[18] On the emergence of the 'amateur prostitute' in the 1910s and 1920s, see Sue Thomas, *The Worlding of Jean Rhys* (Westport: Greenwood Press, 1999), 67–93, 104–05, 108–09.

[19] Letter to Evelyn Scott, 18 February 1934; *Letters*, 24.

[20] Letter to Diana Athill, 16 August 1963; *Letters*, 233. In a letter of 6 November 1957 to Selma Vaz Dias, Rhys notes that the original title of *Voyage in the Dark* was '"Two Tunes"': '[t]hat's what I meant. Past and Present. Then Past got altered and cut to an echo' (*Letters*, 149).

[21] Jean Rhys, *Voyage in the Dark* (London: Penguin, 2000), 97. All further references are to this edition.

crying about nothing, saying 'I believe you're going to be like me, you poor little devil' (81). Using her characteristically simple vocabulary—Rhys remarks that the novel was written 'almost entirely in words of one syllable. Like a kitten mewing perhaps'—Anna comments on her own sadness.[22] Although she upbraids Walter for having the 'soppy idea' that she's always sad, she herself thinks that 'in my heart I was always sad', and describes lying awake at night and remembering things: 'that was when it was sad, a lonely feeling, a hopeless feeling' (33, 14, 49, 64). When Walter leaves her, it precipitates a particularly deep depression: she reflects on her 'depressed feeling', and describes not going out, lying in bed until late, and taking long baths in the afternoon (77–8). Other characters comment on her depressed and vacant appearance. Carl suggests that she looks as though she has been taking ether (131). With considerably less sympathy, Ethel asks '[w]hat do you want to look so miserable about?', and later remarks that '[y]ou always look half asleep and people don't like that' (94, 110).

Anna's melancholic states involve a feeling of dislocation, which stems partly from her experience as a colonial migrant. Bahun identifies the experience of dislocation as one of the key features of the clinical picture of melancholia, and suggests that modernists responded with a range of innovative aesthetic forms to such an experience and the associated feeling of homelessness. While Bahun diagnoses a widespread modernist performance of 'transcendental homelessness', Anna's feeling of dislocation in *Voyage in the Dark* can be understood more specifically in terms of her migration from the West Indies to England.[23] The opening line of the novel—'[i]t was as if a curtain had fallen, hiding everything I had ever know'— conveys the importance of this migration. However, the complete break suggested by the theatrical simile is modified by Anna's following account which makes clear that her past in Dominica is not completely hidden, but rather that the parts of her life are somehow incommensurate or disjointed: she thinks of Dominica and England alternately as real and the other a dream, 'but I could never fit them together' (7–8). In turn, there is a discontinuity in Anna's identity, as she is spatially and temporally 'stretched' between Dominica and England. In a letter many years later, Rhys writes of Anna: '[t]he girl is *divided*, two people really', which suggests an identity divided between her West Indian past and her present in England.[24] Anna's difficulty in assimilating her past to her present is exacerbated by the hostility that she faces as a migrant. She is subjected to a series of hostile comments including being called 'the Hottentot' by the girls at work, and is forced to negotiate Ethel's hatred of 'dirty foreigners' (12, 95). When Joe mocks her West Indian past, she declares angrily 'I'll never tell you anything real about myself', and claims instead that 'I was born in Manchester' (107).

[22] Letter to Evelyn Scott, 18 February 1934; *Letters*, 24.
[23] Bahun, *Melancholia*, 5, 45–6.
[24] Letter to Selma Vaz Dias, 17 September 1963; *Letters*, 241.

Anna's melancholic states of distraction can be explicated as examples of what Flatley calls 'moods'. Flatley understands 'mood' on the model of Martin Heidegger's concept of '*Stimmung*': it is an affective atmosphere in which intentions are formed, projects are pursued, and particular affects attach to particular objects.[25] Much as Heidegger in the second division of *Being and Time* (1927) offers an analysis of moods as temporal structures, so Rhys's narrative renders Anna's states of distraction as having a particular temporal structure, in which time seems to slide past her.[26] And much as Heidegger and Flatley hold that moods fluctuate and can be altered by means of 'counter-moods' which change the world in which we exist at any given moment, so Anna sometimes manages to change her mood.[27] Mostly, she is able to do so by shopping, which is associated in the novel with an affectively-charged, future-oriented temporality of hope. Standing in a shop in Shaftesbury Avenue amid rows of dresses, she thinks: '[t]his is a beginning. Out of this warm room that smells of fur I'll go to all the lovely places I've ever dreamed of'. In turn, this more hopeful mood changes her world: '[t]he streets looked different that day, just as a reflection in the looking-glass is different from the real thing' (25).[28] Similarly, she later watches women looking at clothes in shop-windows on Oxford Street, and notes that 'their eyes were fixed on the future': '[i]f I could buy this, then of course I'd be quite different'. However, the better future promised by shopping and fashion proves to be illusory, and Anna remains trapped within the repetitive temporality of her working life.

While Walter Benjamin characterizes the temporality of modernity as 'the new as the ever-same', Anna experiences a similar temporality when working in England, initially as a music hall entertainer and then as an amateur prostitute.[29] Describing touring around the country as a chorus girl, she comments that '[y]ou were perpetually moving to another place which was perpetually the same' (8). The various towns that she visits become indistinguishable, as do the rooms in the boarding houses in which she stays, and even the meals that are served there: 'the shapes of slices of meat were the same, and the way the cabbage was heaped was the same' (128, 89). In a sentence in which her experience of numbing repetition is conveyed by a concatenation of clauses joined by polysyndeton, temporal repetition blends into a form of spatial repetition: 'all the houses outside in the street were the same', as were 'the streets going north, east, south, west, all exactly the same' (89). She never escapes from these monotonous patterns. For example, the

---

[25] Flatley, *Mapping*, 19.

[26] Heidegger describes the task of establishing the ontological structure of having a mood in its existential-temporal constitution as a matter of 'making the temporality of moods visible' (*Being and Time*. trans. John Macquarrie and Edward Robinson (Oxford: Blackwell Publishing, 2006), 340).

[27] Heidegger, *Being and Time*, 136; Flatley, *Mapping*, 23.

[28] Italics removed. Anna's mood also changes when Walter visits her early in their relationship: the 'room looked different, as if it had grown bigger' (29).

[29] On Benjamin's characterization of the temporality of modernity, see Peter Osborne, *The Politics of Time: Modernity and Avant-Garde* (London: Verso, 1995), 137, 143.

better future promised by shopping proves to be an illusion, and the new 'beginning' she yearns for appears in the form of the ever-same. As Terri Mullholland notes, in exchanging Walter's money for clothes to transform herself, Anna is also transformed into a commodity that Walter has purchased.[30] Even the revised ending of the novel, in which Anna survives her abortion and thinks about 'starting all over again', is equivocal. It seems just as likely that she will remain trapped within the repetitive rhythms of her working life, as hinted by the repetition of the phrase 'all over again', which undercuts her hope of emerging 'new and fresh' (159).

Although at the level of plot Anna does not escape the repetitive patterns of her working life and fails to change her world in significant ways, her melancholic moods might inspire counter-moods in the novel's readers. Flatley suggests that moods have a historicity, and that novels can provide 'affective maps' that make readers aware of the particular set of historical circumstances from which their moods emerged. This can be an important step on the way to transforming moods—in the case of melancholia, of converting depressive melancholias into more politically efficacious moods.[31] In *Voyage in the Dark*, Anna's melancholia is shaped by a history that includes efforts to reduce wasted time in the Caribbean plantation system. In turn, awareness of the provenance of Anna's moods might inflect structures of feeling that are emerging in relation to the Anthropocene.

Wasted time

While Anna's propensity for distraction forms an aspect of her character, it is also typical of a wider historical phenomenon. Jonathan Crary charts the emergence of states of attention and distraction with the formation of the modern subject in the nineteenth century, and shows how these states evolved with the later '24/7 temporalities' that characterize neoliberal globalization.[32] Anna's states of distraction can be viewed as a by-product of the cultures of attention identified by Crary, although they should also be understood as having a specifically Caribbean provenance, emerging from the regimes of time-discipline operating in the Caribbean

---

[30] See Terri Mullholland, 'Between Illusion and Reality, "Who's to Know": Threshold Spaces in the Interwar Novels of Jean Rhys', *Women: A Cultural Review*, 23/4 (2012), 445–62, 449. Anna herself is cynical about shopping and fashion, remarking about the women in Oxford Street: '[k]eep hope alive and you can do anything, and that's the way the world goes round' (111).

[31] Flatley characterizes an affective map as a representation of one's affective life in its historicity (*Mapping*, 84).

[32] See Jonathan Crary, *24/7: Late Capitalism and the Ends of Sleep* (London: Verso, 2013), 8–9. Crary suggests that one of the forms of disempowerment within '24/7 environments' is 'the incapacitation of daydream or of any mode of absent-minded introspection that would otherwise occur in intervals of slow or vacant time' (88). For him, '24/7', in which life is inscribed into duration without breaks, is 'inseparable from environmental catastrophe in its declaration of permanent expenditure, of endless wastefulness for its sustenance, in its terminal disruption of the cycles and seasons on which ecological integrity depends' (10).

plantation system. In Rhys's later short story 'Temps Perdi', the narrator explains that the term 'Temps Perdi' is 'Creole patois and does not mean, poetically, lost or forgotten time, but, matter-of-factly, wasted time, lost labour'. She reports that when she was a child it used to be said that the island was a hostile place: '[y]ou are getting along fine and then a hurricane comes, or a disease of the crops that nobody can cure, and there you are—more West Indian ruins and labour lost'.[33] This story post-dates *Voyage in the Dark*: it was written some time after Rhys's return to Dominica in 1936, and was first published in 1968. Nevertheless, the concept of 'Temps Perdi' can be applied retrospectively as a means of elucidating the narrative strategies of *Voyage in the Dark*.

The Creole concept of 'Temps Perdi' can be understood in the context of the strict time-discipline that was imposed in the Caribbean plantation system, both before and after the abolition of slavery. Such time-discipline meant that any time that was not used efficiently in production was conceived of as wasted. Rhys's great-grandfather, James Potter Lockhart, instituted one such regime at his Geneva Estate on Dominica, and more widely throughout the island when he was president and commander-in-chief in the 1830s. As Sue Thomas documents, the slave-owning James Lockhart formally opposed the Abolition Act of 1833, and during the apprenticeship period that followed the act, imposed a strict system of surveillance on formerly-enslaved people, inflicting severe punishments on those who broke the law. He even policed the use of time on labour-free weekends by introducing a pass system that allowed him to punish 'vagabondage'.[34] (In the Black Exercise Book, Rhys wrote that looking at portraits of James Lockhart and his wife made her 'feel sick with shame', and evoked stories of plantation slavery: 'ferocious punishments the salt kept ready to rub into the wounds').[35] Such policing of time is characteristic of the apprenticeship system, which functioned to socialize formerly-enslaved people into subordinate estate labourers who could be punished for vagrancy, insubordination, and neglecting work.[36] More generally, the measures taken to avoid what the narrator of 'Temps Perdi' calls 'wasted time' and 'lost labour' are illustrated by an anecdote that C. L. R. James tells of his grandfather being asked to fix an engine on one of the sugar-estate factories on Trinidad near the end of the nineteenth century. He recalls that the factories would often grind cane for twenty hours a day during the season, but if an engine failed it would cause

---

[33] Rhys, *Short Stories*, 257. By mentioning 'lost or forgotten time', Rhys signals a move away from Marcel Proust's concerns in *À la recherche du temps perdu* (1913–27). Édouard Glissant contrasts the temporal experiments of Caribbean literature with those of Proust: 'time in our poetry and novels does not produce the impressive harmony that Proust has for instance put together' (*Caribbean Discourse: Selected Essays*, trans. J. Michael Dash (Charlottesville: University Press of Virginia, 1999), 106).

[34] See Thomas, *Worlding*, 168–70.

[35] Quoted in Sue Thomas, 'Ghostly Presences: James Potter Lockhart and Jane Maxwell Lockhart in Jean Rhys's Writing', *Texas Studies in Literature and Language*, 57/4 (2015), 389–411, 402.

[36] See Emery, 'Caribbean Modernism', 426–7.

a 'general crisis', not least because the quality of the juice deteriorated quickly once the cane had been cut:

> if the big engines stopped and were not repaired pretty quickly the whole process was thrown out of gear, and if the break continued the cutters for miles around had to be signalled to stop cutting, and they sat around and waited for hours.[37]

The 'acute' tension felt when anything went wrong, the frantic efforts of the workers to fix the engine, and the hurrying over of engineers from neighbouring factories, all testify to the imperative of avoiding wasted time in the plantation system.[38]

The concept of 'Temps Perdi' can further be understood in the context of the hurricane insurance scheme promoted by Henry Hesketh Bell, the colonial administrator of Dominica whom Rhys knew when she was young.[39] As Peter Hulme notes, Bell pioneered a scheme of hurricane insurance as part of the modernizing activities that he undertook as Administrator of the island, which in turn formed part of Joseph Chamberlain's 'new imperialism'.[40] As Bell recounts in his memoirs, the single greatest obstacle that he identified to the investment of capital in the West Indies was the fear that hurricanes would destroy property. He therefore compiled data on storms in the region over a seventy-five year period to show that the risk posed by hurricanes was lower than commonly thought, and on this basis convinced underwriters of insurance in London to offer a suitable scheme.[41] While the narrator of 'Temps Perdi' remarks that 'a hurricane comes' and leads to 'more West Indian ruins and labour lost', Bell's insurance scheme aimed to mitigate such damage. Yet the scheme (in line with his general policy of encouraging the development of Dominica by a British planter class) was one that promoted uneven development. As he points out in a letter to *The Times* in 1906, it would not be possible to insure the huts and small tenements of 'the very poor' on whom 'the effects of a hurricane will always fall disastrously': 'the poor in the West Indies' would supposedly have to rely on 'the sympathy and help of the Motherland'.[42] In paraphrasing the letter, the editors of *The Times* render Bell's 'the very poor' as 'the poorest negro inhabitants', and thereby reveal the racial logic of the scheme.[43] While insurance underwriters in general and Lloyd's in particular had long facilitated the transatlantic slave trade, Bell's hurricane insurance scheme perpetuated racial inequality by opening the West Indies for development by a white planter class.

[37] C. L. R. James, *Beyond a Boundary* (London: Yellow Jersey Press, 2005), 17–18.
[38] James, *Boundary*, 18.
[39] See Jean Rhys, *Smile Please: An Unfinished Autobiography* (London: Penguin, 2016), 74–7.
[40] Hulme, *Remnants*, 112.
[41] Hesketh Bell, *Glimpses of a Governor's Life* (London: Sampson Low, Marston & Co., [1946]), 31, 41–3, 96–7.
[42] H. Hesketh Bell, 'Insurance Against Hurricanes in the West Indies', *The Times*, 5 February 1906, 4.
[43] 'Hurricane Insurance', *The Times*, 5 February 1906, 9.

Within the regimes of time-discipline imposed on the Caribbean plantation system, withholding labour and disrupting the time of production could be a political act of resistance. Indeed, Geneva Estate was the site of many such acts of resistance. Labourers rebelled there during the 1844 'Guerre Nègre', and the house was later burned down in 1932. Previously, in 1791, enslaved people in the surrounding Grand Bay area of Dominica stopped work and demanded three days a week rather than the customary day and a half to work on their own plots of land, and staged a revolt when this demand was denied.[44] Again, the widespread practice of marronage, in which enslaved people escaped from plantations, would (from the perspective of the colonial planter class) constitute an instance of 'lost labour'. There is a long history of *grand* and *petit marronage* on Dominica, with Maroons organizing themselves into an army in the woods, and waging two wars against the British colonial authorities.[45] In the case of the plantation system in the United States, James draws on the testimony of Frederick Douglass to note that enslaved people fought to set their own tempo and rhythm of work, and developed practices of periodic absenteeism which served as small equivalents of strike action.[46] Strike action itself was another major form of resistance: the year that *Voyage in the Dark* was published saw the first of a wave of strikes and protests throughout the West Indies, which acted as a catalyst for the rise of national consciousness and movements for self-government.[47]

In contrast to Lockhart's imposition of time-discipline and Bell's scheme of hurricane insurance, both of which were designed to mitigate the effects of 'wasted time', Rhys makes aesthetic use of a type of 'wasted time' by her rendering of Anna's states of distraction in *Voyage in the Dark*. Édouard Glissant suggests that the historical practice of marronage finds an analogue in Caribbean literature, both in the early tales told by enslaved people on plantations and in later literatures in English, Spanish, and French, which 'tended to introduce obscurities and breaks— like so many detours—into the material they dealt with'. On his account, 'historical *marronage* intensified over time to exert a creative *marronage*'.[48] Anna's states of distraction can be read as an example of what Glissant calls 'detours', and the obscurities and breaks of her narrative can be read as a form of creative marronage. Of course, such a reading of *Voyage in the Dark* has to acknowledge that the story is told by Anna, who (like Rhys) comes from a family of slave-owning colonial

[44] See Stephan Lenik, 'Plantation Labourer Rebellions, Material Culture and Events: Historical Archaeology at Geneva Estate, Grand Bay, Commonwealth of Dominica', *Slavery & Abolition*, 35/3 (2014), 508–26, 510–16.

[45] See Ferdinand, *Decolonial Ecology*, 154.

[46] C. L. R. James, 'The Atlantic Slave-Trade', in *The Future in the Present: Selected Writings* (London: Allison & Busby, 1977), 235–64, 245, 257.

[47] See Leah Rosenberg, *Nationalism and the Formation of Caribbean Literature* (Basingstoke: Palgrave Macmillan, 2007), 1.

[48] Édouard Glissant, *Poetics of Relation*, trans. Betsy Wing (Ann Arbor: University of Michigan Press, 2010), 68–71.

planters. Victoria Burrows argues that by portraying Antoinette as 'marooned' in *Wide Sargasso Sea*, Rhys culturally appropriates an African-Caribbean trope of resistance and reassigns it meaning from a white Creole perspective, in a manner that occludes the subaltern history of enslaved people and their historical acts of resistance.[49] A parallel charge could be levelled (on a formal rather than thematic level) against the use of creative marronage in *Voyage in the Dark*. On this interpretation, Rhys would be seen as an heir to what Glissant calls an elitist Caribbean literature of 'delusion' written by planters and colonists, which (although equally discontinuous) tends to 'blot out the shudders of life, that is, the turbulent realities of the Plantation.'[50] However, on the contrary, I suggest that the detours of Anna's melancholic states of distraction form a site of resistance from within the repetitive patterns of her working life, and that they ultimately register rather than obscure the brutal history of the plantations.

Anna's states of distraction and feelings of dislocation—understood as a mood with a particular temporal structure—constitute a 'contramodern temporality', or time out of joint.[51] This is so both in the sense that they arise in tension with the prevailing cultures of attention and imperatives to be productive (and no doubt contribute to Anna's failure to 'get on', as Laurie puts it (110)), and in the sense that from within the repetitive temporality into which Anna is thrown as a musical hall entertainer and amateur prostitute, they open onto a disruptive counter-history in which the Caribbean plantation and its racialized regimes of labour is seen to have underpinned modernity. Not only do Anna's states of distraction open onto a counter-history of modernity, but through their melancholic dynamics they register her own troubled place within that history, and refuse to reconcile the damage wrought by the Caribbean plantation system.

Countermourning and Caribbean history

Voyage in the Dark's relationship to Caribbean history is mediated by its melancholic dynamics. For Bahun, modernist melancholia is distinguished by what she calls the 'practice of countermourning': a memorial articulation of loss that uses the symptomology of melancholia to give form to the very impossibility of mourning lost objects. This practice can be a way of relating to history. Unlike traditional historiography which rests on the premise that everything can be pinned down, countermourning voices incompletion and inconclusiveness, and acknowledges

---

[49] Victoria Burrows, *Whiteness and Trauma: The Mother-Daughter Knot in the Fiction of Jean Rhys, Jamaica Kincaid and Toni Morrison* (Basingstoke: Palgrave Macmillan, 2004), 31–5.

[50] Glissant, *Relation*, 70.

[51] I borrow the term 'contramodern temporality' from Emery, who notes that work in the emergent field of Caribbean modernist studies has drawn attention to a range of such temporalities ('Caribbean Modernism', 52).

unappropriability as a precondition of honest dealing with historical occlusions. While modernist melancholia for Bahun tends to point towards the subversive 'unthought' in history, the countermourning performed by *Voyage in the Dark* should be understood specifically in relation to that which escapes colonialist modes of historiography.[52] Glissant suggests that one of the most disturbing consequences of colonization in the Caribbean was the imposition by the colonizers of the notion of a single 'History' that often relegates other peoples and cultures to the realms of the ahistorical or the prehistorical.[53] The melancholic dynamics of *Voyage in the Dark* unsettle such a notion of history, and countermourn losses that are not therein recorded.

Anna's states of distraction typically link her present to her past in Dominica, and to the history of the Caribbean more generally. Her wandering thoughts contain repeated references to the history of Dominica, albeit a history mediated by colonialist sources. (The island is never explicitly named in the novel, but is identifiable by its coordinates, as illustrated in Figure 5.1). One excursus in which her attention drifts away from her friend Maudie's talking contains a direct quotation from an account of a 1595 voyage to the West Indies that was published in Richard Hakluyt's *The Principal Navigations, Voyages, Traffiques, and Discoveries of the English Nation* (1600), and reproduced in Charles Lucas's *Historical Geography of the British Colonies* (1890). This quotation describes Dominica as a 'goodly island and something highland, but all overgrown with woods' (15).[54] It is juxtaposed with another description of the island as 'all crumpled into hills and mountains as you would crumple a piece of paper in your hand', which echoes the story of Christopher Columbus doing just that when asked by Queen Isabella about the appearance of the Dominica, having landed there on his second voyage in 1493 (15).[55]

Similarly, Anna's thoughts wander back to her family's past in the West Indies. When describing Constance—her mother's family estate—to Walter, Anna thinks of 'the walls of the Old Estate house, still standing, with moss on them': '[o]ne ruined room for roses, one for orchids, one for tree ferns', and 'honeysuckle all along the steep flight of steps that led down to the room where the overseer kept his books' (45). The romantic image of overgrown ruins is a melancholic one. It resonates with Rhys's description in her autobiographical *Smile Please* (1979) of

---

[52] Bahun, *Melancholia*, 8–9, 39.

[53] Glissant, *Discourse*, 93, 75–6.

[54] Charles Prestwood Lucas, *Historical Geography of the British Colonies: Vol. II. The West Indies* (Oxford: Clarendon Press, 1890), 163.

[55] Frederick Ober recounts this story in *Camps in the Caribbees: The Adventures of a Naturalist in the Lesser Antilles* (Boston: Lee and Shepard, 1880), 5. Teresa O'Connor draws attention to another version in Joseph Sturge and Thomas Harvey's *The West Indies in 1837* (1838): see *Jean Rhys: The West Indian Novels* (New York: New York University Press, 1986), 13. Bell recalls having read the story in his *Glimpses* (7). As Yusoff remarks, on his second voyage to the New World, Columbus initiated the first transatlantic slave voyage, a shipment of several hundred Taino people sent from Hispaniola to Spain (*Black Anthropocenes*, 30).

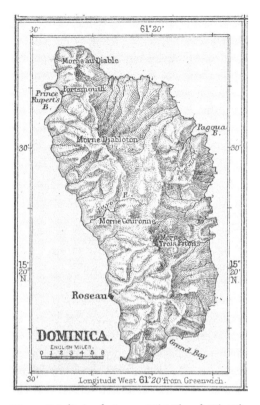

Figure 5.1 'Lying between 15° 10′ and 15° 40′
N. and 61° 14′ and 61° 30′ W.'

Reproduced from Lucas, Charles Prestwood. (1890).
*Historical Geography of the British Colonies: Vol. II. The
West Indies.* Oxford: Clarendon Press.

Geneva Estate, with its 'garden in the ruins' and 'the honeysuckle and the jasmine
and the tall fern trees', as having a 'very strong atmosphere of [...] melancholy'.[56] As
such, the image could be interpreted as typical of a melancholic historical sensibility held by planters, in which the ruin of West Indian plantations was attributed to
the failure of the British government to maintain monopoly rights, and to provide
adequate financial compensation for the loss of slaves following the 1833 Slavery
Abolition Act. Indeed, in the earlier ending of the novel, Anna remembers Uncle
Bo and Hester arguing about the compensation that may or may not have been
paid after Abolition, with Bo remarking 'I'd like to see the rich English give up
their slaves without any compensation like we did'.[57] Such a historical sensibility

---

[56] Rhys, *Smile Please*, 18, 21.
[57] Jean Rhys, 'Voyage in the Dark: Part IV (Original Version)1', in *The Gender of Modernism: A
Critical Anthology*, ed. Bonnie Kime Scott (Bloomington: Indiana University Press, 1990), 381–9, 386.

foregrounds financial loss and discounts the experience of the enslaved, but Rhys's novel complicates such a sensibility as the image of the ruined estate leads Anna to think of Maillotte Boyd. As if following the flight of steps, Anna's thoughts turn to 'an old slave-list' that she saw at Constance once, which was hand-written on parchment and divided into columns: 'Maillotte Boyd, aged 18, mulatto, house servant' (45–6). Later, while having sex with Walter, the reference is notoriously repeated: '*Maillotte Boyd, aged* 18. *Maillotte Boyd, aged* 18. ...' (48). The mention of the slave-list at this point in the narrative is ambiguous: it could be read as Anna identifying with Maillotte Boyd, in a manner that belittles the atrocities of slavery.[58]

However—bearing in mind that modernist melancholia for Bahun characteristically manifests itself through formal inflection rather than description—the parataxis, italicization, repetition, and ellipsis might be read as markers of modernist countermourning. The italicization signals a transition to Anna's thoughts, and the repetition of '*Maillotte Boyd, aged* 18' suggests psychic content that has not been fully worked through—a reading that is reinforced by Anna's admission that she has 'never forgotten' the slave-list with all 'those names written down' (46). The three dots discreetly elide the sexual encounter, yet as a textual marker of absence they also mimic the 'psychic hole' carved by loss.[59] These narrative strategies signal Maillotte Boyd's life to be the site of an irretrievable historical absence, and yet they refuse to forget her experience and those of other enslaved people who were sexually exploited in Caribbean plantations. They thereby constitute a modernist response to what Saidiya Hartman describes as the 'elusiveness of slavery's archive': one in which the manifests of slavers, ledger books of trade goods, itemized lists of bodies, and planters' diaries provide mere traces of enslaved people, whose lives otherwise resist representation.[60] That is, from within a temporality of modernity that is partly shaped by the time-discipline imposed on the Caribbean plantation system, the distracted wandering of Anna's mind makes the history of Dominica momentarily visible as one of forced labour and sexual violence.

Rhys's use of narrative strategies that mimic melancholic symptoms produces a series of textual ambiguities, which reflect Anna's ambivalent attitude as the white daughter of a colonial planter towards black people in Dominica, and towards the history of slavery in in the West Indies. Anna remembers that when she was young she 'always wanted to be black' like Francine, although she later comes to realize the impossibility of this desire when she encounters Francine working in the smoke-filled kitchen: 'she said something in patois and went on washing up.

[58] See Anna Snaith, *Modernist Voyages: Colonial Women Writers in London, 1890–1945* (Cambridge: Cambridge University Press, 2014), 148–9.
[59] See Bahun, *Melancholia*, 10, 65–6.
[60] Saidiya Hartman, *Lose Your Mother: A Journey Along the Atlantic Slave Route* (London: Serpent's Tail, 2021), 17.

But I knew that of course she disliked me too because I was white' (27, 62).[61] Emery notes that in this scene, Anna recognizes that her whiteness was 'produced by the labour of slaves and servants of African descent.'[62] It might be added that this representation of racial identity maps neatly onto contemporary accounts of melancholia.

In a series of writings on the topic, Freud advances an influential account of melancholia as a response to loss, and identifies ambivalence as a distinctive aspect of such a condition. For example, in 'Mourning and Melancholia' (1917), he suggests that such ambivalence stems from the combination of love and hatred that is felt towards the lost object, which the ego initially identified with and then 'assimilated' into the psyche.[63] Anna's early identification with Francine before being rejected by her conforms to this pattern. Again, the use of parataxis when Anna has sex with Walter—in which there are no further connectives or indications given to establish Anna's relationship to Maillotte Boyd—replicates the ambivalence that for Freud characterizes melancholia: it renders Anna's relationship to Maillotte Boyd ambiguous, and leaves opens the possibility that she might identify with her. More generally, Rhys's later description of Anna as 'divided' could be interpreted in psychoanalytic terms. For Freud, melancholia makes evident the more general phenomenon of the division of the ego: in *Group Psychology and the Analysis of the Ego* (1921), he holds that melancholias show us 'the ego divided, fallen apart into two pieces, one of which rages against the second.'[64] Anna's psyche could be seen as thus divided, with her ego having turned the ambivalence she feels towards lost objects (including people from her Caribbean past) against itself. In the Black Exercise Book, Rhys records her own ambivalence when growing up as a white Creole in Dominica towards black people, and towards her West Indian heritage. She recalls being '[s]ick with shame at some of the stories of the slave days', and then '[s]ometimes seeing myself powerful [...] sometimes being proud of my great grandfather, the estate, and the good old days', but 'the end of my thinking about them was a sick revolt and I wanted to be identified with the other side which of course was impossible.'[65] Just as Rhys recognizes that her wish to be identified with 'the other side' is ultimately impossible, so the melancholic dynamics of *Voyage in the Dark* indicate the gulf separating Anna from enslaved people such as Maillotte Boyd, and her inability to speak on their behalf.

---

[61] Similarly, in *Wide Sargasso Sea*, Antoinette's fantasy of living with and being like her black friend Tia is shattered when Tia throws a jagged stone that causes blood to run down her face ((London: Penguin, 1997), 24).

[62] Emery, 'Caribbean Modernism', 424.

[63] Sigmund Freud, 'Mourning and Melancholia', in *The Standard Edition of the Complete Psychological Works of Sigmund Freud*, vol. 14, trans. and ed. James Strachey (London: Hogarth Press, 1957), 237–58, 243.

[64] Sigmund Freud, *Group Psychology and the Analysis of the Ego*, in *The Standard Edition of the Complete Psychological Works of Sigmund Freud*, vol. 18, trans. and ed. James Strachey (London: Hogarth Press, 1955), 65–143, 109; see also 'Mourning', 247.

[65] Quoted in Coral Ann Howells, *Jean Rhys* (Hemel Hempstead: Harvester Wheatsheaf, 1991), 21.

While Anna's wandering thoughts often drift back to Dominica, her melancholic ruminations can be understood in relation to losses that encompass both the personal and the historical. Most immediately, she is devastated by the loss of Walter when he ends their relationship. She thinks of herself as having always lived in fearful anticipation of this event: 'I saw that all my life I had known that this was going to happen, and that I'd been afraid for a long time' (82). Similarly, she seems to be haunted by the loss of her mother. A brief description of a funeral is interposed in a scene in which she tries to convince Walter not to leave her, suggesting the disturbance of a memory; in the earlier version of the novel's ending, her mind again returns to the funeral which is explicitly indicated to be that of her mother (83).[66] Yet *Voyage in the Dark* conveys a sense of loss that is not only personal but that extends to the historical. For example, having written an emotional letter to Walter, Anna tries to recall the words of a music hall song she has started to sing, and her thoughts move from the line 'Oceans away from despair' to the Caribbean Sea, and from there to the indigenous 'Caribs' of Dominica who fiercely resisted British rule but 'are now practically exterminated' (90–1).[67] Ironically, the song is about drifting away from despair, but her thoughts drift back to the Caribbean Sea as a place of extermination. Her thoughts thereby wander from her personal loss to register wider historical losses inflicted by colonization, and suggest the Caribbean Sea to be a site of 'despair' for the Caribs, or Kalinago.

Voyage in the Dark also uses obscure dreams to signal types of loss that escape Anna's fully-conscious thought. Freud holds that melancholics are often unaware of the nature of the loss they have suffered. In one of his earliest writings on the subject, he suggests that melancholic symptoms are caused by repression in the wake of loss, and in 'Mourning and Melancholia' he emphasizes that in many cases 'the patient cannot consciously perceive what he has lost'.[68] As Bahun puts it, cognitive inaccessibility is the crucial trait of melancholia.[69] In Rhys's novel, Anna has recurrent dreams about the sea that point towards inaccessible losses. She dreams that she was on a ship from which she could see small islands, including one that resembles her island; she tries to step ashore, but '[s]omebody had fallen overboard'. A 'little dwarf with a bald head' emerges from a child's coffin, but Anna thinks 'What's overboard?' and has an 'awful dropping of the heart' (140–1). The dream follows a series of allusions to Anna's drowning and possible suicide, so the body falling overboard might be understood as the displaced symbol of a suicidal impulse.[70]

[66] Rhys, 'Original Version', 382.
[67] On the construction of 'Carib' as a colonial category, and its recent contestation by the Kalinago people of Dominica, see Stephan Lenik, 'Carib as a Colonial Category: Comparing Ethnohistoric and Archaeological Evidence from Dominica, West Indies', *Ethnohistory*, 59/1 (2012), 79–107.
[68] See Sigmund Freud, *The Complete Letters of Sigmund Freud to Wilhelm Fliess: 1887–1904*, trans. and ed. Jeffrey Moussaieff Masson (Cambridge, MA: Harvard University Press, 1985), 250; and 'Mourning', 245.
[69] Bahun, *Melancholia*, 25, 19.
[70] When Walter breaks off their relationship, Anna compares the experience to falling back into water and trying to speak when drowned. She later makes a morbid joke about not being able to swim

However, as Thomas points out, with the condensation characteristic of dreams, 'Somebody had fallen overboard' also evokes the history of enslaved people being thrown overboard slaving ships during the Middle Passage. Most infamously, 132 enslaved Africans were killed or pressed to suicide on the *Zong* in 1781, so that the shipowners could claim their insurance value of £30 per slave.[71] The dream thereby functions as a textual strategy for signalling losses that are not fully registered in Anna's conscious thought or colonialist historiography, including the various historical accounts and traveller's reports that are woven into the novel's narrative. Glissant suggests that below the colonizers' conception of a single hierarchical History that would cast many in the Caribbean into a non-historical void can be detected the convergence of a diverse set of histories of different peoples. The emblem of these histories is the invisible presence of 'all those Africans weighed down with ball and chain and thrown overboard whenever a slave ship was pursued by enemy vessels and felt too weak to put up a fight'.[72] Anna's dream gestures towards such a submarine convergence of transversal histories in the Caribbean. By indicating the existence of such repressed histories, the dream performs an act of countermourning for the enslaved Africans lost while making the Middle Passage across the Atlantic. That is, her melancholic feelings of dislocation should be understood as a response not only to her voyage from Dominica to England, but also to what Glissant calls the 'brutal dislocation' of the transatlantic slave trade.[73]

In addition to evoking the loss of enslaved people during the Middle Passage, Anna's dream suggests environmental destruction. The island in her dream 'was home except that the trees were all wrong': '[t]hese were English trees, their leaves trailing in the water' (140). In an instance of what Carol Dell'Amico characterizes as the novel's exploration of 'colonial unhomeliness', the English trees make the otherwise familiar island unfamiliar.[74] Previously, during a trip to Savernake forest in England, Walter asked Anna whether she had similar flowers on her island:

[b]ut when I began to talk about the flowers out there I got that feeling of a dream, of two things that I couldn't fit together, and it was as if I were making up the names. Stephanotis, hibiscus, yellow-bell, jasmine, frangipani, corolita. (67)

Whereas in the forest she has the feeling that the Caribbean flowers are incommensurate with the English flowers, in her later dream English trees have been transferred to her island and superimposed to form a composite dream symbol.

---

well enough when Ethel tells her to clear out of her flat, and imagines someone insensitively asking her why she didn't 'bloody well make a hole in the water' (84, 124, 140).

[71] Sue Thomas, 'Jean Rhys's Piecing of the Local and the Transnational in *Voyage in the Dark*', *Affirmations: of the modern*, 4/1 (2016), 187–207, 203.

[72] Glissant, *Discourse*, 66–7.

[73] Glissant, *Discourse*, 61.

[74] See Carol Dell'Amico, *Colonialism and the Modernist Moment in the Early Novels of Jean Rhys* (New York: Routledge, 2005), 2, 39–55.

The strangeness of this composite symbol conveys the discontinuity that Anna experiences between her life in Dominica and her life in England. Yet the image also suggests the ecological transformations that the island has undergone through its history of colonization. It echoes the contrast between the description of the island at an earlier time being 'all overgrown with woods', and the later 'barren look' of the plantation at Morgan's Rest, where Anna helps her father attempt (with limited success) to grow cocoa, nutmegs, and coffee (62). By doing so, the dream symbol hints at the deforestation that, together with land-grabbing and the massacre of indigenous people, constitute what Ferdinand describes as the foundational acts of colonial inhabitation in the Caribbean.[75] Even Hesketh Bell acknowledged the role of these interconnected forms of violence on Dominica, noting that 'the Caribs found their homes torn from them and their hunting-grounds disappearing under the cane-fields and coffee plantations of the intruders'.[76]

More broadly, the transfer of English trees to the island in Anna's dream evokes the transfer of species between Europe and the Caribbean as part of the Columbian Exchange. This transfer included the export of crops such as sugar cane, coffee, nutmeg, and bananas to be cultivated on plantations, as well as the transmission of diseases such as smallpox, measles, and typhus that—according to Lewis and Maslin—contributed to the deaths of more than 50 million indigenous people.[77] Once again, this is a loss that is largely unarticulated in works of colonial history. For example, Lucas only tentatively approaches the issue of ecological transformations in the Caribbean when he asks whether sugar cane—the principal crop cultivated in the West Indian plantation system—'is indigenous to the West Indies, or whether it was brought there from Europe'. He notes inconclusively that it 'is said by some writers to have been [...] carried by the Spaniards and Portuguese to the New World'.[78] Nevertheless, just as Anna's vague awareness in the dream that somebody has fallen overboard indicates a repressed history of the Middle Passage, so the uncanny image of her island with English trees gestures towards a repressed and unarticulated history of environmental destruction driven by imperial conquest.

By employing literary strategies that replicate melancholic symptoms, *Voyage in the Dark* is able to countermourn losses that are not registered in colonial histories and archives. In 'Mourning and Melancholia' Freud figures the lost object as casting a 'shadow' upon the ego, and in *The Ego and the Id* (1923) he suggests that the character of the ego can be understood as the 'precipitate'

[75] Ferdinand, *Decolonial Ecology*, 28–9.
[76] Bell, *Glimpses*, 18.
[77] See Lewis and Maslin, 'Anthropocene', 175–6.
[78] Lucas, *British Colonies*, 61.

of abandoned object-cathexes.[79] Similarly, social and environmental losses sustained in the Caribbean are registered only indirectly as shadows or residual traces in Anna's consciousness and in the novel more generally: she recalls Maillotte Boyd's name recorded in a plantation register; her mind drifts momentarily to the Kalinago while thinking of the words to a music hall song; and she has a dream in which somebody falls overboard and English trees have been uncannily transplanted to the Caribbean. In this last case, the dream is obscure: Anna tries therein to walk up the deck and get ashore, taking 'huge, climbing, flying strides among confused figures'. Here, 'figures' punningly refers both to bodies—and might thereby suggest bodies packed together in close proximity on slaving ships—and to rhetorical figures, drawing attention to the fact that the symbols in the dream are confused and frustrate meaning. Indeed, the dream 'rose into a climax of meaninglessness' (141). The dream thereby conforms to Bahun's characterization of modernist countermourning as that in which writers make artistic devices into strategies of obstruction, in a manner that accords with the twentieth-century reconceptualization of clinical melancholia as readable not in symbols but in the symptomatic obstructions to the used system of signs.[80] It is precisely through the presence of such textual traces of loss that *Voyage in the Dark* refuses the resolution and closure that Freud associates with successful mourning. By refusing to heal what he portrays as the 'open wound' of the melancholic complex, the novel performs an act of countermourning for the irreconcilable losses of enslaved people during the Middle Passage and in the plantation system, and of indigenous peoples following the colonization of the Americas.[81]

By extension, the countermourning performed by *Voyage in the Dark* can draw attention to losses that are concealed by certain recent accounts of the Anthropocene. As Ferdinand points out, with the concept of the Anthropocene, Paul Crutzen and others 'promote a narrative about the Earth that erases colonial history'. By leaving aside the colonial question in this manner, 'ecologists and green activists overlook the fact that both historical colonization and contemporary structural racism are at the center of destructive ways of inhabiting the Earth'.[82] By contrast, Anna's states of distraction signal losses that are not registered by such versions of the Anthropocene, and point towards counter-histories that would account for the roles of colonialism and the transatlantic slave trade in the current environmental crisis. In turn, by indicating the presence of repressed and unarticulated histories in the Caribbean, Anna's melancholic states promise to inflect Anthropocene structures of feeling and inspire political counter-moods.

---

[79] Freud, 'Mourning', 249; *The Ego and the Id*, in *The Standard Edition of the Complete Psychological Works of Sigmund Freud*, vol. 19, trans. and ed. James Strachey (London: Hogarth Press, 1961), 12–66, 29.
[80] Bahun, *Melancholia*, 42.
[81] Freud, 'Mourning', 253.
[82] Ferdinand, *Decolonial Ecology*, 8, 11.

In their survey of emergent Anthropocene affects, Kyle Bladow and Jennifer Ladino highlight the rise of depression, grief, and 'solastalgia' as states that are oriented towards environmental change and loss, with the last naming the feeling of homesickness that can arise when living in irreparably damaged environments.[83] Reading *Voyage in the Dark* might help to convert such Anthropocene feelings into political action. Flatley argues that by enabling the reader to map the historicity of their affective experience, certain artworks can (through self-estrangement) inspire a counter-mood which is not cathartic, compensatory, or redemptive: such artworks can unite readers into a community, and turn depression into a political response.[84] Indeed, Anna's melancholic moods might estrange us from generalized Anthropocene feelings of depression, grief, and solastalgia by drawing attention to the historical losses that accompanied colonialism and slavery in the Caribbean, as well as to traditions of resistance to those histories. The conclusion to this book explores how the critical counter-moods inspired by the novel might be directed to rethink literary history, and to reconceptualize modernism as a literary and cultural movement that emerged partly in response to the socio-ecological transformations wrought by Caribbean plantations, which were crucial to the formation of the modern world-system. That is, Anna's feelings of dislocation might inspire a similar dislocation in modernist studies, and recognition of the Caribbean plantation as one of its key sites.

[83] Kyle Bladow and Jennifer Ladino, 'Toward an Affective Ecocriticism: Placing Feeling in the Anthropocene', in *Affective Ecocriticism: Emotion, Embodiment, Environment*, ed. Kyle Bladow and Jennifer Ladino (Lincoln: University of Nebraska Press, 2018), 1–22.
[84] Flatley, *Mapping*, 1–7.

Conclusion

Modernist World-Ecology

Until recently, scholars in modernist studies have worked with conceptions of modernity that are largely inattentive to environmental transformations and damage. The concept of the Anthropocene and the debates that it has generated present the opportunity to redress this deficiency. Indeed, the previous chapters have used the concept to assess what might retrospectively be called the 'environmental politics' of British modernism, taking as their main examples novels by H. G. Wells, D. H. Lawrence, Olive Moore, Virginia Woolf, and Jean Rhys. In doing so, this book has operated within a fairly conventional model of British modernism. Yet it has also suggested how modernism might be reshaped in response to the idea of the Anthropocene, in ways that might provide hints to future environmental approaches to modernism. For example, the opening chapter on Wells suggests the value of straying outside the bounds of what was once referred to as 'high modernism' to engage with genres such as the scientific romance and the utopia, to which might be added other genres and modes such as science fiction, horror, and gothic. Lawrence's refiguration of the temporality of modernity in his coalfield fiction invites greater attention to modernist texts in relation to fossil fuel energy systems and their alternatives. Moore's *Spleen* (1930) suggests the value of returning to other texts of modernist queer ecology, which might be explored for the utopian glimpses they afford of a queer environmentalism that is not yet here. And finally, introducing a tension to the book's methodology, the last chapter on Rhys intimates the value of moving beyond a national framework to address environmental transformations that happened on a planetary scale. It thereby corroborates Timothy Clark's argument that the concept of the Anthropocene poses a challenge to literary criticism because it demands new practices of reading, and suggests the insufficiency of national approaches to literature.[1]

Of course, these suggestions for environmental approaches to modernism fit within the broader trajectory of modernist studies over the past few decades, and particularly with work associated with the 'new modernist studies'. For example, to attend to a diverse range of genres is consistent with what Douglas Mao and Rebecca Walkowitz identify as the 'vertical' expansion of modernism into

---

[1] Timothy Clark, *Ecocriticism on the Edge: The Anthropocene as a Threshold Concept* (London: Bloomsbury, 2015), 54–6, 66.

British Modernism and the Anthropocene. David Shackleton, Oxford University Press. © David Shackleton (2023). DOI: 10.1093/oso/9780192857743.003.0007

the realms of the popular, while to move beyond a national framework would be to follow what they describe as modernism's 'spatial' expansion, through a turn described variously as transnational, global, and planetary.[2] Reflecting on this expansion, Paul Saint-Amour notes how a weakening of definitions of modernism—less stringent criteria for what is to count as a work of modernism—has resulted in a 'strong field': one that is 'populous, varied, generative, self-transforming'.[3] And certainly, environmental approaches to modernism should continue to aim for such a strong field.

However, I suspect that environmental approaches to modernism may be best served by using unfashionably 'strong theory' to generate a strong field. Saint-Amour largely welcomes the prospect that various types of 'weak theory'—such as Gianni Vattimo's 'weak thought', Eve Sedgwick's 'reparative reading', and Rita Felski's 'post-critique'—might be used to generate a strong field of modernism. Yet he also expresses some reservations: 'I wonder whether the weakening drift of modernist studies means giving up on totality as a category, either normatively or descriptively, and if so whether we've thought sufficiently about the analytical and political costs of doing so'.[4] Sharing this concern, I agree with Anne Raine and Timothy Wientzen that the costs of giving up the category of totality would be particularly high for ecological approaches to modernism.[5] As Wientzen puts it: '[h]ow else do we think about, read for, and engage with the problem of ecological degradation if not under the sign of the singular and the total'?[6]

Indeed, the idea of the Anthropocene draws much of its power from the way that it articulates a crisis that affects the Earth System as a whole. Moving beyond a narrowly geological understanding of the concept, natural scientists have used Earth System science to characterize the Anthropocene as marking a fundamental shift in the Earth System, understood (by means of systems theory) as a 'total entity': a unified, complex system comprising the lithosphere, hydrosphere, cryosphere, biosphere, and atmosphere.[7] Paying attention to comparable notions of totality in the aesthetic sphere, the previous chapters have highlighted how modernists

[2] Douglas Mao and Rebecca Walkowitz, 'The New Modernist Studies', *PMLA*, 123/3 (2008), 737–48, 737, 739.

[3] Paul Saint-Amour, 'Weak Theory, Weak Modernism', *Modernism/modernity*, 25/3 (2018), 437–59, 441.

[4] Saint-Amour, 'Weak Modernism', 440, 454.

[5] Anne Raine, 'Modernism, Eco-Anxiety, and the Climate Crisis', *Modernism/modernity Print Plus*, 4/3 (2019) <https://modernismmodernity.org/forums/posts/raine-eco-anxiety-and-climate-crisis> [last accessed 25 January 2023]; Timothy Wientzen, 'Strong Ecology, Weak Theory', *Modernism/modernity Print Plus*, 4/1 (2019) <https://modernismmodernity.org/forums/posts/responses-special-issue-weak-theory-part-ii> [last accessed 25 January 2023]. For a converse approach, see Wai Chee Dimock, *Weak Planet: Literature and Assisted Survival* (Chicago: University of Chicago Press, 2020).

[6] Wientzen, 'Strong Ecology'.

[7] See Clive Hamilton, Christophe Bonneuil, and François Gemenne, 'Thinking the Anthropocene', in *The Anthropocene and the Global Environmental Crisis: Rethinking Modernity in a New Epoch*, ed. Clive Hamilton et al. (Abingdon: Routledge, 2015), 1–13, 2.

employ strategies of aesthetic wholeness that start to allow environmental crisis to appear. For example, Wells uses a totalizing form in his utopias, in a manner that parallels the ambition of early ecologists to map 'life communities' on a planetary scale, and thereby starts to make ecological risk visible on similar scales. Or again, Woolf combines the three sections of *To the Lighthouse* into an aesthetic whole, much as Fernand Braudel brings together different registers of history in his conception of 'total history'. This form allows Woolf to unsettle 'great men' conceptions of history, and intimate the presence of other types of historical agency that operate at different speeds and on different scales.

Yet beyond investigating the strategies of aesthetic wholeness that modernists use to make environmental crisis visible, I suggest that we should use strong notions of totality to generate better environmental accounts of modernism. It is not just a question of how certain writers represent (or fail to represent) the environmental transformations that occur on a planetary scale, but also of comparing how writers from different locations in the world register that crisis. To help with this task of scaling-up environmental approaches to modernism, I would like to advertise the theory of world-literature advanced by the Warwick Research Collective (WReC).[8] At the outset, however, it should be acknowledged that there are dangers of appealing to a notion of world literature. Situating the recent debates on world literature within a longer tradition that stretches back to Goethe, Aamir Mufti cautions that the desire for a world literature has often formed part of Orientalist and colonialist projects.[9] More specifically, some of the concepts employed by WReC—such as those of the 'simultaneity of the non-simultaneous', or of economic cores and peripheries—may inadvertently reproduce some facets of the colonialist historiography that they attempt to counteract. In common with other Marxist accounts of the environmental crisis, this approach may run the risk of occluding the importance of race. And finally, like other approaches to transnational, global, and planetary modernisms, the attempt to expand modernism may be suspected of an impulse to 'colonize' other areas and fields of knowledge. In an attempt to counteract such dangers, I will appeal to Malcom Ferdinand's account of the Plantationocene, and his conception of a decolonial ecology.[10] Channelling a critical counter-mood suggested by the reading of *Voyage in the Dark* in the previous chapter, the Caribbean plantation can be identified as a key site for conceptualizing modernist world-literature, and developing a modernist world-ecology.

---

[8] Warwick Research Collective (WReC), *Combined and Uneven Development: Towards a New Theory of World-Literature* (Liverpool: Liverpool University Press, 2015).
[9] Aamir A. Mufti, *Forget English! Orientalisms and World Literatures* (Cambridge, MA: Harvard University Press, 2016).
[10] Malcom Ferdinand, *Decolonial Ecology: Thinking from the Caribbean World*, trans. Anthony Paul Smith (Cambridge: Polity, 2021).

WReC advance a theory of world-literature that holds great potential for modernist studies. Briefly, they reject notions of 'alternative' or 'multiple' modernities, and appeal instead to Fredric Jameson's paradigmatically strong theory of a 'singular modernity'. Specifically, they read world-literature in relation to capitalism, understood by means of Giovanni Arrighi's narrative of the successive Genoese, Dutch, British, and American cycles of capital accumulation that unfold over the *longue durée*, set within a geography of shifting economic cores and peripheries elucidated by Immanuel Wallerstein's world-systems analysis. WReC provide a set of techniques for reading literature within such a system. For example, the different genres, modes, and cultural forms that are typically found sedimented within novels can be read alongside Ernst Bloch's conception of the 'simultaneity of the non-simultaneous' (*die Ungleichzeitigket des Gleichzeitigen*), to elucidate the experiences and processes of combined and uneven development that characterize the capitalist world-system. World-literature is thereby understood as the literature of 'the modern capitalist world-system'.[11] Such a theory of world-literature lends itself to those interested in the environmental transformations wrought by capitalism. Indeed, critics associated with WReC develop new models of world-literature by appealing to the resources of Jason Moore's 'world-ecology', which provides a sophisticated account of the way that the capitalist world-system has transformed nature over the *longue durée*, in what amounts to the 'Capitalocene'.[12]

I propose to build on WReC's theory of world-literature by appealing to Ferdinand's account of the 'Plantationocene'. Undoubtedly, plantations and slavery have long played significant roles in critiques of capitalism. In identifying the 'chief moments of primitive accumulation', Karl Marx famously remarks that the

> discovery of gold and silver in America, the extirpation, enslavement and entombment in mines of the indigenous population of that continent, [...] the conversion of Africa into a preserve for the commercial hunting of blackskins, are all things which characterize the dawn of the era of capitalist production.[13]

Thus it is that capital comes into the world, 'dripping from head to toe, from every pore, with blood and dirt'.[14] As part of her revision of Marx's account of the accumulation of capital, Rosa Luxemburg emphasizes that primitive accumulation

[11] Warwick Research Collective, *Development*, 8.
[12] Jason W. Moore, *Capitalism in the Web of Life: Ecology and the Accumulation of Capital* (London: Verso, 2015). See, for example, Michael Niblett, *World Literature and Ecology: The Aesthetics of Commodity Frontiers, 1890–1950* (Cham: Palgrave Macmillan, 2020); Treasa De Loughry, *The Global Novel and Capitalism in Crisis: Contemporary Literary Narratives* (Cham: Palgrave Macmillan, 2020); and Sharae Deckard, 'Reading the World-Ecology', *Green Letters: Studies in Ecocriticism*, 16/1 (2012), 1–14.
[13] Karl Marx, *Capital: A Critique of Political Economy, Volume 1*, trans. Ben Fowkes (London: Penguin, 1990), 915.
[14] Marx, *Capital*, 926.

occurs not just at the birth of capitalism, but throughout its history, including through its chief political expression of imperialism:

> From the very beginning, the forms and laws of capitalist production aim to comprise the entire globe as a store of productive forces. Capital, impelled to appropriate productive forces for purposes of exploitation, ransacks the whole world, it procures its means of production from all corners of the earth, seizing them, if necessary by force, from all levels of civilisation and from all forms of society.[15]

Illustrating her thesis that 'capitalism in its full maturity [...] depends in all respects on non-capitalist strata and social organisations existing side by side with it', she provides the example of contemporary rubber plantations in African colonies and South America, 'where the institutions of slavery and bondage are combined in various forms'. Amending Marx's figure, she thus claims that dripping with blood and dirt characterizes 'not only the birth of capital but also its progress in the world at every step'.[16] More recently, the persistence of primitive modes of accumulation has been theorized by David Harvey in terms of 'accumulation by dispossession', and by Jason Moore as 'plunder and productivity'.[17] Indeed, following Wallerstein, Moore draws attention to the prominent role of the 'sugar-slave nexus' in the capitalist world-system, tracing the movement of sugar plantations from Madeira to the Atlantic islands, and then to Brazil and the West Indies.[18] However, as Ferdinand points out, by focusing solely on the economic and material dimensions of the ecological crisis, such approaches fail to recognize the Caribbean world as a site of ecological thinking. He therefore proposes the 'Plantationocene' as an alternative to the 'Capitalocene', and identifies the Caribbean as the '[e]ye of modernity's hurricane': 'it was here that the Old World and the New World were first knotted together in an attempt to make the Earth and the world into one and the same totality'.[19]

Supplementing Moore's account of the Capitalocene with Ferdinand's conception of the Plantationocene, world-literature can be understood as that literature which registers the combined and uneven development of the capitalist world-system since 1492 and the colonization of the Americas.[20] Analysis of such literature would pay special attention to the environmental transformations wrought by

[15] Rosa Luxemburg, *The Accumulation of Capital*, trans. Agnes Schwarzschild (London: Routledge, 2003), 338.
[16] Luxemburg, *Capital*, 345, 339, 433.
[17] See Warwick Research Collective, *Development*, 69–70.
[18] Immanuel Wallerstein, *The Modern World-System 1: Capitalist Agriculture and the Origins of the European World-Economy in the Sixteenth Century* (Berkeley: University of California Press, 2011), 88–9; Moore, *Web of Life*, 183–6.
[19] Ferdinand, *Decolonial Ecology*, 18, 45, 12.
[20] This understanding departs slightly from WReC, who suggest that world-literature emerged only in the long nineteenth century (*Development*, 15).

this system, including those that are registered in the geological record. In terms of periodization, modernist world-literature might be seen as coextensive with world-literature, running from 1492 to the present.[21] Or, perhaps more usefully, some temporal boundaries could be imposed to demarcate a modernist subset of a larger body of world-literature.[22] For example, a conventional (although somewhat arbitrary) start date of 1890 might open this modernist phase of world-literature. This phase could then be understood as running until the mid-twentieth century, which marks the beginning of a new phase of capital accumulation with the transition of the economic core from Britain to the United States, and the start of the 'Great Acceleration', associated with nuclear testing and rapid increases in greenhouse gas emissions. In turn, this scheme leaves open the possibility of a 'late modernism' that extends beyond the mid-twentieth century.

On this conception of modernist world-literature, modernism is not thought of as a cultural and artistic movement that first develops in European and American cities, and then spreads to the economic periphery. Rather, modernism occurs simultaneously in the economic peripheries and semi-peripheries of the world-system, reflecting a logic of combined and uneven development. Indeed, complementing existing approaches that shift attention from the modernist metropolis to the Caribbean plantation, the Caribbean should be acknowledged as a key site of modernism.[23] C. L. R. James, Édouard Glissant, and Malcom Ferdinand all emphasize the modernity of the Caribbean, and particularly of the sugar plantation, which for James was a 'modern system' that produced the 'Negro' as a quintessentially modern subject, and for Glissant was a focal point where 'the tendencies of our modernity begin to be detectable'.[24] So too it should be recognized

---

[21] For example, Christopher Columbus's journal might be read as an early text of modernist world-literature. Although it may seem vertiginous, such a temporal expansion of modernism is nevertheless modest compared to Susan Stanford Friedman's proposal for 'planetary modernisms' that would extend back through 'deep' time (*Planetary Modernisms: Provocations on Modernity Across Time* (New York: Columbia University Press, 2015)), 70. As Saint-Amour notes, Friedman's attempts to weaken modernism by 'defining it as any aesthetic rupture engaged with rapid change in any historical period [...] entirely decouple modernity, and consequently modernism, from capitalism' ('Weak Modernism', 454).

[22] Modernist world-literature would still be read in the context of a history that stretches across more than five centuries, and that is itself set within a longer geological history. A distinctive feature of works of modernist world-literature is that they reach—albeit confusedly and from their own perspectives—to the whole. For example, Wells's and Woolf's strategies of aesthetic wholeness might be compared to those of works of Caribbean literature, which for Édouard Glissant strive for totality through their poetics of Relation (*Poetics of Relation*, trans. Betsy Wing (Ann Arbor: University of Michigan Press, 2010), 32–5). Herein can be detected what might be called modernism's 'planetary imagination'.

[23] See, for example, Mary Lou Emery, 'Caribbean Modernism: Plantation to Planetary', in *The Oxford Handbook of Global Modernisms*, ed. Mark Wollaeger and Matt Eatough (Oxford: Oxford University Press, 2012), 48–77; and Amy Clukey and Jeremy Wells, 'Introduction: Plantation Modernity', *The Global South*, 10/2 (2016), 1–10.

[24] C. L. R. James, *The Black Jacobins: Toussaint L'Ouverture and the San Domingo Revolution* (London: Penguin, 2001), 305–06; Glissant, *Relation*, 65. Ferdinand also draws attention to the production of the so-called 'Negro' as a modern subject by identifying the 'Negrocene' as the counterpart of the 'Plantationocene'. For him, the 'Negrocene names the era when the productive work of the Negro,

that plantation modernity gave rise to a distinctive Caribbean or plantation modernism. For example, Rhys's *Voyage in the Dark* could be read alongside Eric Walrond's 'The Vampire Bat' (1926), which reworks tales of duppy spirits to provide a gothic counter-narrative to the development that was envisaged as part of the 'new imperialism'. Again, Claude McKay's *Banana Bottom* (1933) is—to use Sylvia Wynter's distinction between novels of plantation and novels of plot—a novel of plot that subverts the racial hierarchies of the colonial plantation; Jacques Roumain's *Masters of the Dew* (1943) employs realist narrative strategies to render the slow violence of drought, and thereby politicize what might otherwise be construed as a 'natural' phenomenon; and Miguel Ángel Asturias's *Banana Trilogy* (1950–60) registers the damage inflicted by the monocultural plantations run by corporations supported by US military power.[25]

More broadly, a plantation modernism might be traced through the various cultural forms that emerged after the disintegration of the colonial plantation system in the Caribbean. Glissant draws attention to the 'second plantation matrix' that spread through the Caribbean, Latin America, and the United States to end up 'in mazes of sheet metal and concrete': it includes the Black southerners in the United States who followed the underground railroad to places such as Harlem, where writers 'wrote their Renaissance upon the walls of solitude', as well as those who produced urban literature in Bahia, Jacmel, and Fort-de-France.[26] Certainly, as Amy Clukey makes clear, approaches to plantation modernism should distinguish between different kinds of plantation, and the ways in which they evolved over time. They should, for instance, recognize differences between the Munster and Ulster plantations that were used to impose imperial control in Ireland and that led to famines and forced migrations; the colonial sugar plantations in the Caribbean and the cotton plantations in the US South; and the banana plantations run by multinational corporations backed by US gunboat diplomacy.[27] Yet by considering such examples together, studies of plantation modernism promise to elucidate how plantations have wrought profound socio-ecological transformations over the *longue durée* of the capitalist world-system, and have functioned as a defining feature of what Ferdinand calls 'colonial inhabitation'.[28] More generally, to expand the investigation of modernism to a global scale by means of a world-literature that registers the combined and uneven development of the modern world-system would help address what Frantz Fanon describes as the scandal of 'European opulence': such opulence has 'been founded on slavery, it has been

directed at expanding colonial inhabitation, played a fundamental role in the Earth's ecological and environmental changes' (*Decolonial Ecology*, 58–62).

[25] Sylvia Wynter, 'Novel and History, Plot and Plantation', *Savacou*, 5 (1971), 95–102.

[26] Glissant, *Relation*, 72–3.

[27] Amy Clukey, 'Dreaming of Palestine: James Joyce's *Ulysses* and Plantation Modernism', *Modernism/modernity*, 26/1 (2019), 167–84, 170–1.

[28] Ferdinand, *Decolonial Ecology*, 26, 32.

nourished with the blood of slaves and it comes directly from the soil and from the subsoil of that under-developed world'.[29]

Although such an approach to modernist world-literature would employ strong theory, it need not involve completely paranoid reading practices—ones in which modernist texts are read as endlessly confirming the insights offered by world-systems and world-ecological analysis. For those unmoved by WReC's structural homologies—in which the often-uneven mixture of content and form in works of world-literature monadologically reflects the unevenness of the world-system that has been shaped by capitalist development—there are no doubt other ways of proceeding. World-literature might be read not only for the way that it reflects combined and uneven development in the modern world-system, but also in terms of its ability to produce knowledge about the uneven distribution of environmental risk within that system. Again, marking a shift from Moore's 'world-ecology' to Ferdinand's 'worldly-ecology', works of world-literature should be recognized as sites of ecological thinking, which provide resources for what Ferdinand calls 'world-making': ways of living with human and non-human others on the Earth.[30] Indeed, narrative's ability to configure different ways of being in the world makes literature an excellent candidate for such a role. The spatial expansion of modernism by means of a conception of world-literature—and the generation of different geographies of modernism, which might be organized around commodity frontiers or socio-ecological subunits of the world-system such as the Caribbean—would thereby provide a diverse range of perspectives for rethinking environmental politics.

Notably, studies of modernist world-ecology can open new possibilities for environmental justice. Ferdinand points out that many narratives of the Anthropocene seek to account for the environmental crisis without addressing issues of colonialism and race, and thereby perpetuate modernity's 'colonial fracture'. By contrast, a modernist world-ecology would confront modernity's colonial fracture alongside its environmental fracture, and thereby support what Ferdinand calls a 'decolonial ecology'—one that promises to transform the conceptual and political implications of the environmental crisis.[31] Such an undertaking is even more important at a time when environmentalist rhetoric is increasingly being mobilized to support racist and ethnonationalist agendas. A modernist world-ecology promises to counteract such a danger by reconceptualizing the ecological crisis as a series of ongoing catastrophes in which the ruptures of the Middle Passage and settler colonialism have played central roles, and drawing attention to traditions of ecological concern from the peripheries and semi-peripheries of the modern world-system. In Glissant's terms, a modernist world-ecology might revive an aesthetic connection to

---

[29] Frantz Fanon, *The Wretched of the Earth*, trans. Constance Farrington (London: Penguin, 2001), 76.
[30] Ferdinand, *Decolonial Ecology*, 18, 230.
[31] Ferdinand, *Decolonial Ecology*, 4.

the Earth based on relational rather than root-identity thinking, and thereby support an ecological politics of the poor.[32] Or in Ferdinand's terms, it might help to rethink environmental politics from 'modernity's hold': this is a politics that would foreground the interests and perspectives of those dispossessed by slavery and settler colonialism; pursue reparations; establish new interspecies alliances; and draw inspiration from ecological movements led by women, especially women of colour from the Global South.[33] To pursue such a possibility would be to continue the project started in this book: of returning to modernism to assess its environmental politics, and to use its resources to shape new structures of care and concern in response to the urgent environmental challenges of the present.

To proceed in this manner would transform our conceptions of modernism and modernity, in ways that could not be specified in advance. Harry Harootunian provides a helpful understanding of modernity as 'a specific cultural form and consciousness of lived historical time that differs according to social forms and practices', an idea that allows for 'differing inflections of the modern'.[34] World-literature might then be understood—following WReC—as registering a range of different temporal experiences of modernity within the modern world-system.[35] These include the distinctive experiences of time that arose in the Caribbean following the dislocations of the Middle Passage, and that are expressed in Caribbean literature through strategies of detour and obscurity.[36] Indeed, Mary Lou Emery notes that the recent spatial expansion of modernism 'takes us back to time, or rather, to newly modern times'.[37] Appealing to Paul Ricoeur's account of three-fold mimesis, we can add that the configurations of time in works of modernist world-literature can refigure our conceptions of modernity, which might then be used to generate new accounts of modernism. Notably, modernist world-literature can produce conceptions of modernity that are more attentive to environmental transformations; these conceptions might in turn reshape models of modernism by placing greater emphasis on peripheral and semi-peripheral modernisms. Like Neurath's ship, modernism and modernity can be used to rebuild each other, with the difference that at the end of the voyage both might end up looking very different. Overall, this process suggests how modernist literature can contribute to the project of 'world-ecology' and its understanding of capitalist modernization: by providing an archive of experiences of modernity, it might generate a specifically 'modernist world-ecology'.

---

[32] See Glissant, *Relation*, 143–8.

[33] Ferdinand, *Decolonial Ecology*, 3, 242–3.

[34] Quoted in Warwick Research Collective, *Development*, 14.

[35] Warwick Research Collective, *Development*, 12.

[36] See Édouard Glissant, *Caribbean Discourse: Selected Essays*, trans. J. Michael Dash (Charlottesville: University Press of Virginia, 1999), 61–2; and *Relation*, 71–2.

[37] Emery, 'Caribbean Modernism', 48.

Of course, any spatial expansion of modernism should consider the institutional context in which it is undertaken, and particularly the conditions of labour in neoliberal universities. The shift to modernist world-literature would likely require new comparative and collaborative methodologies, alongside a range of linguistic competencies. Recognizing the danger that such projects might be led by researchers in the Global North in a manner that exploits the labour of precariously-employed scholars of colour in the Global South, such projects should develop strategies to resist the academic precarity and systemic racism that characterizes neoliberal universities, and particularly what Christina Sharpe describes as their 'pervasive climate of anti-blackness'.[38] By pursuing such strategies, approaches to modernist world-literature can best contribute to efforts to decolonize modernist studies.

Paradoxically, using strong theory to conceptualize modernist world-ecology would counteract the universalism of many narratives of the Anthropocene. Dipesh Chakrabarty controversially appeals to a form of universalism when he claims that accounts of anthropogenic climate change necessitate a rethinking of history at the level of the species, and warns that no one will escape the current crisis: 'there are no lifeboats here for the rich and the privileged'.[39] By contrast, Wynter takes issue with an Intergovernmental Panel on Climate Change (IPCC) report that suggests that 'global warming is the result of *human* activities'. She points out that such a claim misrepresents the causes of global warming, and will lead to inequitable responses: the 'proposals that they're going to give for change are going to be devastating', and 'most devastating of all for the global poor, who have already begun to pay the greatest price'.[40] Reading modernist world-literature alongside accounts of the Capitalocene and Plantationocene can help to counteract the universalism of many Anthropocene narratives by elucidating the roles of capitalism and colonialism in causing the environmental crisis, revealing the uneven distribution of environmental risk on a global scale, and rethinking environmental politics from a range of places and perspectives.

Reading works of modernist world-literature can thereby generate a better understanding of the environmental crisis. In Ricoeur's terms, the narratives of the Anthropocene might be described as a competing set of 'poetic resolutions' to the intractable differences between lived time and geological time, yet they are poetic resolutions that have real political consequences: they open and close different ways of being in the world, and different possibilities of political action.[41] By virtue

---

[38] Christina Sharpe, *In the Wake: On Blackness and Being* (Durham, NC: Duke University Press, 2016), 106, 115.

[39] Dipesh Chakrabarty, *The Climate of History in a Planetary Age* (Chicago: University of Chicago Press, 2021), 45.

[40] Sylvia Wynter, *On Being Human as Praxis*, ed. Katherine McKittrick (Durham, NC: Duke University Press, 2015), 20–4.

[41] See Paul Ricoeur, *Time and Narrative*, trans. Kathleen McLaughlin and David Pellauer, 3 vols (Chicago: University of Chicago Press, 1984–8), III, 99.

of their concerns with time and history that make them so adept at rendering different experiences of modernity, works of modernist world-literature promise to enrich the understanding of the environmental crisis supplied by the Capitalocene and the Plantationocene, in what would constitute a distinctively modernist world-ecology. Reading works of modernist world-literature can thereby open better ways of being in the world, and better possibilities of political action.

Images Used by Permission

Figure 1.1
H. G. Wells at the Normal School of Science. Reproduced with permission from Alpha Historica/Alamy Stock Photo.

Figure 3.1
The Great Acceleration. Reproduced with permission from Steffen, Will, et al. (2015). The Trajectory of the Anthropocene: The Great Acceleration. *The Anthropocene Review*, 2(1): 81–98.

Figures 1.6 and 1.7
Figures SPM.1 and SPM.3(a). Reproduced with permission from IPCC (2018). 'Summary for Policymakers', in *Global Warming of 1.5°C. An IPCC Special Report on the Impacts of Global Warming of 1.5°C Above Pre-Industrial Levels and Related Global Greenhouse Gas Emission Pathways, in the Context of Strengthening the Global Response to the Threat of Climate Change, Sustainable Development, and Efforts to Eradicate Poverty*, ed. V. Masson-Delmotte et al. Cambridge: Cambridge University Press, pp. 3–24.

Bibliography

Primary

Aristotle, *Poetics*, trans. I. Bywater, in *The Complete Works of Aristotle*, ed. Jonathan Barnes, 2 vols (Princeton: Princeton University Press, 1984), I, 2316–40.

Aquinas, Thomas, *Summa Theologiae: Questions on God*, ed. Brian Davies and Brian Leftow (Cambridge: Cambridge University Press, 2006).

Bell, Hesketh, *Glimpses of a Governor's Life* (London: Sampson Low, Marston & Co., [1946]).

Bell, Hesketh 'Insurance Against Hurricanes in the West Indies', *The Times*, 5 February 1906, 4.

Benjamin, Walter, *The Arcades Project*, ed. Rolf Tiedemann, trans. Howard Eiland and Kevin McLaughlin (Cambridge, MA: Belknap Press, 2002).

Benjamin, Walter *Selected Writings*, ed. Michael W. Jennings et al., trans. Edmund Jephcott et al., 4 vols (Cambridge, MA: Belknap Press, 1996–2003).

Bonney, T. G., *The Story of Our Planet* (London: Cassell, 1893).

Braudel, Fernand, 'History and the Social Sciences: The *Longue Durée*', in *On History*, trans. Sarah Matthews (London: Weidenfeld and Nicolson, 1980), 25–54.

Braudel, Fernand *The Mediterranean and the Mediterranean World in the Age of Philip II*, trans. Siân Reynolds, 2 vols (London: Collins, 1972–73).

Burke, Edmund, *A Philosophical Enquiry into the Origin of Our Ideas of the Sublime and Beautiful*, 2nd edn (London: R. and J. Dodsley, 1759).

Butts, Mary, *Warning to Hikers* ([London]: Wishart, 1932).

Carlyle, Thomas, *Critical and Miscellaneous Essays*, 5 vols (London: Chapman and Hall, 1904).

Carlyle, Thomas *On Heroes, Hero-Worship & the Heroic in History: Six Lectures* (London: J. Fraser, 1841).

Carpenter, Edward, *The Intermediate Sex: A Study of Some Transitional Types of Men and Women* (London: Swan Sonnenschein, 1908).

Caudwell, Christopher, *Studies in a Dying Culture* (London: John Lane, 1938).

Coleridge, Samuel Taylor, *Coleridge's Miscellaneous Criticism*, ed. T. M. Raysor (London: Constable, 1936).

Collier, J. Payne, 'The Life of Spenser', in *Works of Edmund Spenser*, ed. J. Payne Collier, 5 vols (London: Bell and Daldy, 1862), I, ix–clxxviii.

Conrad, Joseph, *The Nigger of the Narcissus* (New York: Doubleday, 1914).

Darwin, Charles, *On the Origin of Species by Means of Natural Selection, Or the Preservation of Favoured Races in the Struggle for Life* (London: John Murray, 1859).

Demant, V. A. et al., *Coal: A Challenge to the National Conscience*, ed. Alan Porter (London: Hogarth Press, 1927).

Ellis, Havelock, *Studies in the Psychology of Sex: Sexual Inversion* (Philadelphia: F.A. Davis, 1901).

Extinction Rebellion, *Rebel Starter Pack*, 14 March 2019.

Forster, E. M., *Abinger Harvest* (London: Edward Arnold, 1936).

Forster, E. M. *England's Pleasant Land: A Pageant Play* (London: Hogarth Press, 1940).

Forster, E. M. 'A Great History', *Athenaeum*, 2 July 1920, 8.

Forster, E. M. *Maurice*, ed. P. N. Furbank (London: Penguin, 2005).

Freud, Sigmund, *The Complete Letters of Sigmund Freud to Wilhelm Fliess: 1887–1904*, trans. and ed. Jeffrey Moussaieff Masson (Cambridge, MA: Harvard University Press, 1985).

Freud, Sigmund *The Ego and the Id*, in *The Standard Edition of the Complete Psychological Works of Sigmund Freud*, vol. 19, trans. and ed. James Strachey (London: Hogarth Press, 1961), 12–66.

Freud, Sigmund *Group Psychology and the Analysis of the Ego*, in *The Standard Edition of the Complete Psychological Works of Sigmund Freud*, vol. 18, trans. and ed. James Strachey (London: Hogarth Press, 1955), 65–143.

Freud, Sigmund 'Mourning and Melancholia', in *The Standard Edition of the Complete Psychological Works of Sigmund Freud*, vol. 14, trans. and ed. James Strachey (London: Hogarth Press, 1957), 237–58.

Froude, James Anthony, *The English in the West Indies or The Bow of Ulysses* (London: Longmans, Green and Co., 1888).

Geikie, Archibald, *The Scenery of Scotland Viewed in Connection with Its Physical Geology*, 2nd edn (London: MacMillan, 1887).

Gregory, R. A. and H. G. Wells, *Honours Physiography* (London: Joseph Hughes, 1893).

Hannington, Wal, *Unemployment Struggles 1919–1936: My Life and Struggles Amongst the Unemployed* (London: Lawrence and Wishart, 1936).

Hegel, Georg Wilhelm Friedrich, *Lectures on the Philosophy of World History: Introduction: Reason in History*, ed. Duncan Forbes, trans. H. B. Nisbet (Cambridge: Cambridge University Press, 1984).

Heidegger, Martin, *Being and Time*, trans. John Macquarrie and Edward Robinson (Oxford: Blackwell Publishing, 2006).

Heidegger, Martin *Discourse on Thinking*, trans. John M. Anderson and E. Hans Freund (New York: Harper & Row, 1966).

Heidegger, Martin *Nietzsche*, ed. and trans. David Farrell Krell, 4 vols (New York: Harper Collins, 1991).

Heidegger, Martin, *The Question Concerning Technology and Other Essays*, trans. William Lovitt (New York: Harper & Row, 1977).

'Hurricane Insurance', *The Times*, 5 February 1906, 9.

Hutton, James, *Theory of the Earth, with Proofs and Illustrations*, 2 vols (Edinburgh: William Creech, 1795).

Huxley, Julian, 'Biology in Utopia', *Nature*, 111 (1923), 591–4.

Huxley, Julian *Essays in Popular Science* (London: Chatto & Windus, 1926).

Huxley, Thomas H., *Evolution & Ethics and Other Essays* (London: Macmillan, 1894).

James, C. L. R., 'The Atlantic Slave-Trade', in *The Future in the Present: Selected Writings* (London: Allison & Busby, 1977), 235–64.

James, C. L. R. *Beyond a Boundary* (London: Yellow Jersey Press, 2005).

James, C. L. R. *The Black Jacobins: Toussaint L'Ouverture and the San Domingo Revolution* (London: Penguin, 2001).

Joyce, James, *Finnegans Wake*, ed. Finn Fordham (Oxford: Oxford University Press, 2012).

Joyce, James *Letters of James Joyce*, ed. Stuart Gilbert and Richard Ellmann, 3 vols (London: Faber and Faber, 1957–66).

Kant, Immanuel, *Critique of Judgement*, ed. Nicholas Walker, trans. James Creed Meredith (Oxford: Oxford University Press, 2007).

Kant, Immanuel *Kant's Principles of Politics, Including his Essay on Perpetual Peace: A Contribution to Political Science*, ed. and trans. W. Hastie (Edinburgh: T. & T. Clark, 1891).

Kay, James Phillips, *The Moral and Physical Condition of the Working Classes Employed in the Cotton Manufacture in Manchester*, 2nd edn (London: James Ridgway, 1832).

Krafft-Ebing, R. von, *Psychopathia Sexualis, With Especial Reference to Contrary Sexual Instinct*, trans. Charles Gilbert Chaddock (Philadelphia: F. A. Davis, 1892).

Lawrence, D. H., *Apocalypse and the Writings on Revelation*, ed. Mara Kalnins (Cambridge: Cambridge University Press, 1980).

Lawrence, D. H. *The First and Second Lady Chatterley Novels*, ed. Dieter Mehl and Christa Jansohn (Cambridge: Cambridge University Press, 1999).

Lawrence, D. H. *Introductions and Reviews*, ed. N. H. Reeve and John Worthen (Cambridge: Cambridge University Press, 2005).

Lawrence, D. H. *Lady Chatterley's Lover and A Propos of 'Lady Chatterley's Lover'*, ed. Michael Squires (Cambridge: Cambridge University Press, 1993).

Lawrence, D. H. *Late Essays and Articles*, ed. James T. Boulton (Cambridge: Cambridge University Press, 2004).

Lawrence, D. H. *The Letters of D. H. Lawrence*, ed. James T. Boulton et al., 8 vols (Cambridge: Cambridge University Press, 1979–2000).

Lawrence, D. H. *Movements in European History*, ed. Philip Crumpton (Cambridge: Cambridge University Press, 1989).

Lawrence, D. H. *Reflections on the Death of a Porcupine and Other Essays*, ed. Michael Herbert (Cambridge: Cambridge University Press, 1988).

Lawrence, D. H. *Study of Thomas Hardy and Other Essays*, ed. Bruce Steele (Cambridge: Cambridge University Press, 1985).

Lawrence, D. H. *Women in Love*, ed. David Farmer, Lindeth Vasey, and John Worthen (Cambridge: Cambridge University Press, 1987).

Lucas, Charles Prestwood, *Historical Geography of the British Colonies: Vol. II. The West Indies* (Oxford: Clarendon Press, 1890).

Luxemburg, Rosa, *The Accumulation of Capital*, trans. Agnes Schwarzschild (London: Routledge, 2003).

Lyell, Charles, *A Manual of Elementary Geology: Or, the Ancient Changes of the Earth and Its Inhabitants as Illustrated by Geological Monuments*, 3rd edn (London: John Murray, 1851).

Lyell, Charles *Principles of Geology: Being an Attempt to Explain the Former Changes of the Earth's Surface, by Reference to Causes Now in Operation*, 3 vols (London: John Murray, 1830–33).

McKay, Claude, *A Long Way from Home* (New York: Lee Furman, 1937).

Marvin, F. S., *The Living Past: A Sketch of Western Progress* (Oxford: Clarendon Press, 1913).

Marx, Karl, *Capital: A Critique of Political Economy, Volume 1*, trans. Ben Fowkes (London: Penguin, 1990).

Marx, Karl *Capital: A Critique of Political Economy, Volume 1*, ed. Frederick Engels, trans. Samuel Moore and Edward Aveling (Chicago: Charles H. Kerr, 1906).

Merleau-Ponty, Maurice, *Phenomenology of Perception*, trans. Colin Smith (London: Routledge, 2002).

Moore, Olive, *Collected Writings* (Elmwood Park, IL: Dalkey Archive Press, 1992).

Moore, Olive 'Man of the Month: Le Corbusier', *Scope*, August 1951, 60–73.

Moore, Olive *Spleen* (Normal, IL: Dalkey Archive Press, 1996).

Murchison, Roderick, *The Silurian System*, 2 vols (London: John Murray, 1839).

Nietzsche, Friedrich, *The Anti-Christ, Ecce Homo, Twilight of the Idols and Other Writings*, ed. Aaron Ridley and Judith Norman, trans. Judith Norman (Cambridge: Cambridge University Press, 2005).

Nietzsche, Friedrich 'Eternal Recurrence', in *The Twilight of the Idols*, ed. Oscar Levy, trans. Anthony M. Ludovici (Edinburgh: T. N. Foulis, 1911), 237–56.

Nietzsche, Friedrich *On the Genealogy of Morality*, ed. Keith Ansell-Pearson, trans. Carol Diethe (Cambridge: Cambridge University Press, 2008).

Nietzsche, Friedrich *The Gay Science: With a Prelude in Rhymes and an Appendix of Songs*, ed. and trans. Walter Kaufmann (New York: Vintage Books, 1974).

Nietzsche, Friedrich *Thus Spoke Zarathustra: A Book for All and None*, ed. Adrian Del Caro and Robert Pippin, trans. Adrian Del Caro (Cambridge: Cambridge University Press, 2006).

Nietzsche, Friedrich *The Will to Power*, ed. Walter Kaufmann, trans. Walter Kaufmann and R. J. Hollingdale (New York: Vintage Books, 1968).

Ober, Frederick, *Camps in the Caribbees: The Adventures of a Naturalist in the Lesser Antilles* (Boston: Lee and Shepard, 1880).

'Onlooker', 'Why Not Sanctuaries for Us?', *Daily Sketch*, 23 January 1929, 4.

Orwell, George, *The Complete Works of George Orwell*, ed. Peter Davison, 20 vols (London: Secker & Warburg, 1998).

Pascal, Blaise, *Pensées and Other Writings*, ed. Anthony Levi, trans. Honor Levi (Oxford: Oxford University Press, 2008).

Plato: Complete Works, ed. John Cooper, trans. G. M. A. Grube et al. (Indianapolis: Hackett, 1997).

Playfair, John, 'Biographical Account of the Late Dr James Hutton, F. R. S. Edin.', *Transactions of the Royal Society of Edinburgh*, 5/3 (1805), 39–99.

Rhys, Jean, *The Collected Short Stories* (London: Penguin, 2017).

Rhys, Jean *Jean Rhys: Letters, 1931–1966*, ed. Francis Wyndham and Diana Melly (London: André Deutsche, 1984).

Rhys, Jean *Smile Please: An Unfinished Autobiography* (London: Penguin, 2016).

Rhys, Jean *Voyage in the Dark* (London: Penguin, 2000).

Rhys, Jean 'Voyage in the Dark: Part IV (Original Version)', in *The Gender of Modernism: A Critical Anthology*, ed. Bonnie Kime Scott (Bloomington: Indiana University Press, 1990), 381–89.

Rhys, Jean *Wide Sargasso Sea* (London: Penguin, 1997).

Roberts, R. D., *The Earth's History: An Introduction to Modern Geology* (London: John Murray, 1893).

Shelley, Percy Bysshe, *The Major Works*, ed. Zachary Leader and Michael O'Neil (Oxford: Oxford University Press, 2009).

Spenser, Edmund, *Works of Edmund Spenser*, ed. J. Payne Collier, 5 vols (London: Bell and Daldy, 1862).

Stapledon, W. Olaf, *Last and First Men: A Story of the Near and Far Future* (London: Methuen, 1930).

Stephen, Leslie, *Hours in a Library* (London: Smith, Elder, 1874).

Stephen, Leslie *Hours in a Library*, new edn, 3 vols (London: Smith, Elder, 1892).

Stephen, Leslie *Sir Leslie Stephen's Mausoleum Book* (Oxford: Clarendon Press, 1977).

Swinnerton, Frank, '"Men Hate Women", New Arlen Book for Coming Spring', *Chicago Daily Tribune*, 3 January 1931, 9.

Tennyson, Alfred, *In Memoriam*, ed. Susan Shatto and Marion Shaw (Oxford: Clarendon Press, 1982).

Things to Come, dir. William Cameron Menzies (United Artists, 1936).

Thomson, William, 'On a Universal Tendency in Nature to the Dissipation of Mechanical Energy', in *Mathematical and Physical Papers*, I (Cambridge: Cambridge University Press, 1882), 511–14.

'An Unhappy Life', *New York Times Book Review*, 2 November 1930, 6–7.

Ure, Andrew, *A New System of Geology* (London: Longman et al., 1829).

Vaerting, Mathilde, and Mathias Vaerting, *The Dominant Sex: A Study in the Sociology of Sex Differentiation*, trans. Eden and Cedar Paul (London: George Allen and Unwin, 1923).

Wells, H. G., *After Democracy: Addresses and Papers on the Present World Situation* (London: Watts, 1932).

Wells, H. G. *The Definitive Time Machine: A Critical Edition of H. G. Wells's Scientific Romance*, ed. Harry M. Geduld (Bloomington: Indiana University Press, 1987).

Wells, H. G. *The Discovery of the Future* (London: T. Fischer Unwin, 1902).

Wells, H. G. *Early Writings in Science and Science Fiction*, ed. Robert M. Philmus and David Y. Hughes (Berkeley: University of California Press, 1975).

Wells, H. G. *Experiment in Autobiography: Discoveries and Conclusions of a Very Ordinary Brain (Since 1866)*, 2 vols (London: Victor Gollancz and The Cresset Press, 1934).

Wells, H. G. *The Fate of Homo Sapiens* (London: Secker & Warburg, 1939).

Wells, H. G. *H. G. Wells's Literary Criticism*, ed. Patrick Parrinder and Robert M. Philmus (Brighton: Harvester, 1980).

Wells, H. G. *Men Like Gods* (London: Cassell, 1923).

Wells, H. G. *A Modern Utopia* (London: Chapman & Hall, 1905).

Wells, H. G. *The New World Order* (London: Secker and Warburg, 1940).

Wells, H. G. *The Outline of History* (London: Cassell, 1920).

Wells, H. G. 'Reminiscences of a Planet', *Pall Mall Gazette*, 15 January 1894, 4.

Wells, H. G. *The Shape of Things to Come: The Ultimate Revolution* (London: Hutchinson, 1933).

Wells, H. G. *A Short History of the World* (London: Cassell, 1922).

Wells, H. G. *The Time Machine: An Invention*, ed. Stephen Arata (New York: Norton, 2009).

Wells, H. G. *The Time Machine*, ed. Roger Luckhurst (Oxford: Oxford University Press, 2017).

Wells, H. G. *Travels of a Republican Radical in Search of Hot Water* (Harmondsworth: Penguin, 1939).

Wells, H. G., Julian S. Huxley, and G. P. Wells, *The Science of Life: A Summary of Contemporary Knowledge about Life and Its Possibilities*, 3 vols (London: Amalgamated Press, 1929–30).

Williams-Ellis, Clough, *England and the Octopus* (London: Geoffrey Bles, 1928).

Woolf, Virginia, '"Anon" and "The Reader": Virginia Woolf's Last Essays', ed. Brenda R. Silver, *Twentieth Century Literature*, 25 (1979), 356–441.

Woolf, Virginia *Between the Acts*, ed. Susan Dick and Mary S. Millar (Oxford: Blackwell, 2002).

Woolf, Virginia *Between the Acts*, ed. Mark Hussey (Cambridge: Cambridge University Press, 2011).

Woolf, Virginia *The Essays of Virginia Woolf*, ed. Andrew McNeillie and Stuart N. Clarke, 6 vols (London: Hogarth Press, 1986–2011).

Woolf, Virginia *Jacob's Room*, ed. Stuart N. Clarke and David Bradshaw (Cambridge: Cambridge University Press, 2020).

Woolf, Virginia *Orlando*, ed. Brenda Lyons (London: Penguin, 2000).

Woolf, Virginia *Pointz Hall: The Earlier and Later Typescripts of Between the Acts*, ed. Mitchell A. Leaska (New York: University Publications, 1983).

Woolf, Virginia 'Reading Notebook XLV', Sussex, Monks House Papers, B.2m.

Woolf, Virginia A Room of One's Own; Three Guineas, ed. Morag Shiach (Oxford: Oxford University Press, 1992).Woolf, Virginia *To the Lighthouse*, ed. Stella McNichol (London: Penguin, 1992).

Woolf, Virginia *To the Lighthouse: The Original Holograph Draft*, ed. Susan Dick (London: Hogarth Press, 1983).

Woolf, Virginia *The Waves*, ed. Michael Herbert and Susan Sellars (Cambridge: Cambridge University Press, 2011).

Secondary

Adkins, Peter, *The Modernist Anthropocene: Nonhuman Life and Planetary Change in James Joyce, Virginia Woolf and Djuna Barnes* (Edinburgh: Edinburgh University Press, 2022).

Adorno, Theodor, 'Reconciliation Under Duress', trans. Rodney Livingstone, in Theodor Adorno and others, *Aesthetics and Politics*, ed. Ronald Taylor (London: Verso, 2007), 151–76.

Alaimo, Stacy, *Undomesticated Ground: Recasting Nature as Feminist Space* (Ithaca, NY: Cornell University Press, 2000).

Alaimo, Stacy 'Your Shell on Acid: Material Immersion, Anthropocene Dissolves', in *Anthropocene Feminism*, ed. Richard Grusin (Minneapolis: University of Minnesota Press, 2017), 89–120.

Alt, Christina, 'Extinction, Extermination, and the Ecological Optimism of H. G. Wells', in *Green Planets: Ecology and Science Fiction*, ed. Gerry Canavan and Kim Stanley Robinson (Middletown: Wesleyan University Press, 2014), 25–39.

Alt, Christina *Virginia Woolf and the Study of Nature* (Cambridge: Cambridge University Press, 2010).

Anderson, Perry, 'From Progress to Catastrophe', *London Review of Books*, 33/15 (2011), 24–8.

Anker, Peder, *Imperial Ecology: Environmental Order in the British Empire, 1895–1945* (Cambridge, MA: Harvard University Press, 2001).

Annales, Les, 'Anthropocene', *Annales HSS (English Edition)*, 72/2 (2017), 161–3.

Armiero, Marco, and Wilko Graf Von Hardenberg, 'Green Rhetoric in Blackshirts: Italian Fascism and the Environment', *Environment and History*, 19 (2013), 283–311.

Arrighi, Giovanni, *The Long Twentieth Century: Money, Power, and the Origins of Our Times* (London: Verso, 1994).

Asafu-Adjaye, John, and others, *An Ecomodernist Manifesto* (2015), 6. <https://www.ecomodernism.org/manifesto-english> [last accessed 25 January 2023]

Auerbach, Erich, *Mimesis: The Representation of Reality in Western Literature*, trans. Willard R. Trask (Princeton: Princeton University Press, 2013).

Bahun, Sanja, *Modernism and Melancholia: Writing as Countermourning* (Oxford: Oxford University Press, 2014).

Barrows, Adam, *The Cosmic Time of Empire: Modern Britain and World Literature* (Berkeley: University of California Press, 2011).

Bateman, Benjamin, 'Avian, Anal, Outlaw: Queer Ecology in E. M. Forster's *Maurice*', *ISLE*, 28/2 (2021), 622–40.

Bateman, Benjamin *The Modernist Art of Queer Survival* (Oxford: Oxford University Press, 2017).

Beaumont, Matthew, *The Spectre of Utopia: Utopian and Science Fictions at the Fin de Siècle* (Oxford: Peter Lang, 2012).

Beck, Ulrich, *Risk Society: Towards a New Modernity*, trans. Mark Ritter (London: Sage, 1992).

Becket, Fiona, *D. H. Lawrence: The Thinker as Poet* (Basingstoke: MacMillan, 1997).

Bell, Michael, *D. H. Lawrence: Language and Being* (Cambridge: Cambridge University Press, 1992).

Beer, Gillian, *Darwin's Plots: Evolutionary Narrative in Darwin*, George Eliot, *and* Nineteenth-Century Fiction, 3rd edn (Cambridge: Cambridge University Press, 2009).

Beer, Gillian *Virginia Woolf: The Common Ground* (Edinburgh: Edinburgh University Press, 1996).

Bennett, Jane, *Vibrant Matter: A Political Ecology of Things* (Durham, NC: Duke University Press, 2010).

Berlant, Lauren, and Michael Warner, 'Sex in Public', *Critical Inquiry*, 24/2 (1998), 547–66.

Bersani, Leo, 'Is the Rectum a Grave?', *October*, 43 (1987), 197–222.

Björkén, Cecilia, *Into the Isle of Self: Nietzschean Patterns and Contrasts in D. H. Lawrence's The Trespasser* (Lund: Lund University Press, 1996).

Bladow, Kyle, and Jennifer Ladino, 'Toward an Affective Ecocriticism: Placing Feeling in the Anthropocene', in *Affective Ecocriticism: Emotion, Embodiment, Environment*, ed. Kyle Bladow and Jennifer Ladino (Lincoln: University of Nebraska Press, 2018), 1–22.

Bonneuil, Christophe, 'The Geological Turn: Narratives of the Anthropocene', in *The Anthropocene and the Global Environmental Crisis*, ed. Clive Hamilton and others (Abingdon: Routledge, 2015), 17–31.

Bonneuil, Christophe, and Jean-Baptiste Fressoz, *The Shock of the Anthropocene: The Earth, History and Us*, trans. David Fernbach (London: Verso, 2017).

Bradshaw, David, 'Red Trousers: *Lady Chatterley's Lover* and John Hargrave', *Essays in Criticism*, 55/4 (2005), 352–73.

Buckland, Adelene, *Novel Science: Fiction and the Invention of Nineteenth-Century Geology* (Chicago: University of Chicago Press, 2013).

Burrows, Victoria, *Whiteness and Trauma: The Mother-Daughter Knot in the Fiction of Jean Rhys, Jamaica Kincaid and Toni Morrison* (Basingstoke: Palgrave Macmillan, 2004).

Canavan, Gerry, 'Memento Mori: Richard McGuire's *Here* and Art in the Anthropocene', *Deletion*, 13 (2017). <https://www.deletionscifi.org/episodes/episode-13/memento-mori-richard-mcguires-art-anthropocene/> [last accessed 25 January 2023]

Cavey, Sophie, 'Olive Moore: A New Biography', *Feminist Modernist Studies*, 5/1 (2022), 1–20.

Chakrabarty, Dipesh, 'Anthropocene Time', *History and Theory*, 57/1 (2018), 5–32.

Chakrabarty, Dipesh 'Climate and Capital: On Conjoined Histories', *Critical Inquiry*, 41/1 (2014), 1–23.

Chakrabarty, Dipesh *The Climate of History in a Planetary Age* (Chicago: University of Chicago Press, 2021).

Chakrabarty, Dipesh 'Postcolonial Studies and the Challenge of Climate Change', *New Literary History*, 43/1 (2012), 1–18.

Chakrabarty, Dipesh *Provincializing Europe: Postcolonial Thought and Historical Difference* (Princeton: Princeton University Press, 2000).

Chambers, Jessie, *D. H. Lawrence: A Personal Record by E. T.* (Cambridge: Cambridge University Press, 1980).

Christian, David, *Maps of Time: An Introduction to Big History*, 2nd edn (Berkeley: University of California Press, 2011).

Clark, Timothy, *Ecocriticism on the Edge: The Anthropocene as a Threshold Concept* (London: Bloomsbury, 2015).

Clark, Timothy 'Scale', in *Telemorphosis: Theory in the Era of Climate* Change, Vol. 1, ed. Tom Cohen (Michigan: Open Humanities Press, 2012), 148–66.

Clarke, Stuart, 'The Horse with a Green Tail', *Virginia Woolf Miscellany*, 34 (1990), 3–4.

Clukey, Amy, 'Dreaming of Palestine: James Joyce's *Ulysses* and Plantation Modernism', *Modernism/modernity*, 26/1 (2019), 167–84.

Clukey, Amy, and Jeremy Wells, 'Introduction: Plantation Modernity', *The Global South*, 10/2 (2016), 1–10.

Cobley, Evelyn, *Modernism and the Culture of Efficiency: Ideology and Fiction* (Toronto: University of Toronto Press, 2009).

Cole, Sarah, *Inventing Tomorrow: H. G. Wells and the Twentieth Century* (New York: Columbia University Press, 2019).

Cole, Stewart, 'Sex in a Warming World: *Lady Chatterley's Lover* as Fossil Fuel Fiction', *Studies in the Novel*, 52/3 (2020), 288–304.

Coole, Diana, and Samantha Frost (eds), *New Materialisms: Ontology, Agency and Politics* (Durham, NC: Duke University Press, 2010).

Corton, Christine L., *London Fog: The Biography* (Cambridge, MA: Harvard University Press, 2015).

Crary, Jonathan, *24/7: Late Capitalism and the Ends of Sleep* (London: Verso, 2013).

Crist, Eileen, 'On the Poverty of Our Nomenclature', *Environmental Humanities*, 3 (2013), 129–47.

Crutzen, Paul J., 'Geology of Mankind', *Nature*, 415 (2002), 23.

Crutzen, Paul J., and Eugene F. Stoermer, 'The "Anthropocene"', *Global Change Newsletter*, 41 (2000), 17–18.

Davies, Jeremy, *The Birth of the Anthropocene* (Oakland: University of California Press, 2016).

Davion, Victoria, 'Is Ecofeminism Feminist?', in *Ecological Feminism*, ed. Karen Warren (London: Routledge, 1994), 8–28.

Deckard, Sharae, 'Reading the World-Ecology', *Green Letters: Studies in Ecocriticism*, 16/1 (2012), 1–14.

Deer, Jemma, *Radical Animism: Reading for the End of the World* (London: Bloomsbury, 2021).

De Grazia, Victoria, *How Fascism Ruled Women: Italy, 1922–1945* (Berkeley: University of California Press, 1992).

Del Caro, Adrian, *Grounding the Nietzsche Rhetoric of Earth* (Berlin: De Gruyter, 2004).

Dell'Amico, Carol, *Colonialism and the Modernist Moment in the Early Novels of Jean Rhys* (New York: Routledge, 2005).

De Loughry, Treasa, *The Global Novel and Capitalism in Crisis: Contemporary Literary Narratives* (Cham: Palgrave Macmillan, 2020).

Diaper, Jeremy (ed), *Eco-Modernism: Ecology, Environment and Nature in Literary Modernism* (Clemson: Clemson University Press, 2022).

Dickinson, Renée, *Female Embodiment and Subjectivity in the Modernist Novel: The Corporeum of Virginia Woolf and Olive Moore* (New York: Routledge, 2009).

Dimock, Wai Chee, *Weak Planet: Literature and Assisted Survival* (Chicago: University of Chicago Press, 2020).

Edelman, Lee, *No Future: Queer Theory and the Death Drive* (Durham, NC: Duke University Press, 2004).

Emery, Mary Lou, 'Caribbean Modernism: Plantation to Planetary', in *The Oxford Handbook of Global Modernisms*, ed. Mark Wollaeger and Matt Eatough (Oxford: Oxford University Press, 2012), 48–77.

Emery, Mary Lou 'The Poetics of Labor in Jean Rhys's Caribbean Modernism', *Women: A Cultural Review*, 23/4 (2012), 421–44.

Esty, Jed, *A Shrinking Island: Modernism and National Culture in England* (Princeton: Princeton University Press, 2004).

Evans, Rebecca, 'Nomenclature, Narrative and the Novum: The "Anthropocene" and/as Science Fiction', *Science Fiction Studies*, 45/3 (2018), 484–99.

Fanon, Frantz, *The Wretched of the Earth*, trans. Constance Farrington (London: Penguin, 2001).

Ferdinand, Malcom, *Decolonial Ecology: Thinking from the Caribbean World*, trans. Anthony Paul Smith (Cambridge: Polity, 2021).

Fernihough, Anne, *D. H. Lawrence: Aesthetics and Ideology* (Oxford: Clarendon Press, 1993).

Ferrall, Charles, and Dougal McNeill, *Writing the 1926 General Strike: Literature, Culture, Politics* (New York: Cambridge University Press, 2015).

Fjågesund, Peter, *The Apocalyptic World of D. H. Lawrence* (Oslo: Norwegian University Press, 1991).

Flatley, Jonathan, *Affective Mapping: Melancholia and the Politics of Modernism* (Cambridge, MA: Harvard University Press, 2008).

Foucault, Michel, *The Will to Knowledge: The History of Sexuality Volume 1*, trans. Robert Hurley (London: Penguin, 1998).

Franks, Matt, 'Mental Inversion, Modernist Aesthetics, and Disability Exceptionalism in Olive Moore's *Spleen*', *Journal of Modern Literature*, 38/1 (2014), 107–27.

Friedman, Susan Stanford, *Planetary Modernisms: Provocations on Modernity Across Time* (New York: Columbia University Press, 2015).

Funke, Jana, 'Intersexions: Dandyism, Cross-Dressing, Transgender', in *Late Victorian into Modern*, ed. Laura Marcus and others (Oxford: Oxford University Press, 2016), 414–27.

Funke, Jana *Sexological Modernism: Queer Feminism and Sexual Science* (Edinburgh: Edinburgh University Press, 2022).

Gaard, Greta, 'Ecofeminism Revisited: Rejecting Essentialism and Re-Placing Species in a Material Feminist Environmentalism', *Feminist Formations*, 23/2 (2011), 26–53.

Gaard, Greta 'Toward a Queer Ecofeminism', *Hypatia*, 12/1 (1997), 114–37.

Garrard, Greg, 'Heidegger Nazism Ecocriticism', *ISLE*, 17/2 (2010), 251–71.

Garrard, Greg 'Nietzsche *Contra* Lawrence: How to Be True to the Earth', *Colloquy*, 12 (2006), 9–27.

Garrity, Jane, 'Olive Moore's Headless Woman', *Modern Fiction Studies*, 59/2 (2013), 288–316.

Garrity, Jane *Step-Daughters of England: British Women Modernists and the National Imaginary* (Manchester: Manchester University Press, 2003).

Gay, Jane de, *Virginia Woolf's Novels and the Literary Past* (Edinburgh: Edinburgh University Press, 2006).

Ghosh, Amitav, *The Great Derangement: Climate Change and the Unthinkable* (Chicago: University of Chicago Press, 2016).

Glissant, Édouard, *Caribbean Discourse: Selected Essays*, trans. J. Michael Dash (Charlottesville: University Press of Virginia, 1999).

Glissant, Édouard *Poetics of Relation*, trans. Betsy Wing (Ann Arbor: University of Michigan Press, 2010).

Grogan, Jane, 'Introduction', in *Celebrating Mutabilitie: Essays on Edmund Spenser's Mutabilitie Cantos*, ed. Jane Grogan (Manchester: Manchester University Press, 2010), 1–23.

Grusin, Richard, 'Introduction. Anthropocene Feminism: An Experiment in Collaborative Theorizing', in *Anthropocene Feminism*, ed. Richard Grusin (Minneapolis: University of Minnesota Press, 2017), vii–xix.

Habermas, Jürgen, *The Philosophical Discourse of Modernity: Twelve Lectures*, trans. Frederick Lawrence (Cambridge: Polity, 1990).

Hadfield, Andrew, *Edmund Spenser: A Life* (Oxford: Oxford University Press, 2012).

Haffey, Kate, *Literary Modernism, Queer Temporality: Eddies in Time* (Cham: Palgrave Macmillan, 2019).

Halberstam, Judith [Jack], *The Queer Art of Failure* (Durham, NC: Duke University Press, 2011).

Halberstam, Judith [Jack] *In a Queer Time and Place: Transgender Bodies, Subcultural Lives* (New York: New York University Press, 2005).

Hamilton, Clive, Christophe Bonneuil, and François Gemenne, 'Thinking the Anthropocene', in *The Anthropocene and the Global Environmental Crisis: Rethinking Modernity in a New Epoch*, ed. Clive Hamilton and others (Abingdon: Routledge, 2015), 1–13.

Haraway, Donna, *Staying with the Trouble: Making Kin in the Chthulucene* (Durham, NC: Duke University Press, 2016).

Hartman, Saidiya, *Lose Your Mother: A Journey Along the Atlantic Slave Route* (London: Serpent's Tail, 2021).

Harvey, David, *The Condition of Postmodernity: An Enquiry into the Origins of Cultural Change* (Malden, MA; Oxford: Blackwell, 1990).

Hatab, Lawrence J., *Nietzsche's Life Sentence: Coming to Terms with Eternal Recurrence* (New York: Routledge, 2005).

Haule, James, '*To the Lighthouse* and the Great War: The Evidence of Virginia Woolf's Revisions of "Time Passes"', in *Virginia Woolf and War: Fiction, Reality and Myth*, ed. Mark Hussey (Syracuse: Syracuse University Press, 1991), 164–79.

Hegglund, Jon, and John McIntyre (eds), *Modernism and the Anthropocene: Material Ecologies of Twentieth-Century Literature* (Lanham: Lexington Books, 2021).

Heise, Ursula, *Imagining Extinction: The Cultural Meanings of Endangered Species* (Chicago: University of Chicago Press, 2016).

Heise, Ursula 'Science Fiction and the Time Scales of the Anthropocene', *ELH*, 86/2 (2019), 275–304.

Heringman, Noah, *Romantic Rocks, Aesthetic Geology* (Ithaca, NY: Cornell University Press, 2004).

Hillegas, Mark R., *The Future as Nightmare: H. G. Wells and the Anti-Utopians* (New York: Oxford University Press, 1967).

Holderness, Graham, *D. H. Lawrence: History, Ideology and Fiction* (Dublin: Gill and Macmillan, 1982).

Hovanec, Caroline, *Animal Subjects: Literature, Zoology, and British Modernism* (Cambridge: Cambridge University Press, 2018).

Howell, Edward H., 'Modernism, Ecology, and the Anthropocene' (unpublished doctoral dissertation, Temple University, 2017).

Howells, Coral Ann, *Jean Rhys* (Hemel Hempstead: Harvester Wheatsheaf, 1991).

Hulme, Peter, *Remnants of Conquest: The Island Caribs and their Visitors, 1877–1998* (Oxford: Oxford University Press, 2000).

Hyde, H. Montgomery (ed.), *The Lady Chatterley's Lover Trial: Regina v. Penguin Books Limited* (London: Bodley Head, 1990).

Iovino, Serenella, and Serpil Opperman (eds), *Material Ecocriticism* (Bloomington: Indiana, 2014).

IPCC, *Global Warming of 1.5°C*, ed. Valérie Masson-Delmotte and others (2018). <https://www.ipcc.ch/sr15/> [last accessed 25 January 2023]

Jackson, Dennis, 'Literary Allusions in *Lady Chatterley's Lover*', in Michael Squires and Dennis Jackson (eds), *D. H. Lawrence's 'Lady': A New Look at 'Lady Chatterley's Lover'* (Athens: University of Georgia Press, 1985), 170–96.

James, Simon J., *Maps of Utopia: H. G. Wells, Modernity, and the End of Culture* (Oxford: Oxford University Press, 2012).

Jameson, Fredric, *The Antinomies of Realism* (London: Verso, 2015).

Jameson, Fredric *Archaeologies of the Future: The Desire Called Utopia and Other Science Fictions* (London: Verso, 2005).

Jameson, Fredric 'Modernism and Imperialism', in *Nationalism, Colonialism, and Literature*, ed. Terry Eagleton and others (Minneapolis: University of Minnesota Press, 1990), 43–66.

Jameson, Fredric *The Political Unconscious* (London: Routledge, 2002).

Jameson, Fredric *A Singular Modernity: Essay on the Ontology of the Present* (London: Verso, 2002).

Johnson, Erica L., and Patricia Moran, 'Introduction: The Haunting of Jean Rhys', in *Jean Rhys: Twenty-First-Century Approaches*, ed. Erica L. Johnson and Patricia Moran (Edinburgh: Edinburgh University Press, 2015), 1–17.

Kalaidjian, Andrew, *Exhausted Ecologies: Modernism and Environmental Recovery* (Cambridge: Cambridge University Press, 2020).

Kantorowicz, Ernst H., *The King's Two Bodies: A Study in Medieval Political Theology* (Princeton: Princeton University Press, 1997).

Kermode, Frank, *Lawrence* ([London]: Fontana, 1973).

Kermode, Frank *The Sense of an Ending: Studies in the Theory of* Fiction, new edn (Oxford: Oxford University Press, 2000).

Koselleck, Reinhart, *Futures Past: On the Semantics of Historical Time*, trans. Keith Tribe (Cambridge: MIT Press, 1985).

Krockel, Carl, *D. H. Lawrence and Germany: The Politics of Influence* (Amsterdam: Rodopi, 2007).

Lacivita, Alison, *The Ecology of* Finnegans Wake (Gainesville: University of Florida Press, 2015).

Laniel, Marie, 'Revisiting a Great Man's House: Virginia Woolf's Carlylean Pilgrimages', *Carlyle Studies Annual*, 24 (2008), 117–32.

Landuyt, Inge, and Geert Lernout, 'Joyce's Sources: *Les grands fleuves historiques*', *Joyce Studies Annual*, 6 (1995), 99–137.

Latour, Bruno, 'Agency at the Time of the Anthropocene', *New Literary History*, 45/1 (2014), 1–18.

Lenik, Stephan, 'Carib as a Colonial Category: Comparing Ethnohistoric and Archaeological Evidence from Dominica, West Indies', *Ethnohistory*, 59/1 (2012), 79–107.

Lenik, Stephan 'Plantation Labourer Rebellions, Material Culture and Events: Historical Archaeology at Geneva Estate, Grand Bay, Commonwealth of Dominica', *Slavery & Abolition*, 35/3 (2014), 508–26.

Lewis, Simon L., and Mark A. Maslin, 'Defining the Anthropocene', *Nature*, 519 (2015), 171–80.

Lewis, Simon L., and Mark A. Maslin *The Human Planet: How We Created the Anthropocene* (London: Penguin, 2018).

Linett, Maren Tova, *Bodies of Modernism: Physical Disability in Transatlantic Modernist Literature* (Ann Arbor: University of Michigan Press, 2017).

Löwith, Karl, *Nietzsche's Philosophy of the Eternal Recurrence of the Same*, trans. J. Harvey Lomax (Berkeley: University of California Press, 1997).

Lukács, Georg, *The Historical Novel*, trans. Hannah and Stanley Mitchell (Lincoln: University of Nebraska Press, 1983).

Lukács, Georg *The Meaning of Contemporary Realism*, trans. John and Necke Mander (London: Merlin Press, 1963).

McCabe, Richard A., *The Pillars of Eternity: Time and Providence in 'The Faerie Queene'* (Blackrock: Irish Academic Press, 1989).

McCabe, Richard A. *Spenser's Monstrous Regiment: Elizabethan Ireland and the Poetics of Difference* (Oxford: Oxford University Press, 2002).

McCarthy, Jeffrey Mathes, *Green Modernism: Nature and the English Novel, 1900 to 1930* (Basingstoke: Palgrave Macmillan, 2015).

McConnell, Frank, *The Science Fiction of H. G. Wells* (New York: Oxford University Press, 1981).

MacDuffie, Allen, *Victorian Literature, Energy, and the Ecological Imagination* (Cambridge: Cambridge University Press, 2014).

McFarland, James, *Constellation: Friedrich Nietzsche and Walter Benjamin in the Now-Time of History* (New York: Fordham University Press, 2013).

McGurl, Mark, 'The Posthuman Comedy', *Critical Inquiry*, 38/3 (2012), 533–53.

McLean, Steven, *The Early Fiction of H. G. Wells: Fantasies of Science* (Basingstoke: Palgrave Macmillan, 2009).

Malm, Andreas, *Fossil Capital: The Rise of Steam Power and the Roots of Global Warming* (London: Verso, 2016).

Malm, Andreas '"This Is the Hell that I have Heard Of"': Some Dialectical Images in Fossil Fuel Fiction', *Forum for Modern Language Studies*, 53/2 (2017), 121–41, 127–8.

Mao, Douglas, and Rebecca Walkowitz, 'The New Modernist Studies', *PMLA*, 123/3 (2008), 737–48.

Marcus, Jane, *Virginia Woolf and the Languages of Patriarchy* (Bloomington: Indiana University Press, 1987).

Marshall, Kate, 'What Are the Novels of the Anthropocene? American Fiction in Geological Time', *American Literary History*, 27/3 (2015), 523–38.

Maslen, Cathleen, *Ferocious Things: Jean Rhys and the Politics of Women's Melancholia* (Newcastle: Cambridge Scholars Publishing, 2009).

Matz, Jesse, *Literary Impressionism and Modernist Aesthetics* (Cambridge: Cambridge University Press, 2001).

Matz, Jesse *Modernist Time Ecology* (Baltimore: John Hopkins University Press, 2018).

Miller, Elizabeth, *Extraction Ecologies and the Literature of the Long Exhaustion* (Princeton: Princeton University Press, 2021).

Millett, Kate, *Sexual Politics* (London: Rupert Hart-Davis, 1971).

Milton, Colin, *Lawrence and Nietzsche: A Study in Influence* (Aberdeen: Aberdeen University Press, 1987).

Mitchell, Timothy, *Carbon Democracy: Political Power in the Age of Oil* (London: Verso, 2011).

Montgomery, Robert E., *The Visionary D. H. Lawrence: Beyond Philosophy and Art* (Cambridge: Cambridge University Press 1994).

Moore, Jason W., 'Capitalism as World-Ecology: Braudel and Marx on Environmental History', *Organization & Environment*, 16/4 (2003), 431–58.

Moore, Jason W. *Capitalism in the Web of Life: Ecology and the Accumulation of Capital* (London: Verso, 2015).

Moore, Jason W. (ed.), *Anthropocene or Capitalocene?: Nature, History, and the Crisis of Capitalism* (Oakland: PM Press, 2016).

Morgan, Benjamin, 'How We Might Live: Utopian Ecology in William Morris and Samuel Butler', in *Ecological Form: System and Aesthetics in the Age of Empire*, ed. Nathan K. Hensley and Philip Steer (New York: Fordham University Press, 2019), 139–60.

Mortimer-Sandilands, Catriona, 'Masculinity, Modernism, and the Ambivalence of Nature: Sexual Inversion as Queer Ecology in *The Well of Loneliness*', *Left History*, 13/1 (2008), 35–58.

Mortimer-Sandilands, Catriona, and Bruce Erickson, 'Introduction: A Genealogy of Queer Ecologies', in *Queer Ecologies: Sex, Nature, Politics, Desire*, ed. Catriona Mortimer-Sandilands and Bruce Erickson (Bloomington: Indiana University Press, 2010), 1–47.

Morton, Timothy, *The Ecological Thought* (Cambridge, MA: Harvard University Press, 2010).

Mufti, Aamir A., *Forget English! Orientalisms and World Literatures* (Cambridge, MA: Harvard University Press, 2016).

Mullholland, Terri, 'Between Illusion and Reality, "Who's to Know": Threshold Spaces in the Interwar Novels of Jean Rhys', *Women: A Cultural Review*, 23/4 (2012), 445–62.

Muñoz, José Esteban, *Cruising Utopia: The Then and There of Queer Futurity* (New York: New York University Press, 2009).

Nally, David P., *Human Encumbrances: Political Violence and the Great Irish Famine* (Notre Dame: University of Notre Dame Press, 2011).

Niblett, Michael, *World Literature and Ecology: The Aesthetics of Commodity Frontiers, 1890–1950* (Cham: Palgrave Macmillan, 2020).

O'Connor, Ralph, *The Earth on Show: Fossils and the Poetics of Popular Science, 1802–1856* (Chicago: University of Chicago Press, 2007).

O'Connor, Teresa, *Jean Rhys: The West Indian Novels* (New York: New York University Press, 1986).

Osborne, Peter, *The Politics of Time: Modernity and Avant-Garde* (London: Verso, 1995).

Page, Michael R., *The Literary Imagination from Erasmus Darwin to H. G. Wells: Science, Evolution and Ecology* (Farnham: Ashgate, 2012).

Parkes, Adam, *A Sense of Shock: The Impact of Impressionism on Modern British and Irish Writing* (New York: Oxford University Press, 2011).

Parrinder, Patrick, 'From Rome to Richmond: Wells, Universal History, and Prophetic Time', in George Slusser, Patrick Parrinder and Daniele Chatelain (eds), *H. G. Wells's Perennial Time Machine* (Athens: University of Georgia Press, 2001), 110–21.

Parrinder, Patrick *Shadows of the Future: H. G. Wells, Science Fiction and Prophecy* (Liverpool: Liverpool University Press, 1995).

Partington, John S., *Building Cosmopolis: The Political Thought of H. G. Wells* (Aldershot: Ashgate, 2003).

Pinkney, Tony, *D. H. Lawrence and Modernism* (Iowa City: University of Iowa Press, 1990).

Pong, Beryl, *British Literature and Culture in Second World Wartime: For the Duration* (Oxford: Oxford University Press, 2020).

Prince, John, 'The "True Riddle of the Sphinx" in *The Time Machine*', *Science Fiction Studies*, 27/3 (2000), 543–6.

Rabaté, Jean-Michel, and Angeliki Spiropoulou, (eds), *Historical Modernisms: Time, History and Modernist Aesthetics* (London: Bloomsbury, 2022).

Raine, Anne, 'Ecocriticism and Modernism', in *The Oxford Handbook of Ecocriticism*, ed. Greg Garrard (Oxford: Oxford University Press, 2014), 98–117.

Raine, Anne 'Modernism, Eco-Anxiety, and the Climate Crisis', *Modernism/modernity Print Plus*, 4/3 (2019). <https://modernismmodernity.org/forums/posts/raine-eco-anxiety-and-climate-crisis> [last accessed 25 January 2023]

Ricoeur, Paul, *Time and Narrative*, trans. Kathleen McLaughlin and David Pellauer, 3 vols (Chicago: University of Chicago Press, 1984–8).

Rosenberg, Aaron, 'Romancing the Anthropocene: H. G. Wells and the Genre of the Future', *Novel*, 51/1 (2018), 79–100.

Rosenberg, Leah, *Nationalism and the Formation of Caribbean Literature* (Basingstoke: Palgrave Macmillan, 2007).

Ross, William T., *H. G. Wells's World Reborn: 'The Outline of History' and Its Companions* (Selinsgrove: Susquehanna University Press, 2002).

Rubenstein, Michael, and Justin Neuman, *Modernism and Its Environments* (London: Bloomsbury, 2020).

Rudwick, Martin J. S., *Bursting the Limits of Time: The Reconstruction of Geohistory in the Age of Revolution* (Chicago: University of Chicago Press, 2005).

Rudwick, Martin J. S. *Scenes from Deep Time: Early Pictorial Representations of the Prehistoric World* (Chicago: University of Chicago Press, 1992).

Rudwick, Martin J. S. 'The Strategy of Lyell's *Principles of Geology*', *Isis*, 61/1 (1970), 4–33.

Rudwick, Martin J. S. *Worlds Before Adam: The Reconstruction of Geohistory in the Age of Reform* (Chicago: University of Chicago Press, 2008).

Saint-Amour, Paul, 'The Medial Humanities: Toward a Manifesto for Meso-Analysis', *Modernism/modernity* Print Plus, 3/4 (2019). <https://doi.org/10.26597/mod.0092>

Saint-Amour, Paul *Tense Future: Modernism, Total War, Encyclopedic Form* (New York: Oxford University Press, 2015).

Saint-Amour, Paul 'Weak Theory, Weak Modernism', *Modernism/modernity*, 25/3 (2018), 437–59.

Sanders, Scott, *D. H. Lawrence: The World of the Five Major Novels* (New York: Viking Press, 1974).

Sandilands, Catriona, 'Queer Ecology', in *Keywords for Environmental Studies*, ed. Joni Adamson and others (New York: New York University Press, 2016), 169–71.

Saunders, Max, *Self Impression: Life-Writing, Autobiografiction, and the Forms of Modern Literature* (Oxford: Oxford University Press, 2010).

Savory, Elaine, 'Jean Rhys's Environmental Language: Oppositions, Dialogues, and Silences', in *Jean Rhys: Twenty-First-Century Approaches*, ed. Erica L. Johnson and Patricia Moran (Edinburgh: Edinburgh University Press, 2015), 85–106.

Scheckner, Peter, *Class, Politics, and the Individual: A Study of the Major Works of D. H. Lawrence* (London: Associated University Presses, 1985).

Scherr, Barry J., *D. H. Lawrence's Response to Plato: A Bloomian Interpretation* (New York: Peter Lang, 1996).

Schneider, Daniel J., 'Psychology in Lawrence's *Movements in European History*', *Rocky Mountain Review of Language and Literature*, 39/2 (1985), 97–106.

Schuster, Joshua, *The Ecology of Modernism: American Environments and Avant-Garde Poetics* (Tuscaloosa: University of Alabama Press, 2015).

Scott, Bonnie Kime, *In the Hollow of the Wave: Virginia Woolf and the Modernist Uses of Nature* (Charlottesville: University of Virginia Press, 2012).

Seymour, Nicole, *Strange Natures: Futurity, Empathy, and the Queer Ecological Imagination* (Urbana: University of Illinois Press, 2013).

Sharpe, Christina, *In the Wake: On Blackness and Being* (Durham, NC: Duke University Press, 2016).

Sheehan, Paul, *Modernism, Narrative and Humanism* (Cambridge: Cambridge University Press, 2002).

Shyrock, Andrew, and others, *Deep History: The Architecture of Past and Present* (Berkeley: University of California Press, 2011).

Silver, Brenda, *Virginia Woolf's Reading Notebooks* (Princeton: Princeton University Press, 1983).

Skelton, Matthew, 'The Paratext of Everything: Constructing and Marketing H. G. Wells's *The Outline of History*', *Book History*, 4 (2001), 237–75.

Snaith, Anna, *Modernist Voyages: Colonial Women Writers in London, 1890–1945* (Cambridge: Cambridge University Press, 2014).

Spier, Fred, *Big History and the Future of Humanity*, 2nd edn (Chichester: Wiley Blackwell, 2015).

Spiropoulou, Angeliki, *Virginia Woolf, Modernity and History: Constellations with Walter Benjamin* (Basingstoke: Palgrave Macmillan, 2010).

Steffen, Will, Paul J. Crutzen, and John R. McNeill, 'The Anthropocene: Are Humans Now Overwhelming the Great Forces of Nature?', *Ambio*, 36/8 (2007), 614–21.

Steffen, Will, and others, 'The Anthropocene: Conceptual and Historical Perspectives', *Philosophical Transactions of the Royal Society A*, 369 (2011), 842–67.

Steffen, Will, and others, 'The Trajectory of the Anthropocene: The Great Acceleration', *The Anthropocene Review*, 2/1 (2015), 81–98.

Stevenson, Randall, *Reading the Times: Temporality and History in Twentieth-Century Fiction* (Edinburgh: Edinburgh University Press, 2018).

Sultzbach, Kelly, *Ecocriticism in the Modernist Imagination: Forster, Woolf and Auden* (Cambridge: Cambridge University Press, 2016).

Suvin, Darko, *Metamorphoses of Science Fiction: On the Poetics and History of a Literary Genre* (New Haven: Yale University Press, 1979).

Szeman, Imre, and Dominic Boyer, 'Introduction: On the Energy Humanities', in *Energy Humanities: An Anthology*, ed. Imre Szeman and Dominic Boyer (Baltimore: John Hopkins University Press, 2017), 1–13.

Taylor, Jesse Oak, *The Sky of Our Manufacture: The London Fog in British Fiction from Dickens to Woolf* (Charlottesville: University of Virginia Press, 2016).

Thomas, Sue, 'Ghostly Presences: James Potter Lockhart and Jane Maxwell Lockhart in Jean Rhys's Writing', *Texas Studies in Literature and Language*, 57/4 (2015), 389–411.

Thomas, Sue 'Jean Rhys's Piecing of the Local and the Transnational in *Voyage in the Dark*', *Affirmations: of the modern*, 4/1 (2016), 187–207.

Thomas, Sue *The Worlding of Jean Rhys* (Westport: Greenwood Press, 1999).

Thompson, E. P., 'Time, Work-Discipline and Industrial Capitalism', *Past and Present*, 38 (1967), 56–97.

Tung, Charles, 'Baddest Modernism: The Scales and Lines of Inhuman Time', *Modernism/modernity*, 23/3 (2016), 515–38.

Tung, Charles *Modernism and Time Machines* (Edinburgh: Edinburgh University Press, 2019).

Tung, Charles 'Second Modernism and the Aesthetics of Scale', in Jon Hegglund and John McIntyre (eds), *Modernism and the Anthropocene: Material Ecologies of Twentieth-Century Literature* (Lanham: Lexington Books, 2021), 133–50.

Vergès, Françoise, 'Racial Capitalocene', in *Futures of Black Radicalism*, ed. Gaye Theresa Johnson and Alex Lubin (London: Verso, 2017), 72–82.

Voelker, Joseph C., 'The Spirit of No-Place: Elements of the Classical Ironic Utopia in D. H. Lawrence's *Lady Chatterley's Lover*', *Modern Fiction Studies*, 25/2 (1979), 223–39.

Wagner, Johanna M., 'Unwomanly Intellect: Melancholy, Maternity, and Lesbianism in Olive Moore's *Spleen*', *Journal of Language, Literature and Culture*, 64/1 (2017), 42–61.

Wallace, Diana, *Writing the Past: Modernism and Historical Fiction*, forthcoming.

Wallerstein, Immanuel, *The Modern World-System 1: Capitalist Agriculture and the Origins of the European World-Economy in the Sixteenth Century* (Berkeley: University of California Press, 2011).

Warner, Michael, *The Trouble with Normal: Sex, Politics, and the Ethics of Queer Life* (Cambridge, MA: Harvard University Press, 2000).

Warwick Research Collective (WReC), *Combined and Uneven Development: Towards a New Theory of World-Literature* (Liverpool: Liverpool University Press, 2015).

Waters, Colin N., and others, 'The Anthropocene Is Functionally and Stratigraphically Distinct from the Holocene', *Science*, 351/6269 (2016), 137.

Watt, Ian, *Conrad in the Nineteenth Century* (Berkeley: University of California Press, 1979).

Whyte, Kyle, 'Indigenous Science (Fiction) for the Anthropocene: Ancestral Dystopias and Fantasies of Climate Change Crises', *Environment and Planning E: Nature and Space*, 1/1–2 (2018), 224–42.

Wientzen, Timothy, 'Strong Ecology, Weak Theory', *Modernism/modernity Print Plus*, 4/1 (2019). <https://modernismmodernity.org/forums/posts/responses-special-issue-weak-theory-part-ii> [last accessed 25 January 2023]

Wilkerson, Dale Allen, 'The Root of Heidegger's Concern for the Earth at the Consummation of Metaphysics: The Nietzsche Lectures', *Cosmos and History*, 1/1 (2005), 27–34.

Williams, Raymond, *Keywords: A Vocabulary of Culture and Society* (London: Fontana, 1976).

Wolkovich, E. M., and others, 'Temporal Ecology in the Anthropocene', *Ecology Letters*, 17 (2014), 1365–79.

Woods, Derek, 'Scale Critique for the Anthropocene', *the minnesota review*, 83 (2014), 133–42.

Wright, T. R., *D. H. Lawrence and the Bible* (Cambridge: Cambridge University Press, 2002).

Wynter, Sylvia, 'Novel and History, Plot and Plantation', *Savacou*, 5 (1971), 95–102.

Wynter, Sylvia *On Being Human as Praxis*, ed. Katherine McKittrick (Durham, NC: Duke University Press, 2015).

Yoshino, Ayako, 'Between the Acts and Louis Napoleon Parker—the Creator of the Modern English Pageant', *Critical Survey*, 15 (2003), 49–60.

Yusoff, Kathryn, *A Billion Black Anthropocenes or None* (Minneapolis: University of Minnesota Press, 2018).

Zalasiewicz, Jan, and Kim Freedman, *The Earth After Us: What Legacy Will Humans Leave in the Rocks?* (Oxford: Oxford University Press, 2008).

Zalasiewicz, Jan, and others, 'Colonization of the Americas, "Little Ice Age" Climate, and Bomb-Produced Carbon: Their Role in Defining the Anthropocene', *The Anthropocene Review*, 2/2 (2015), 117–27.

Zalasiewicz, Jan, and others 'The Technofossil Record of Humans', *The Anthropocene Review*, 1/1 (2014), 34–43.

Zalasiewicz, Jan, and others (eds), *The Anthropocene as a Geological Time Unit: A Guide to the Scientific Evidence and Current Debate* (Cambridge: Cambridge University Press, 2019).

Index